The Uncensored History of Television's Wildest Talent Show

ADAM NEDEFF

Gong This Book! The Uncensored History of Television's Wildest Talent Show
© 2024 Adam Nedeff. All Rights Reserved.

No part of this book may be reproduced in any form or by any means, electronic, mechanical, digital, photocopying or recording, except for the inclusion in a review, without permission in writing from the publisher.

Published in the USA by:
BearManor Media
4700 Millenia Blvd.
Suite 175 PMB 90497
Orlando, Florida 32839
www.bearmanormedia.com

Hardcover: ISBN 979-8-88771-364-9
Paperback: ISBN 979-8-88771-363-2

Printed in the United States of America.
Book design by Brian Pearce | Red Jacket Press.

Table of Contents

Acknowledgments 5
Major Talent... 6
A Closet In Beverly Hills........................ 18
If It Ain't Fun, Don't Do It 30
Look To The Stars 56
Up To Chuck 72
Bang The Gong Quickly 86
Gary Gets Gonged 120
The Family That Gongs Together.............. 136
Gong Bananas!................................... 168
More Stuff.. 184
The Horror…The Horror....................... 198
Where Did They Come From?.................. 226
Hey…Aren't You… 258
NBC Bangs The Gong 276
Gong To The Movies 298
Respect... 332
The Gong Shall Rise Again 344
Bibliography....................................... 361
Index.. 365

ACKNOWLEDGMENTS

From the beginning, I knew that photos would be critical to the printing of a book about the history of *The Gong Show*. No author could capture the unique flavor of this show in words alone. *The Gong Show* simply had to be seen, so my strongest gratitude is for the people who provided photos:

For starters, there's the man who snapped the vast majority of the photos in this book, Vince Longo, the staff photographer for Chuck Barris Productions, who attended every taping of every episode and snapped pictures of all the zaniness happening around him. His collection is a treasure, and Mr. Longo personally provided many of the shots found in this book and on its cover.

For their generosity in sharing photos and videos from their personal collections: Bob Boden, Robert Burroughs, Shelley Herman, John Ricci, Jr., and Fred Wostbrock. Special nod to Mark Sweet for putting me in touch with Mr. Burroughs.

For their assistance in research: Brendan McLaughlin, David Schwartz, and Elise Thrasher.

And most of all, the people who took the time to sit down and share their memories:

Kurt and Athens Abell, Alan Arnopole, Jefferson Beeker, Michael Brockman, Joey "Dr. Flame-O" D'Auria, Big Chuck D'Imperio, Jamie Farr, Albert Fisher, Larry Gotterer, Sean Hannon, Shelley Herman, John Hill, Mountain John Hilligoss, Larry Keen, Jaime Klein, Al Lampkin, Murray Langston, Danny Lies, Vince and Yvonne Longo, Mike and Ellen Metzger, Raymond Michael, Howard Nugent, Jim Richardson, Jeff Schimmel, John Schneiderman, Michael "Mike The Vike" Sherman, Susan Simons, Fred Spencer, Larry Spencer, Andy Swan, Arte Tedesco, Jim Tobin, JoAnne Worley, and Paul Zeglar. Thanks to Will Harris and Robert Malcolm, who guided me to Jamie Farr, thanks again to John Ricci, Jr. for helping to make contact with the Metzgers, and to the incomparable and generous Art Alisi for reaching out to JoAnne Worley.

CHAPTER 1

Major Talent

Above: Major Bowes at the gong. AUTHOR'S COLLECTION

Maybe you've already heard the history of this show: a businessman who worked behind the scenes, thrust into the national spotlight in a job he had no business doing, hosting an amateur talent contest in which the less remarkable performers were ushered offstage by the clang of a gong. The part that might surprise you is that this show premiered in 1935.

Nearly 30 years before that, in 1908, a former Marine-turned-traveling salesman named Samuel Rothafel — he went by the nickname "Roxy" — got a new job as a bartender at a saloon in the middle of a coal mining town in Pennsylvania. Seeing potential in the large storage area in the back, Roxy asked for, and received, permission to turn it into a performance venue. Vaudeville shows and even roller-skating exhibitions were held in the Family Theater, as Roxy had dubbed it, but the movies proved most successful. Over the next decade, he snapped up theaters across the country and refurbished them into movie houses.

In Manhattan, another theater owner, Messmore Kendall, teamed up with a successful real estate prospector, Edward Bowes, to build what was eagerly touted as the largest movie theater in New York City. The Capitol Theater, which opened its doors in 1919, boasted 5,300 seats. Unfortunately, most nights, they didn't boast 5,300 paying customers, so within a few years, Samuel Goldwyn and a consortium of investors bought the theater and put Roxy Rothafel in charge of it. Bowes kept his job, and was even given a raise, but he had some of his responsibilities taken away in the process.

Meanwhile, radio materialized. After years of being the domain of hobbyists, radio became a commercial endeavor, with the FCC issuing licenses for broadcasting, and the business of radio launched on November 2, 1920. Two years later, AT&T asked Roxy about the possibility of airing the live performances at the Capitol Theater live. The program came to be known as *Roxy and His Gang*, radio's first variety show.

Capitol Theater was not only rescued by *Roxy and His Gang*, but it also became a must-see destination in New York. Tourists to New York made it a point to include a night at the Capitol Theater, either to see *Roxy and His Gang* in person or just take in a movie and hang onto the ticket to show friends back home that they had been to the theater that they heard every week on the radio.

In 1925, Roxy Rothafel, more than aware of his own popularity as master of ceremonies and of his escalating clout in the theater industry, opened up his own, larger theater (5,920 seats), named it The Roxy Theater, and took *Roxy and His Gang* with him, overseeing his show and his business from the new edifice.

The three years of success that came from hosting *Roxy and His Gang* convinced Capitol Theater that the exposure of radio was just too valuable to give up, so they continued the weekly radio show in their own venue; it just wasn't going to be called *Roxy and His Gang* anymore. They arranged with a nascent enterprise called the National Broadcasting Company to pick up their weekly variety show. The search for a new host was a short one; Capitol Theater appointed Edward Bowes to emerge from his office once a week to helm the show.

Edward Bowes had grown up in a poor family, helping to support them himself, even in childhood, with his unusually beautiful handwriting. Wealthier families would recruit the boy to pen their dinner party invitations and Christmas cards with his unique calligraphy. As an adult, a natural disaster unintentionally helped him build his fortune. After the 1906 San Francisco earthquake, he bought up the real estate amongst the ruins for a fraction of its former value and built new properties. A retired army reserve major, Edward Bowes was so obsessed with his own ranking that for years, he had demanded that his own employees at Capitol Theater address him as Major Bowes, and now, for the relaunched variety show, he would use it as his billing. The series was titled *Major Bowes' Capitol Family*.

Bowes was a businessman by trade, not a performer. The people he introduced every week were the performers. But from the beginning, Bowes clearly saw *Major Bowes' Capitol Family* as a vehicle for himself. To compensate for his own absence of talent, he asked his performers to submit their routines in advance, and he re-wrote the script for that week to give himself the best lines, which he'd deliver in a sleepy but folksy tone utterly devoid of spontaneity.

Bowes continued operating the theater. In the early 1930s, movie theaters struggled in the grip of the Great Depression, and Bowes went searching for ways to boost attendance. One of his more successful ideas was "Plate Night." One Wednesday night, you could go to the movies and get a free dinner plate. The following Wednesday, you'd get a free salad plate. And so on and so on…if you went to the movies on Wednesday night often enough, eventually you'd have a full set of china. The bigger hit he stumbled upon was Amateur Night. People could sign up and perform whatever type of act they like on the glorious stage of the theater. The audience got a show, and people bitten by the performing bug could feel like stars for one night.

By 1934, *Capitol Family* was nearing the end of its run and Bowes, who had tasted celebrity for the past nine years now and liked it quite a bit, looked for another radio show to call his own. CBS Radio had a successful Sunday night series called *National Amateur Night* and Bowes thought he'd make a good host in a similar program. Bowes made his own tweaks to the format; while *National Amateur Night* was just a showcase, Bowes would host a competition between the performers, with listeners invited to cast votes by telephone or telegram. Bowes convinced a single radio station in New York City to air his program, with a bit of a wink and a nudge in the spirit of his title, *Major Bowes' Original Amateur Hour*. In 1935, NBC picked it up for a national version.

Each week, Major Bowes would open the show by spinning his wheel of fortune with his poetic incantation "Round and round and round she goes, where she stops, nobody knows." The wheel didn't serve any actual function on the show, except to serve as a symbol of potential. As the amateurs took the stage, they had no idea that just the right person might be tuning in tonight. Maybe a recording company executive chanced to be listening right as a contestant went onstage to sing an old ragtime tune. Maybe a casting director would hear a hopeful actor delivering Prince Hamlet's soliloquy. Week after week, that wheel spun to remind the contestants and the listeners that there were rewards at stake far beyond what Bowes himself was offering. A contestant would step onstage, and Bowes would have a witty conversation with them, with the major tossing in a few supposedly off-the-cuff quips, but the contestant and Major Bowes were both so consistently stilted and awkward in their "spontaneous" chat that more than a few listeners figured out the conversations were rigidly scripted.

Twenty amateur acts per week would tap dance, sing, tell jokes, do bird calls, whistle, play the spoons, recite dramatic monologues, and anything else, while listeners at home called in to pick their favorite act. But Bowes himself acted as gatekeeper. Near his microphone was an ominous gong. If Bowes was underwhelmed by an act, he'd interrupt them by banging the gong and ushering them offstage, muttering "All right, all right" until they were gone. The gong was inspired by the hook that theaters used in amateur nights around the country. When an act was bombing and the audience was letting them know it, someone off stage would pick up a shepherd's crook and use it to hook the arm or the neck of the performer, forcing them offstage. Bowes had done the same thing during his own theater amateur nights, but once he entered the planning stages and realized he was doing a radio show, he decided that the hook was too much of a visual element to translate. The distinctive toll of a gong worked much better.

The willingness to perform, knowing that an embarrassing clang of the gong could end the exhibition, struck many listeners as unfathomable. It had to be a ruse. The off-key singers and the dancers with no twinkles in their toes? Phonies, surely. Bowes and his staff were coy when confronted with the accusation, saying that they tried to "average" two gongs per broadcast, and that while they didn't set out to gong anybody deliberately,

The official Major Bowes alarm clock with the quintessential wake-up call: a built-in gong. PHOTO BY THE AUTHOR; ALARM CLOCK PROPERTY OF ALBERT FISHER

they made it a point to give some performers a heads-up if they "suspected" that Bowes might, just might, gong them.

But if that was the case, why even put any unqualified participants in front of the microphone? Major Bowes affectionately called them "radio meat." Sure, he could have classically trained singer after classically trained singer after classically-trained singer belting out beautiful renditions of standards, but how much fun would that be? If you missed a week, would you feel like you really missed anything at all? Bowes was much more interested in bringing on a truck driver who could sing kind-of-okay. For the same reason, he encouraged the audition staff to give preferential consideration to acts that were just a little off kilter. A spoon player, an organ grinder, a man who played a harmonica attached to a garden hose, a "three-voiced" singer, musicians with feather-duster banjos, broomstick violins, or bamboo flutes, and Harold Moy "The Chinese Hillbilly" got moved to the front of the line ahead of arguably much more deserving tryouts, knowing that the trade-off was they were much more likely to be laughed off stage at the sound of the gong.

Any contestant who survived without a gong was eligible to receive votes from the home audience. The winning act received the Major Bowes Medal of Honor, which looked from a distance exactly like something presented to a soldier for acts of valor but was actually a purple ribbon festooning a medal bearing the face of Major Bowes himself, plus an inscription with the name of the act and the year they appeared on the show.

The show became a national phenomenon, becoming the first radio show to hold the #1 overall spot in the ratings for ten consecutive months. As the popularity of *Original Amateur Hour* grew, Major Bowes came to recognize the value of merchandise and turned himself and his show into a brand. There were Major Bowes highball glasses, a Major Bowes alarm clock (A small gong clanged to interrupt the slumber), Major Bowes linens, *Major Bowes Amateur* Magazine, a Major Bowes board game, and twice a month in your neighborhood movie house, *Major Bowes' Original Amateur Hour* short films. H.L. Mencken, the noted linguist, even coined a word inspired by the show: "gong-meat" for one who's unqualified. It didn't catch on.

A few legitimate stars launched their careers as contestants. Ventriloquist Paul Winchell and his dummy Jerry Mahoney debuted on the show, as did opera stars Beverly Sills and Maria Callas. But in terms of sheer star power and enduring fame, the biggest success to emerge from *Major Bowes' Original Amateur Hour* was Frank Sinatra. In 1935, Sinatra was a member of a quartet called Frank Sinatra and the Three Flashes. Bowes' staff told them that it was too strange a name to use on the show; Sinatra was unknown at the time, so giving him a star-like billing would sound odd to the audience. Bowes himself noticed that the members of the group had listed Hoboken, New Jersey as their hometown on their contestant application, and listeners tended to react strongly when they heard their own hometowns mentioned on the radio. Bowes suggested that they could skew the voting in their favor by changing their name to The Hoboken Four.

They took the advice and used that name when they went on the air. Sinatra delivered his prepared lines well during his interview with Bowes: "We're looking for jobs, how about it?"

The Hoboken Four delivered such a remarkable performance of "Shine" that it was later rumored that Bowes secretly met with the group and encouraged them to continue appearing on the show, under different names each time so the home audience wouldn't catch on.

Bowes, keenly aware that he had created a vehicle for stardom, wanted to ensure that he was the first to cash in on any careers that he launched. Performers were signed to contracts giving Bowes a one-year option to use their service. The contract prohibited performers from promoting themselves by mentioning Bowes or his show, while at the same time promising Bowes payment of 15% of any income that the singer received as a result of their appearance on the show. At the apex of popularity, Bowes assembled a traveling caravan consisting of past winners from the show, performing in theaters across America. With more winners than he had spots on the road show, and with sell-out houses convincing Bowes that there were more ticket sales where that came from, he called up more past winners and set up a concurrent second traveling show... then a third...then a fourth. Eventually, there were fourteen simultaneous Major Bowes road shows going all over the country.

With America still mired in the Great Depression, Major Bowes' expanding tours convinced thousands of desperately poor and unemployed people that if they could carry a tune at all, *Major Bowes' Original Amateur Hour* was a ticket to financial salvation. They all spent their last dollars on train tickets to New York City. 10,000 hopefuls per week applied for an audition, even though the staff was only equipped to handle 500 auditions per week. The doormen at the office complex were deputized by the production staff to weed people out as they showed up. Blind and disabled applicants were turned away because Bowes didn't want his audience to be swayed by sympathy. But even if they got on the show, contestants were only promised a $10 fee plus dinner at a cafeteria across the street. After that, they were on their own again.

As a result, *Major Bowes' Original Amateur Hour* accidentally clogged New York's welfare department. In a single month, 1,200 failed singers and dancers signed up for government assistance after their tryouts had come and gone. If they had known how little they stood to gain from the major, they probably wouldn't have even bothered making the move.

The performers in the traveling shows were paid $50 per week plus a stipend for their train tickets. Other than the train tickets, no other expenses were covered. That $50 had to cover hotel rooms, food, taxis, and anything else that came up along the way, all as Major Bowes himself collected, by one estimate, $30,000 a week from his empire. Frank Sinatra briefly joined one of the tours but was so insulted by the paydays that he quickly figured out that Bowes was taking advantage of the performers and dropped out.

Major Bowes with the Hoboken Four. That's Frank Sinatra on the right.
AUTHOR'S COLLECTION

For someone who presented himself with low-key approachability, Bowes ironically became very well-known for his open contempt for contestants, auditionees, and peers. Bowes' bodyguard manhandled an NBC executive who tried to enter during a rehearsal for the show. A magazine profiling Bowes quoted him looking down from his office window at the line of people waiting for their tryouts, and saying, "Look at those poor boobs down there."[1]

An undercover reporter posing as a singer auditioned for the program and filed a thoroughly unflattering portrait of the experience. He was made to audition three times; Bowes attended the third audition and

1. Ramsberg, Jim. "Major Bowes' Original Money Machine." *Jim Ramsberg's Gold Time Radio.* http://www.jimramsburg.com/major-bowes-original-money-machine.html visited 11 May. 2019.

grilled the singer with questions afterward, with a stenographer transcribing the conversation. On show night, the singer was given a script for the introductory chat with Bowes, with a change made at the last minute. The singer was originally to name the song he was singing and the opera it came from. He was then told only to name the song, with Bowes planning to interrupt him and name the opera himself, to show the audience how cultured he was. Once on stage, the singer received the dreaded gong and got shooed off-stage by Major Bowes. On his way out, he got a glimpse of the format sheet for that night's broadcast, with minute-by-minute details of how the show should play out. For his own performance, only one minute had been allotted; Bowes and his staff had decided in advance to give him the gong.

The show was being hit in different directions with backlash over the gong. People who saw the article were irked by what they saw as fakery. People who didn't see it just found the gong mean-spirited. It was a quandary for Bowes; listeners were becoming increasingly upset about the gong, but it had become such a calling card for the show that he couldn't bring himself to get rid of it.

Bowes soon realized that a calling card was all the gong needed to be. Contestants no longer suffered the indignity of having their act cut off. Everyone got to perform their whole routine. Bowes only sounded the gong as a beacon at the opening of the broadcast.

In the coming years, the show's popularity waned. By one account, the death nell came in 1943, when the traveling caravans lost performer after performer to better-paying USO tours and even factory jobs in US defense plants. In 1944, the former #1 series on radio placed 71st in the ratings each week. Major Bowes took the hint and voluntarily canceled his own show to save himself the embarrassment of having the network do it for him. Eleven months after the final broadcast, Major Bowes died.

Enter William Edward Maguiness. Maguiness was a bandleader who took his orchestra on tour with one of Major Bowes' caravans and was effectively charged with overseeing that entire unit of performers. During one stop on the tour, a theater owner complained about the amount of space that the name "Edward Maguiness" took up on the marquee. He came up with a more concise version of the name, "Ted Mack," which Maguiness liked so much he kept it for the rest of his life.

Ted Mack had become a trusted advisor to Major Bowes late in the major's life, serving as a talent scout and even guest-hosting the show on weeks when Bowes needed to tend to his health. After Bowes died, Mack ended up with the rights to the show and the format as a result.

In 1948, he brought the show to television on the Dumont Network. In the next 22 years, it would find its way onto every network's schedule. More careers would launch on the television incarnation. Seven-year-old Gladys Knight was asked to return for three shows (on the application that the young girl had originally filled out, the staffer who auditioned her scribbled a note about an "unusual voice" for a child her age). A singer who boasted that he was the great-great-great-great grandson of Daniel Boone, Pat Boone, got his big break from Ted Mack, too. At a vastly different time in his life, Louis Farrakhan appeared on the program, playing the violin. Connie Francis made her TV debut with Ted Mack. Comedian Robert Klein showed up, not as a comic, but as a member of a singing group called the Teen Tones. Raul Julia did a comedic monologue about choking on a marble.

In its 22 years on television, it was a show firmly entrenched in its own traditions. There was a gong on Ted Mack's lectern, even though on many weeks he may not have even bothered sounding it. The series started with a wheel of fortune on stage, then switched to a prepared film of a spinning wheel of fortune superimposed on the screen. Eventually, they discarded the wheel altogether and just had the orchestra play a fluttering jingle that suggested the visual of a spinning wheel. But week after week, Ted Mack still said "Round and round and round she goes…" It remained *The Original Amateur Hour* even as networks plugged it into 45-minute time slots, and then 30-minute time slots.

Albert Fisher was a talent coordinator during the show's last eight years on the air. "We always looked for good stories; we liked people who had gone through a challenging time in life and overcame it. We also liked BIG acts; every week had to have a band of some sort, or an ensemble from a dance school; a group that had an exceptionally large number of people. Every week needed someone in uniform, quite literally. It could be a military man, or a cop, or a nurse, someone performing in uniform. The feeling was that showing people performing in their uniforms would make the viewers feel like they were seeing a wide range of people. I also want to say Ted Mack, to his credit, wanted people of color on every episode. In those days, that was not a common attitude among people in television, but Ted wanted people of color, not just because they were talented performers, but for the same reason he liked the uniforms. If you saw different ethnic groups, it made the viewers feel that they were seeing variety. And this was a variety show, after all."[2]

2. Personal interview. 10 Nov. 2018.

During his many years at the helm of *The Original Amateur Hour*, Ted Mack would launch careers just as Major Bowes had. But for every Gladys Knight and Pat Boone that graced the stage, Mack would welcome a man who played the piano with his nose or an old lady who removed her dentures and then slapped her cheeks repeatedly to create music.

Ted Mack's Original Amateur Hour stabilized into a regular Sunday afternoon slot on CBS in 1960. The TV landscape for Sundays would change significantly during the upcoming decade because of the emerging dominance of football. The show was subjected to pre-emptions increasingly frequently. The pre-emptions were a source of irritation for Mack because CBS didn't pay him during the off weeks, yet Mack retained a full staff and needed to pay them. In other words, he lost money every time he was pre-empted for a football game. During a period in 1970, he was pre-empted for four consecutive weeks, and at that point, Mack pulled the plug himself, after 22 years. The gong was silent.

CHAPTER 2

A Closet In Beverly Hills

Above: Chuck Barris, as seen in his high school yearbook.
ROBERT BURROUGHS COLLECTION

Every Sunday in 1957, the streetlamps throughout America illuminated only vacant sidewalks and parked cars. The windows of every house gave off a different glow, from the living room TV. *The Ed Sullivan Show* was on the air. Sullivan, a gossip columnist, became the unlikely star of a weekly variety series in 1948, and somehow, nine years later, he still hosted every broadcast with the deportment of a man who had never seen a TV camera or an audience in his life. He stared, dour and unblinking, shuffling his feet, and grasping for something to say, even with his cue cards near him. He introduced the Three Stooges as "The Three Ritz Brothers" and announced that as a token of the show's appreciation, The Singing Nun's convent would receive "a new Jew" — he meant to say "Jeep."

Sullivan's own absence of talent belied the sharp eye he had for the talent of others. *The Ed Sullivan Show* was perhaps the greatest, purest variety show in the history of television — Ed Sullivan booked acts on the show if they were good at what they did, regardless of what they did. The guest line-up for Sullivan's Sunday night spectaculars in 1957 included the high wire-walking Wallenda family, impressionist Sue Carson, the Crew-Cuts singing "Sh-Boom," the Flying Zacchinis being shot out of cannons, accordionist Dick Contino, a song from Cab *("Hi-de-hi-de-hi-de-ho")* Calloway, unicyclist Lola Dobritch, pianist Roger Williams, comedy magician Carl Ballentine, ventriloquist Professor Backwards, knife throwers Elizabeth and Collins, opera singer Anna Maria Alberghetti, and the dance team of Chaquita & Johnson. The eclectic blend of performances, overseen by a man who had no business standing on a stage, made *The Ed Sullivan Show* the number-two series on television that year. Only the final season of *I Love Lucy* outshone it.

In that same year, Lyn Levy, the daughter of a co-founder of CBS, married a shiftless clothing factory employee named Charles Hirsch Barris. His friends called him Chuck. Chuck, born June 3, 1929, and raised in Philadelphia by a dentist and a homemaker that passed down absolutely no traits that he could think of, never really had any sense of direction about what to do with his life. He drifted through high school, a firm underachiever. For a little pocket money, he sold sodas at the Phillies' home games in Shibe Park, where his most memorable day on the job was the day he injured his finger removing a bottle cap at the same time that pitcher Bubba Church got hit by a line drive. Sitting in the first aid station next to the pitcher, Chuck waited patiently for treatment until the attendant finally noticed his mangled finger and asked, "What do you want?"

Chuck wrote for the student newspaper at Drexler University, but once he was out of college, it was off to the factory, with no other plans popping into his mind.

For the first time in his life, Chuck had a goal once he married Lyn: get out of Philadelphia. There were certainly good respectable careers in Philadelphia, and had he stayed, he might have figured out some route into the good graces of the Levy family, but the urge to get away from the city tugged harder and harder.

Chuck and Lyn Barris headed to New York, a city that appealed to the newlyweds solely because it wasn't Philadelphia. Chuck was keenly aware that his in-laws thought he was beneath the family that he had married into, and living in the 1950s, when radio was overtaken by the small flickering screens of television, he reasoned that he needed to earn the Levy family's respect, and that one line of work above all others would earn it. He applied for the most prestigious of entry-level jobs: a page at NBC's famed 30 Rockefeller Plaza studios. Yes, it was just sorting through the incoming mail and fetching coffee, and seating befuddled tourists row by row into their seats for a live broadcast, but even then, the NBC page program was a famed gateway. The host of NBC's *Today*, Dave Garroway, had been an NBC page. So had Gene Rayburn, the hammy announcer for Steve Allen's prime time variety show.

Chuck conned his way into the job, listing a number of NBC executives as references, and somehow, he got hired without anybody in charge calling his bluff. For the first time in his life, Chuck was motivated. And funnily, he was motivated in the one situation where everyone around him had low expectations. At an office Christmas party, a supervisor admitted that Chuck had been hired solely because of his references, and that they really didn't think he had much to offer beyond friends in high places.

But, the supervisor admitted, "You turned out to be a pretty good hire."[1]

Chuck spent 1958 enrolled in the NBC management training program. That same year, Ann-Margret made her first appearance on television, as a contestant on *Ted Mack's Original Amateur Hour*. She lost to a man who played "Lady of Spain" on a leaf.

Chuck performed so well in the training program that he came out of it fully confident that in a matter of years, he'd be the president of the network. Not only did he believe the job was within his grasp, but as

---

1. Archive of American Television interview with Chuck Barris. 10 Jun. 2010. *https://interviews.televisionacademy.com/interviews/chuck-barris visited May 11, 2019.*

a bonus, it would come with respect. How could the Levy family hate Chuck for following the same career path as his father-in-law?

Given a choice of departments within the network, Chuck took a position in Daytime TV Sales. Having assessed the network's inner workings during the training program, Daytime TV Sales seemed to be the most direct path to the president's office...until the entire department was fired. Shutting down the department, Chuck could understand, even if he didn't agree with it. But he was aghast that they were firing him. After putting so much time and effort into training Chuck, why wouldn't the network reassign him, instead of just cutting him adrift but with a puffed-up resume that made him employable for a competitor? For added insult, the respect Chuck was hoping to earn never would come, and he was dismayed that he couldn't get an interview for a job — any job — at CBS.

That left ABC. The third-place network. The DISTANT third place network. The network whose broadcasting day didn't even begin until 11:30 a.m., four and a half hours after the other guys. But it was a network. And they were willing to interview him.

And they were willing to hire him.

Getting a job at ABC proved comically bittersweet. The network hired him to be a standards and practices representative for one of their few hits, the afternoon dance party *American Bandstand*. The job required a daily ninety-minute train ride to the city where the show emanated live... Philadelphia.

Whatever feelings Chuck had about the assignment were assuaged when he realized how surprisingly low-pressure the job was, thanks mostly to that daily train ride. That was a chunk of ninety minutes where nobody could realistically expect him to do anything, so he'd spend ninety minutes reading on the way to Philadelphia and then take a ninety-minute nap on the way back to New York City, leaving him well-rested to do whatever he wanted during his off-hours.

ABC was serious-minded about Chuck's task, though, even if he felt it was a silly assignment. He was in charge of watching Dick Clark. Payola had been used as a broadly sweeping term to refer to any number of ethically questionable business deals in the radio industry. The most common form had been the practice of making certain songs popular by paying disc jockeys to favor them. Dick Clark, only 30 years old when called to speak to the House Committee on Legislative Oversight, had built an empire from practices that the committee found extremely questionable. Clark, by that point, owned stakes in 33 record companies, all of which had their songs featured on *American Bandstand*. The show's staff was aware of this, but didn't recognize it as ethically questionable. One admitted to thinking that it was a brilliant idea for the boss to use his show that way.

In his own words, Dick Clark explained it this way to the Archive of American Television: "Since I only got $1500 a week to produce seven and a half hours of television for ABC, I went into the music business. I was a manager of artists, a publisher of music, a manufacturer of recordings...horizontally, vertically, every single way you can think of, I made money from that show.

"One day, a man offered me a hundred-dollar bill to play a certain record. It was the only time anyone ever tried to bribe me. People who worked for my record company were commissioned to pay disc jockeys. It was normal. It was legal. We declared it. It was not illegal at that point. It became illegal...It still goes on to this day, except it isn't as blatant. It's much more subtle."[2]

Clark candidly told *Rolling Stone* in 1989, "Protect your ass at all times."[3]

With that in mind, he sold off every investment he had in the music industry, including the royalties he collected for some 150 songs on which he was credited as a co-writer. And then he spoke to Congress, as did legendary disc jockey Alan Freed. Freed looked haggard, behaved brusquely throughout the hearing, and was uncooperative. His career was ruined. Dick Clark, well-rested, sharply dressed, and confident, killed the committee with kindness. The committee chair, Representative Oren Harris, dubbed him "a fine young man" and sent him on his way.

ABC now felt that the network and the show would be targeted, and they wanted somebody to keep a sharp eye on the production. Chuck called the assignment ridiculous because ABC only had him working an eight-hour day. If he left the studio every day at 6 p.m., what was he going to do about whatever meetings Dick Clark might have at 6:15 pm? Chuck also suspected that ABC only wanted him down there for the sake of plausible deniability — being able to tell people that they had somebody down there. Chuck filled out reports each day documenting what he had seen — which was nothing — and delivered them to the network, fully confident that nobody even bothered reading them.

---

2. Archive of American Television interview with Dick Clark. 29 Jul. 1999. *https://interviews.televisionacademy.com/interviews/dick-clark* visited May 11, 2019.

3. Demain, Bill. "Paying the Piper a Little Something Extra. A Short History of Payola." 7 Nov. 2011. *Mental Floss. http://mentalfloss.com/article/29183/paying-piper-little-something-extra-short-history-payola* visited 16 Jun. 2019.

Eddie Kelly was a dancer on *American Bandstand*. "When the Payola scandal first broke, Dick called one of the dancers, Carmen, and told her, 'Don't believe anything about this.' And she spread the word to us that Dick was denying everything. Even before word got out, there were some things about the show that made me wonder. For example, every week, we had the Top Ten. And it wasn't the top ten songs according to *Billboard* or anything else. It was just *American Bandstand*'s Top Ten songs, and you'd think to yourself, 'Says who? Who told you that this song is the #1 song in America?' There was also a certain song that we must have played on every episode of the show for two or three weeks straight, and during the Payola investigation, we found out Dick owned a stake in the company that released the song. So that kind of thing made ABC want to keep an eye on the show. And of all people, they sent Chuck Barris down to keep an eye on it."[4]

But Chuck was surprised at the way the assignment made him feel. For the first time in his life, he was the heavy, the bad guy. He sensed palpable hatred from some on the *Bandstand* staff. A notable exception to that was Dick Clark himself. Chuck Barris may have been there as a watchdog, but Clark quickly realized that Chuck was the greatest source of protection he had. A network employee rubber-stamped a form daily saying that there was nothing wrong with the way he was conducting his business; who could criticize Clark when he had official approval like that? But as worthless as Chuck found the job at its core, he realized the future potential it held.

Eddie Kelly adds, "I remember really liking Chuck. One of the other dancers, Myrna, introduced us, and explained to me why Chuck was there. I just remember him being very pleasant and saying hello to everybody every day. Chuck had a warm, inviting personality. But I also remember he made it a point to keep some space between himself and us. He was there to do a certain job, and he really was very professional about it. He was friendly, but he also kept us at a distance because he felt he needed to."[5]

Inspiration struck unexpectedly for Chuck one night during a drive in New Jersey. Chuck passed the bustling Palisades Park and just took in the sight for a few minutes. Chuck had no musical background or training, nor any inkling that it was anything that he'd ever want to pursue. But for some reason, the sight of that amusement park caused a melody to start swirling in his head. Fragmented phrases assembled themselves

---

4. Personal interview. 28 Nov. 2018.

5. Ibid.

into poetry. Even though it was little more than a lark, Chuck was smart enough not to let the idea go to waste. He scribbled down the lyrics the moment he had the chance. Chuck, who couldn't read a note of music, went to a friend who played the piano and sang the song. The friend transcribed it as sheet music.

Rock & roller Freddie Cannon was in a meeting with his manager, poring through songs for his next album, when the phone rang. Cannon took the call — he had crossed paths with Chuck at *American Bandstand* and remembered the name — and was puzzled when Chuck greeted him by saying, "I got a song I'd like you to hear."[6]

Freddie and his manager liked it. They liked it a lot. They liked it enough to run it by the staff at Swan Records, which was releasing Freddie's next album. They loved the song too; they just didn't care for the title Chuck had given his creation: "Amusement Park." The source of Chuck's inspiration had a catchier name, so they suggested retitling it "Palisades Park." Freddie released it as a single — it spent 15 weeks on the Billboard Hot 100, peaking at #3. "The first creative thing I ever did in my life," as Chuck dubbed it,[7] was a resounding success.

ABC was gobsmacked, not so much that one of their employees showed prowess in another field, but that Chuck had pursued something that created such an obvious conflict of interest. The network had hired him to make sure that no one on *American Bandstand* had a personal stake in any of the songs the show featured. Now he was writing his own song, performed by a *Bandstand* guest, and collecting royalties from it! Even further than that, Chuck was taking the stage with Cannon. They performed the song as a duet during an Independence Day concert at Palisades Park. And despite ABC's objections, Chuck made it known that he bought a guitar and was learning to play it by ear, so he could keep writing songs in his off-hours from the network.

In the fall of 1963, *American Bandstand* switched from the weekday schedule to once a week on Saturday afternoons. Dick Clark, who was now overseeing an *American Bandstand* concert tour, began taping multiple episodes of the now-weekly show in one day to open his schedule, which drastically reduced the need for Chuck Barris to supervise him. Fortunately, an opening came up at ABC at the same time, and Chuck made his move, in more ways than one. Chuck, Lyn and their new daughter, Della, born on Christmas Eve 1962, all moved to California. Chuck

---

6. Archive of American Television Interview with Chuck Barris.
7. Ibid.

had been given a job title as lengthy as the distance between New York and Los Angeles: He was now the American Broadcasting Company's Director of Daytime Television, West Coast Division.

Barris was primarily charged with building the network's daytime schedule and greenlighting new series, and ABC's line-up under his watch was a fairly eclectic blend of entertainment: a daytime variety

Chuck Barris, TV executive. It wouldn't take long for him to conclude that the neatly combed and straightened hair with the suit and tie were a bad look for him. ROBERT BURROUGHS COLLECTION

show called *Hello Peapickers,* a scripted series called *Day in Court* which dramatized actual trials; the news department presented *News with the Women's Touch;* and there were a few soap operas, like *The Young Marrieds* and *A Flame in the Wind.*

Mike Metzger was a videotape clerk at ABC at the time that Chuck was in charge. "Chuck had a reputation at that time for being a maverick. Very anti-establishment. Word got around about how he'd sometimes show up at his office barefoot and just work that way."[8]

As an executive, Chuck found that he had a certain fondness for game shows. He found certain advantages to them that other programs didn't have. Game shows remained absolutely the cheapest form of programming available — and again, since ABC was in last place by quite a few furlongs, Chuck was very aware of show costs. Because game shows didn't have massive casts of high-paid actors with guaranteed contracts, they were easy to cancel, too. When one game show failed, you could just as easily plug in another one.

Although Chuck liked game shows as an executive, as a viewer he couldn't have been less enamored with them. He found them dull and mechanical, and the feeling that he could do a better job nagged at him. There was one on ABC that he disdained, *Camouflage,* in which the contestants viewed hidden-picture puzzles, akin to what you'd find in *Highlights* Magazine, and locate, say, a candy cane embedded in a parade scene. He thought it was the most boring thing he had ever seen.

Fortunately, a change in management at the network would give him a chance to put his faith in his own sensibilities to the test. Edward Bleier, an ABC sales manager, was promoted to Vice President of Daytime Television, and with ABC's perpetual shoestring budget in mind, Bleier had an idea for a cost-cutting measure: drastically cutting back on shows from independent production companies. If the network produced its own shows, it would mean less expense to shell out for other companies and less to pay out in royalties. A federal law prevented ABC from producing every show on their own schedule — that was considered restraint of trade — but Bleier wanted as many ABC shows as possible to be shows that were developed within the network itself.

Chuck stepped forward with an idea for a game show that he named *Poker People.* The premise was that the contestants would face 15 people, some of whom shared common occupations. Some might be lawyers, some might be physicians, some might be grocery baggers. Players would

---

8. Personal interview. 13 May 2019.

choose five people at a time to build poker hands — three doctors and two lawyers would be a full house, for example. Chuck's bosses were intrigued and allowed him to produce a pilot.

"It was a disaster," Chuck remembered later.[9]

There were two big problems with *Poker People*. Viewers liked to play along with game shows, and as the pilot taped, Chuck looked at the studio monitors and realized that was impossible. The players in the studio could study the 15 mystery people from head to toe and examine their faces carefully, looking for any tells about who or what they were. On a TV screen, 15 people's bodies were completely indistinguishable. Maybe you could fix that by shooting each of the fifteen people one at a time for a viewer to really look at them, but that would be so time-consuming that you'd barely have time for the game itself.

The other problem was that Chuck decided to do something just a little daring for one round of the pilot. He hired prostitutes. He thought it would be funny to have a round where the contestants were told that among the 15 people were prostitutes and female police officers. The police officers didn't learn until after taping had started what they were expected to be a part of, and they refused to go onstage. Taping was delayed while Chuck tried to reason with them, but to no avail. They didn't budge. ABC passed on *Poker People*, and even Chuck conceded that it was the right call.

In May 1965, Chuck resigned from ABC to establish his own independent company, Chuck Barris Productions. The first step was setting up an office. Chuck wanted an office in Beverly Hills; not so much for bragging rights but because he had learned a lesson about the importance of image while he was an executive at ABC. A few years earlier, when he was still based in New York, the network had sent him on a business trip in California. ABC, still hampered by the finances that came with being a distant dead last in the ratings, put Chuck in a motel in the middle of Los Angeles. For the first few days of the trip, Chuck made numerous phone calls, leaving a message with every secretary he reached, asking people to call him back, and telling them the name of the motel in Los Angeles where he was staying. The phone never rang. As it happened, Chuck had a little extra money because he had just received his first "Palisades Park" royalties, so he checked out of the motel and spent the remainder of the business trip in the lavish Beverly Hills Hilton. Again, he hit the phones as needed for network business over the next few days. But now, people

---

9. Archive of American Television Interview with Chuck Barris.

were calling back. "I'm staying at the Beverly Hills Hilton" gave him an air of credibility that the motel didn't.

Now, with a business to get off the ground, Chuck felt he needed to be in Beverly Hills. He rented an office in the Beverly Hills Writers and Artists Building for $25 a month. If you're wondering what $25 a month in Beverly Hills could possibly rent, it wasn't much. Chuck named his office "The Closet." But what mattered to him was that all his outgoing mail would read "Chuck Barris, c/o Beverly Hills Writers and Artists Building," and that when he talked to potential new business contacts, he could tell them "I'm at the Beverly Hills Writers and Artists Building."

Barris had enough money to pay the rent on The Closet and keep his family afloat for about six months. He later said of those months, "It was awfully lonely. I read a lot, developed guilt complexes, and napped. After a while I started to get frightened."[10]

Within months, Chuck was back at ABC. Not to grovel for his old job, but to sell them a big idea. Barris would later claim that on the day of his big meeting, he only had $75 left in the bank.

---

10. Inman, Julia. "Barris Struck It Rich in 'Games.'" *The Indianapolis Star.* 17 Sep. 1967.

CHAPTER 3

If It Ain't Fun, Don't Do It

Above: Does this look like a mogul to you? Chuck Barris, sitting in his office in the months after his ideas finally started to sell. AUTHOR'S COLLECTION

It was originally a radio show that attracted an audience by putting real people in front of the microphone. It was called *Blind Date*.

The host was Arlene Francis, a talented stage actress whose dramatic career seemed to take a backseat to a formidable list of credits she would amass in the 1950s and 1960s in unscripted television, as hostess of NBC's *Home* and perennial panelist on CBS's *What's My Line?* Prior to those credits, she hosted *Blind Date* for the NBC Blue Network on radio, earning herself a spot in broadcasting history as the first woman to host a game show, a novelty that led the press to dub her a "femcee."

On *Blind Date*, six servicemen on furlough in New York were brought onstage and given a telephone. They spoke on the phone with each of three lovely young women, as the audience listened in to the servicemen using the best pick-up lines in their arsenals to woo the bevy of models and local actresses that the show recruited. One man, boasting about his athletic prowess, ill-advisedly told a model that he was known for being "a ten-second man" in college. Another guy took a diabolical approach, talking up one of his competitors during the conversation.

"A wonderful guy. He looks like a zombie, but he more than makes it up with his personality," he gushed.

The woman on the other end of the line replied, "Is he a gentleman of the old school?"

"He's old school, yes, but it's summer vacation time."

After all the conversations were finished, each woman picked a guy, who earned himself a modest $5 plus a chaperoned date at the Stork Club in Manhattan. Amazingly, the "ten-second man" was one of the lucky winners.

Blind Date riveted audiences. Everyone who agonized over dialing a phone, with one half of the brain hoping she'd answer and the other half of the brain hoping she wouldn't answer, listened each week to what would have otherwise been private conversations from men who were alternately cocky, outgoing, stammering, weak, inept, bold, and creepy.

We don't know if Chuck Barris ever listened to *Blind Date*. Taking him at his word, he didn't. He maintained that his major achievement of 1965 was stirred by a Dick Clark series. Clark's *American Bandstand* had moved off the weekday schedule on ABC and was now airing once a week on Saturdays. But ABC turned right around and put Clark back on the weekday afternoon schedule with a show titled *Where the Action Is*. There was a heavier emphasis on live performances, as opposed to the records favored by *Bandstand*, but in many ways, it was fundamentally the same show. The pop music blared as teens danced and smiled for the cameras, with Dick Clark supervising the proceedings.

Chuck Barris was taken by the way young viewers flocked to ABC in the afternoon in a way that they just plain didn't for the other networks — mainly because NBC and CBS didn't program anything on their daytime schedules that aggressively courted youth the way ABC did. Chuck wanted to create something for ABC that could be paired with *Where the Action Is* as a one-hour block of teenage programming for the network. While watching *Where the Action Is* one afternoon, Chuck, struck by inspiration from we-don't-know-exactly-what, thought it might be interesting to watch three young guys competing for a date with a woman who couldn't see any of them.

The Dating Game premiered on December 20, 1965, not in the afternoons with *Where the Action Is*, but slotted at 11:30 a.m, following another new game show, *Supermarket Sweep*. Amidst a television landscape still populated by Ozzie & Harriett, Donna Reed, and Lawrence Welk, *The Dating Game* looked like something from another dimension. The set was splashed with far-out flower designs, and a live rock band strummed the theme music while dancing girls gyrated across the set. The band and dancers were phased out early on in favor of recorded music, but even that change came with purpose; pop tunes were used instead of generic elevator music, and announcer Johnny Jacobs could often be heard describing the prizes over the unmistakable sound of a Beatles hit.

The host, San Francisco disc jockey Jim Lange, put his own stamp on the show by introducing the bachelors with a drawn-out "Heeeeeeeeeere they are!" And the college-aged guys were suitably flirty and flummoxed as they tried to win the affections of the stranger on the other side of the wall.

The first problem with the show was that some guys and gals will say anything to get a potential date's attention. And by "anything," we mean that, according to Chuck, the first three episodes taped weren't suitable for broadcast. The second problem was that when contestants behaved themselves, it was dreadful.

Mike Metzger, the former ABC videotape clerk, was searching for a job in late 1965 and acting on a tip, he went to Chuck Barris' office. "At the time I arrived, they had taped two weeks' worth of episodes and none of them had aired yet. My first day on the job was the day that ABC aired the first episode. Chuck gathered everybody to watch the premiere. And we did that the whole week. Everybody dropped what they were doing to watch *The Dating Game* in Chuck's office. I noticed how repetitive the show was. Every woman asked the same questions. 'Bachelor #1, what's your favorite sport?' Every game had that question. And she would ask every question to all three bachelors and there was no variety in the answers. 'Football.'"[1]

In the nascent stage of *The Dating Game*, women were on their own to prepare the lists of questions that they would ask. Every woman was

Jim Lange welcomes America to The Dating Game. AUTHOR'S COLLECTION

preparing nearly the same questions. Metzger stuck his neck out on day five and asked the boss to consider having the women write their questions under the supervision of some of his staffers.

To his surprise, Chuck told him, "You're right, this show is duller than owl shit."[2]

He gave Metzger some homework; come in on Monday with fifty questions that would make the show more entertaining. Metzger, who admits to giving himself some herbal assistance for the writing process, turned in fifty questions on Monday, and in an instant, the new guy

1. Personal interview with Mike Metzger. 13 May 2019.

2. Ibid.

had reinvented the show. Metzger, a self-described "aspiring hippie," was paired with a 19-year-old kindred spirit named Jonathan Debin, and the two of them had their permanent assignment. Every woman booked for *The Dating Game* was asked to prepare a list of her own questions, and then brought in for a one-hour workshop with Metzger and Devin to tinker with them. Generally, the workshop consisted of Metzger and Debin just

Jonathan Debin and Mike Metzger, masters of the Creative Abstraction.
PHOTO COURTESY OF MIKE AND ELLEN METZGER

tearing up the woman's list and giving her totally new material.

The questions were now, as Metzger put it, "creative abstractions." A question like "What piece of sporting equipment is sexiest?" is a weird question, but it gets a viewer's attention, and best of all, it forces the men to show a creative side.

This solution still didn't make the show perfect. Three stage-frightened contestants grasping about for just the right ad-libbed pick-up lines could still be dreary television. Chuck needed some ringers. While most game shows preferred "real people" for their contestants, Chuck encouraged members of AFTRA (American Federation of Television and Radio Actors, a prominent performers' union in Hollywood) to apply to be contestants, on the promise that if they did, he was willing to pay "scale," the minimum fee required of actors for a television performance. Actors and improv theater performers from all over Los Angeles, who never thought of going anywhere near a game show, suddenly lined up to be on *The Dating Game* because, win or lose, they would get the rent paid that month. The actors gave Chuck exactly what he was looking for; they were lightning-quick with ad-libs, they were funny more often than not, and they were far more cautious of what lines couldn't be crossed. When Chuck was truly happy with a contestant's performance on the show, he would even encourage them to appear again on a future episode, using an alias. Given that

And he sings too! Chuck and some of his more musically inclined staffers really did release singles in the late 1960s, under the name The Chuck Barris Syndicate. Their songs included "Too Rich" and "I Know a Child."
AUTHOR'S COLLECTION

the premise of the show was that contestants didn't know each other's identities while the game was in progress, there was nothing excessively unethical about Jim Lange announcing a fake name and a fake hometown for the home viewers, and it kept *The Dating Game* watchable.

So successful was *The Dating Game* that when two veteran TV producers, Roger Muir & Nick Nicholson (formerly of *Howdy Doody*) arrived at ABC with a game show idea, the network bought the idea from them and handed it over to Chuck Barris to let him produce it instead. Muir and Nicholson collected royalties, while Chuck Barris and his motley crew received all the credit for *The Newlywed Game*.

The Newlywed Game pitted four couples, all wed less than two years, against each other to determine which couple knew each other the best.

They tried to match answers to questions that ranged from innocuous — What color is your husband's favorite shirt? — to lascivious; couples struggled to come up with adjectives for each other's body parts, described their lovemaking techniques…excuse me…whoopie techniques ("whoopie" was the only term for sexual intercourse that ABC would allow), and dished on which in-laws they truly couldn't stand. For 30 full

Bob Eubanks asks the questions that titillated America on The Newlywed Game. AUTHOR'S COLLECTION

minutes, couples shared things that were absolutely nobody's business in front of a nationwide audience, all for a grand prize that was usually no more lavish than a refrigerator or a washing machine. It was a spectacle that dismayed Howard Hughes so much that he canceled his plans to purchase ABC after watching a single episode.

It would be wrong to say that Chuck Barris had a Midas touch. He actually missed far more than he hit; Chuck Barris Productions flopped with there-and-gone shows like *The Parent Game*, *How's Your Mother-in-Law?*, and *Dream Girl of '67*. And sometimes Chuck was told no — ABC rejected a game show idea that appalled them, titled *Three of a Kind*. The premise was that a husband, a wife, and the husband's secretary would play the game together and answer *Newlywed Game*-style questions. The object of the game was to determine if it was the wife or the secretary who matched more answers with the husband.

The results of all these efforts could be described without mentioning any ratings data. Chuck conspicuously forked over more rent to the office complex in Beverly Hills to make room for the staff of 82 that he was now overseeing, although he himself stayed modest and remained in The Closet.

It only took a cursory glance around the offices to notice that something was different about Chuck Barris Productions. Barris, who wanted to court a young audience, hired almost exclusively from the age range he was targeting. The average age of a Chuck Barris Productions employee in 1967 was only 24. They drifted through the building in t-shirts, blue jeans, and sandals. A staff photo from that period shows Chuck and his employees crowded around a Volkswagen Beetle with flags bearing the logos of the company's shows. The hairstyles are afros, mop tops, bobs, and beehives. The wardrobes are mini-skirts, love beads, denim vests, fringe, and cowboy boots. Chuck is in a Nehru jacket, leaning against the car and showing off his guitar. This was the staff and the CEO of a multimillion-dollar company.

Vince Longo was hired in 1967 to join the "bandits," Chuck's preferred term for contestant coordinators, the people who found and booked players for game shows. Longo remembers, "I walked in on my first day dressed for business. I was wearing a suit and tie. Everybody laughed at me. Somebody grabbed a pair of scissors, cut up my tie, and said 'We don't do that here. Go home and change.'

"My job was to greet people as they arrived for *The Newlywed Game* auditions. I was to hand them forms for them to fill out. Once they did that, I was to snap a Polaroid picture and attach it to their form. And then I had to check their marriage license and make sure they actually were legally married. All these young married couples are arriving, and in come these two men, and both are slobs. One is tall and has a beard, the other is short and scruffy; his hair wasn't combed. Their clothes were dirty and rumpled. I told them 'I'm sorry, you two are going to have to leave, we're doing business for *The Newlywed Game*.' And both guys just walked away and left without saying anything. I found out later that the short, scruffy guy was Chuck Barris and that the tall, bearded guy was Mike Metzger, one of his producers. Neither of them said a thing to me!'

"When it was time for my lunch break, two staffers, Alan Welch and Steve Friedman, took me to lunch at this really nice restaurant. We were seated in a booth next to a window. Some guy walks by the window and starts making faces while we're talking to each other. Steve Friedman has a big glass of milk in front of him. Without a break in his sentence, he just picks up the glass of milk and heaves all of it right at the window. I thought 'My god, what kind of people am I working with?!'"[3]

Ellen Halpern joined the staff shortly after Vince Longo. She remembers, "I was 18, so I was straight out of high school. I was scared shitless. I wore a yellow suit with a silk shirt for my job interview, and I got off that elevator and everybody I could see was a hippie. I felt so out of place. I walked into Chuck's office, and he motioned for me to have a seat and wait for him because he was finishing up a phone call. He was eating an ice cream sandwich and while he's still on the phone, he holds the ice cream sandwich out and motions toward me. He was offering a bite. Well, I was wearing yellow with white silk, so I said no."[4]

Chuck loved using his unkempt crew to perplex the occasional interlopers who showed up from ABC. Network executives occasionally came in for meetings, wearing the expected gray flannel suits and bryllcremed hair befitting the 1960s American businessman. The elevator doors would open, and the staff would be lined against the walls, all wearing matching *Dating Game* t-shirts and saluting.

The boss amassed a steady collection of oversized hats, including an army helmet with a peace sign painted on it, and walked up and down the halls wearing them just to watch the employees react. As a ritual, any time he had good news to announce, he gathered the staff and had them watch as he poured beer over his own head and gave them the update. Chuck's office looked like the interior of a TGI Friday's crammed into a single tiny room; Stained glass lamps, neon clocks, bells, horseshoes, a

---

3. Personal interview. 7 May 2019.

4. Personal interview. 15 May 2019.

jack-o-lantern, a bullhorn, framed magazine covers, records, signs reading PRIVATE and CLERGY and AMERICAN LEGION, the framed motto "The Eternal Struggle in Art is to Forget Everything but the Essential," photos, inside jokes (a cue card reading "John Wayne can kiss my ass!" for some reason), and musical instruments, including guitars, bongos, a trombone, and a piano.

A promotional photo of the boss promoting his musical endeavors. He built his empire on game shows, but Chuck kept looking to expand. ROBERT BURROUGHS COLLECTION

The definitive decoration in that office was a laminated sign bearing a quote, allegedly from Chuck's grandmother: "IF IT AIN'T FUN, DON'T DO IT." The staff adopted it as their mantra. It guided every idea and every show.

Chuck later explained his television philosophy. "All I hoped was that I could stop a person's fork once or twice in every show. That's the moment when you're eating dinner, you raise your fork to your mouth and something you see or hear on TV halts you mid-mouthful."[5]

Though Barris' company had grown exponentially, staff meetings always truly involved the entire staff. Janitors and switchboard operators were roped in for the discussions, because Barris felt that their opinions were just as valid as the writers' and producers'. He openly detested words like "company" and "corporation," asking the staff to refer to Chuck Barris Productions as "our place."

John Hill says, "I was a Fine Arts major, and I needed a summer job, and a friend worked for Chuck Barris. My first impression of the man was that Chuck was definitely the boss. You could see that Chuck was in charge. But he really seemed to be having a good time. He wasn't heavy-handed. He wasn't mean. And I noticed that his employees liked being around him.

"We all had deadlines to meet and work to do. It was a job, to be clear. But we had water fights in the office. And I'm not talking water pistols. I'm talking full buckets of water. One of my first days on the job, I was sitting at my desk and a guy came over and just dumped a bucket of water on me and my desk and walked away. And nobody seemed to notice! It was just right back to work!"[6]

Mike Metzger remembers, "Chuck ran the company like a summer camp. If you walked in, you would see some employees playing foosball, and some employees lying on the floor and just spacing out to relax. Sometimes, he'd put on a record and play it so everyone could hear it. You could grab an instrument that he had lying around and play along with the music."[7]

Ellen Halpern tells this story: "Chuck had to go to New York for a business meeting with the ABC executives. On the day he came back, we found out what flight he was on and when he was scheduled to land. We all left the office, went to the airport, and greeted him. We made signs

---

5. Gilbey, Ryan. "The Hit Man." *The Guardian.* London, Greater London, England. 3 Mar. 2003.

6. Personal interview. 14 May 2019.

7. Personal interview. 13 May 2019.

and cheered when we saw him come into view. And some people brought along their instruments, so there was music too."[8]

Lynnette Pope, now Lynnette Karnes, says, "Mike Metzger invited me to join the company because I was working at the studio complex where they were taping a pilot. I had heard lots of stories about how Chuck was a wild guy. Before he was a celebrity in the eyes of the public, that was his reputation inside the television business. We had all heard stories about how he rode ATVs throughout the office floors.[9]

"I met Chuck for the first time, and I remember thinking he was really interesting to look at. He wasn't ugly or handsome — just really interesting-looking. When I began working for him, the thing that stood out was not just his quirkiness, but his level of energy. He had a lot of energy. He had trouble sitting still."

Working for Chuck Barris was a daily party. Occasionally, everyone would gather musical instruments for what Chuck called "The Stompers," a ritual in which they'd march around the halls playing songs for a mini-parade. Sometimes Chuck would rent a school bus and take his entire staff to Pink's Hot Dogs on La Brea Avenue for lunch.

Ellen Halpern, who climbed the ladder quickly and became an associate producer for many of Chuck Barris' shows, remembers, "Chuck walked into the middle of the offices one day and just yelled 'Everybody stop what you're doing! Stop it right now!' And we all got off our phones and put our paperwork down to listen, and Chuck announces, 'We're going to the movies!' And we left the office at once and just spent the whole afternoon at the movies. I look back and think 'Wow, this was my job?'"[10]

Chuck could be a taskmaster though. The bandits in charge of *The Dating Game* had to meet a weekly quota; each one had to book 100 people to come in for contestant auditions — people who came in for auditions had to write the name of the bandit who contacted them — and if you didn't meet the quota one week, you were replaced. Fights would break out in the bandits' office whenever the phone rang; people would dive to answer it so they could take credit for the contestant hopeful on the other end of the call, and there would be a tug-of-war for the receiver.

Chuck seemed to be uneasy with that level of authority sometimes. Threatening employees with pay cuts or replacement was such a deviation from the boss who had hallway parades and school bus trips to hot dog

8. Personal interview. 15 May 2019.
9. Personal interview. 3 Oct. 2019.
10. Personal interview. 15 May 2019.

stands that Chuck occasionally needed to channel his frustrations into an alter ego. If the staff saw a memo from "Zachary Grump," it meant the boss was in a particularly bad mood. Proceed with caution. And if he was really angry, the memo was signed "HITLAR."

And yes, Chuck Barris did fire people sometimes. Barris staffers took turns at tapings serving as monitors, keeping an eye on the contestants and looking for any sign of cheating. At the start of a taping day at *The Newlywed Game*, a Barris staffer would tell the contestants, "Do not attempt to cheat. There are ways to cheat on *The Newlywed Game*, and we're going to tell you about them now because we want to make sure you know that we know about them." The staffer would rattle off several possible ways to cheat, and that put everybody on their best behavior before they went onstage to play the game. As the show was in progress, that same staffer, plus a few others, would stand just out of view of the cameras and stare at the contestants.

One staffer, named David, was looking at one married couple's hands during the taping and thought he saw something that looked like passing signals back and forth. He told his co-workers what he had seen and was appalled when they brushed off his concern. He raised his voice and declared quite adamantly that taping needed to be stopped because of the possible cheating that was happening onstage. He was so vocal that it left everyone without a choice. They had to shut down taping. Because he had declared it where contestants could hear him, it gave them their own suspicions of the couple David was watching. The situation was so messy that the episode couldn't be finished; they just had to throw out the entire game and send all of the contestants home.

The problem with the indiscrete accusation is that in television, time is money. Crew members are paid by the hour, the studio space is rented, and ABC needed new episodes. Stopping the entire game in progress and causing it to be shut down meant that all the time leading up to that had been a waste, and studio time and crews would need to be reserved to tape a replacement. David was fired.

Vince Longo says, "What's funny is, I don't think David ever got why what he did was wrong, and I don't think he got the point of the pre-show speech, and the staff monitors staring at the contestants. He didn't get that we were making an idle threat!"[11]

Sometimes an illusion of tight security is just as effective as the real thing. If the staffers gave a speech that sounded intimidating, and if those

---

11. Ibid.

staffers remained where the contestants could see them, the truth was, they didn't have to watch for anything. David didn't get that he was just supposed to be faking it.

Chuck felt wary of being nickled-and-dimed out of his growing fortune. It wasn't so much that he was cheap; far from it. But he worried about being taken advantage of. For example, the bandits at *The Dating Game* had a small first aid station to help them cope with the occasional high-stress day, and for some reason, Chuck was irked by the suggestion that he should pay for their aspirin. He nickel-and-dimed them back by instituting "fees and fines" for employees. There were no set guidelines; if Chuck was upset about something you had done on the job, a memo from Chuck's secretary, Loretta, went out announcing that your next paycheck would be docked as a fine for the infraction. If Chuck was impressed, a memo went out announcing a fee, a bonus for your next check. Every few days, a memo went out listing the fines and fees being doled out.

FINE – *$2.00 — Debbie — For Being Angry That I Took Her Last Piece Of Gum*

FEE – *$5.00 — Joe — For Stealing Ernest Hemingway Sign*

FINE – *$0.50 — Joe — For Forgetting Chuck's Tobacco*

FEE – *$3.00 — Louise — For Pooper Scooping Above And Beyond The Call Of Duty*

FINE – *$6.56 — John — For Taking An Umbrella To Get Gift Wrapped And Brought Back To Be Given As A Birthday Present (It Was Supposed To Be Brought Back In An "Hour Or So") And Was Brought Back Three Months And Eight Rainstorms Later*

For each taping day at *The Newlywed Game,* a table was set up with sandwiches and snacks for contestants. Chuck became aware that staffers were helping themselves and sent word out that he didn't want staff eating the food that had been purchased for contestants.

Vince Longo says, "On taping days, you're there the entire day. I went to the table, and there were these horrible sandwiches laid out. They were cut into fourths — some were tuna, some were peanut butter & jelly, and some were some kind of meat. I grabbed one and stuffed the whole thing in my mouth so I wouldn't be there too long. And of course, I turn around, and there's Chuck. Chuck yells 'That's it for you! Loretta! Fine Vince Longo!' I said, 'Chuck, I was testing the food. One of the contestants said something wasn't right with the tuna sandwiches and I just wanted to make sure they were safe to eat.'"[12]

The next day, a memo went out.

Vince Longo Is Fined $25 For Eating Food From Contestants' Table Yesterday.

An hour later, another memo went out.

Vince Longo To Receive $50 Fee For Risking Personal Safety To Test Food On Contestants' Behalf.

Chuck Barris could appreciate a good line of BS from a quick-thinking staffer and turned his penalty into a reward.

John Hill remembers, "The first time I ever got fined, it was my entire paycheck. Literally hundreds of dollars for some offense that I can't even remember now. But I went into Chuck's office and confronted him about it. 'You can't do this! I have to pay rent!' I threatened to call the labor board and make a stink. Chuck just smiled at me and said, 'It'll all work out.' And it did. I got my bills and my rent paid. I got fined and I got fees over the years, and I always came out ahead by the time my bills were due. And that's why we all loved working there so much. Chuck would complain about your shirt. 'That shirt stinks, don't ever wear that to work again.' And there'd be a fine in the next memo, penalizing you for wearing the shirt. But then Chuck would notice you doing something at your desk the next day that he liked, and you'd get a fee that offset that."[13]

Mike Metzger says, "Chuck ran as tight a ship as he needed to. Now remember how television works. The network commits to a certain number of episodes, and you know when these shows are going to air. You have specific times that you must be in the studio and get the shows made in time so they can air when they're supposed to. Television is just constant deadlines. So yes, in that sense, Chuck ran a tight ship.

"On the other hand, there's the way I remember Chuck. On days when the deadlines were looming and for whatever reason, things just weren't coming together, there'd be a staffer hunched over the phone for a

---

12. Ibid.
13. Personal interview. 14 May 2019.

twelve-hour day trying to make something happen. And in the middle of that, Chuck would just go to that employee, wrap his arms around them, and give them a hug. And there'd be a hundred-dollar bonus for them in their next check. That was Chuck Barris to me."[14]

Vince Longo adds, "At the end of a particularly difficult day, right after I got home, there was a knock at the door, and it was a deliveryman with flowers. And with the flowers was a note from Chuck: HANG IN THERE."[15]

Ellen Halpern, who became Ellen Metzger shortly after a whirlwind office romance that Chuck took pride in, said, "At that age, I learned everything from watching how Chuck ran his business. The hours were unbelievable sometimes, but you never questioned anything. You were a little afraid of Chuck because he was The Man, but he wasn't mean or scary. He just wanted you to do your job, but he demanded that of you in such a fun way."[16]

Among the favorite events of the Barris staff were the regular auctions that the boss had. Chuck Barris would need to clear out the clutter sometimes to make room for the new clutter he was acquiring, so Chuck would auction off the items in his office. Chuck had expensive tastes for his own belongings, but when he was ready to be rid of them, he would sell for next to nothing.

Vince Longo recalls, "I won a foosball table. Not a foosball table like you buy for your house. Chuck had this professionally crafted foosball table like you would see at a pub. It had to have cost him a few thousand dollars. He started the bidding at fifty bucks. I wanted that table. I was sitting in front of Pat, the head of the stagehands. I raised my hand and bid $95, and all this stuff really mattered so little to Chuck that instead of conducting it like a real auction, he would just call it at some point. I bid $95 and Chuck immediately yells 'SOLD!' and I got the hardest smack on the back of my head from Pat. But I won Chuck's foosball table."[17]

Lynnette Karnes says, "I won a program from a performance of *Lovers' Vows*, which is a famous play because it figures prominently in the plot of Jane Austen's novel *Mansfield Park*. The program was dated February 14, 1799. Chuck just had that in his office. One of the actors was named Pope, which was the name on my father's side of the family, and I love

14. Personal interview. 13 May 2019.
15. Personal interview. 7 May 2019.
16. Personal interview. 15 May 2019.
17. Personal interview. 7 May 2019.

Jane Austen's novels, so I wanted it for that. And I still have it, framed on my wall."

Mike Metzger said, "Sometimes he didn't even bother with auctions. His office was always packed with stuff, and all the walls were covered. Very often, if you mentioned you liked something, he'd just give it to you. 'Oh, you like that iguana statue? I'm tired of looking at it. Just take it.'"[18]

The Friday awards at Chuck Barris Productions. His employees cherished them and hung onto them for decades after. COURTESY OF ELLEN AND MIKE METZGER

"We had weekly meetings on Fridays where Chuck would give the state of the company. How the shows were doing in the ratings, what ideas he was developing, what ideas had just been pitched to the networks. And he would always end it with the Employee Awards. He would call attention to the work everyone was doing, and he would really make it a point to single out the lesser employees in the pecking order and announce things that he had noticed them doing. And he'd present them with laminated, handwritten award certificates."[19]

Ellen Metzger adds, "I got the MOST HUGGIEST award. Chuck would come over while I was on the phone and yell 'Hi, Ell!' Then he'd give me a pat on the back and hugged me. Chuck was a hugger. And apparently, I was the best at it. He also gave out ribbons, like you'd give to military

18. Personal interview. 13 May 2019.
19. Ibid.

officers. Ribbons went to staffers who had to go on trips to chaperone dates for *Dating Game* contestants. Back then, you had to be at least 21 to be a chaperone, and since I was only 18 when I started, I never got to travel anywhere, so a lot of the staffers who chaperoned a bunch of the dates gave me their extra ribbons because they felt bad for me."[20]

Vince Longo recalls, "Chuck would follow the awards with a rousing speech where he went through every job that everybody had to do and bragged that they were all the best at it. Chuck generated an extremely high level of morale among his employees. And anybody that was a toxic presence and crossed people was shown the door quickly."[21]

Whenever Chuck showed someone the door, replacing them was easy. His own employees admit that he favored nepotism; most of them were hired because they were a friend or relative of somebody who was already there. But if a stranger made a particular impression on Chuck, they were in for a surprise.

Ellen Metzger recalls, "Chuck was at Baskin-Robbins one day and chatted up the employee who was scooping his ice cream. This kid had no idea who he was talking to, but Chuck just really took a liking to him, and as Chuck's paying for his cone, he says, 'Are you sick of this job yet? Come on over to 1313 Vine Street and work for me. You'll have fun there.'"[22]

In 1966, the state of Chuck Barris Productions was thriving. In October of that year, ABC added a sixth episode of *The Dating Game* to their schedule, in prime time once a week, and in color! The ratings were so strong that Chuck signed a deal with ABC for a prime-time *Newlywed Game* starting the following January. For just a moment, Chuck Barris' staff was exposed to the outside world and realized that there were people out there who didn't like what they did.

Mike Metzger says, "We were proud. ABC put us in prime time against Jackie Gleason on CBS. One episode of Jackie Gleason's show cost $400,000 to produce. A *Dating Game* in 1966 was $5,000. We beat Jackie Gleason. And people were angry. We were really shocked by that. There were critics and even people inside the television business who were angry that Jackie Gleason's big show got beaten by our low-cost game. But we followed Chuck's lead, and Chuck never outwardly reacted to any criticism. We didn't either."[23]

20. Personal interview. 15 May 2019.
21. Personal interview. 7 May 2019.
22. Personal interview. 15 May 2019.
23. Personal interview. 13 May 2019.

More shows came and went in the next few years: *The Family Game, The Parent Game,* and even the meta-titled *The Game Game,* plus *Dream Girl of '67,* a prime-time variety show called *Operation: Entertainment* taped on location at military bases all over the US, and a debacle called *How's Your Mother-in-Law?,* in which mothers-in-law were "defended" by comics telling mother-in-law jokes, with one being voted the winner at the end of the

A "miss" for Chuck Barris Productions. How's Your Mother-in-Law? *starring Wink Martindale. Waiting in the shadows are guest comedians Larry Storch and George Carlin.* AUTHOR'S COLLECTION

show and receiving $100. That show disappeared in 13 weeks. Barris concluded later that the problem with the show was that a mother-in-law is, after all, somebody's mother, and that nobody wanted to laugh at a mother.

Barris told *Life* in 1969, "I once created a show idea called *Greed.* I thought, let's get right down to it, let's don't mince words. The idea was this: We'd have a panel of four people, and we'd present them with a problem. We would bring out a boy and his dog. And we would say, 'How little would you take to take the dog away from the boy and shoot it?' The lowest bid took the job and won the money. Or we'd bring out an arthritic old man on crutches, and say 'Who will kick the crutches away from this gentleman?' It was pretty grotesque; it was black humor, but there is truly a game show there somewhere. People would watch it, I know."[24]

24. Barthel, Joan. "King of TV Gamesmanship." *Life.* 10 Oct. 1969.

Barris' plan to expand the empire into films, after buying the rights to several novels he wanted to adapt, didn't come to fruition. But when Barris got something right, he got it right. The pocketful of successes more than off-set the trash can filled with failures.

Vince Longo remembers, "Chuck was frustrated. The company went through a spell where shows were getting on the air, but they weren't lasting. Stuff was getting canceled. And Chuck asked the staff to come up with ideas. I can't really come up with ideas. I'm not the Duke of Daytime, after all. But I brought in three books about strange events in history, UFOs, and paranormal activity. I gave them to Chuck and said, 'This stuff might make for a good TV show.' A few weeks later, I came back, and Chuck just threw the books at me. I said, 'So you didn't like the books?' Chuck says, 'I liked them, I just can't see my way to turning them into a TV show. It would have to be filmed, and it couldn't be done as a five-day-a-week daytime show.' A few years later, *In Search Of...* goes on the air. Somebody else had the same idea — it wasn't stolen from me; somebody just had the same idea — and got it on the air. But that idea was in Chuck's hands first and he didn't do anything with it."[25]

Doing business with Chuck Barris stymied television executives. You want to be in business with a producer who has some enormous successes to his credit (ABC made $100,000 per week profit from *Dating* and *Newlywed* alone) but his ideas were so perplexing that executives found themselves unwilling to gamble. They begged Barris to develop something "more traditional."

Even when he tried to do "more traditional," it came across as something out of the Chuck Barris factory. On *Treasure Hunt*, a contestant was asked to choose one of 30 boxes. Host Geoff Edwards would open the envelope attached to the box and reveal the money contained inside. A contestant could keep the money or take the prize in the box. A simple, pure, traditional-sounding game show…until you watched it. And you saw the prizes being modeled by the Treasure Hunt Chicken, a klutz in a chicken costume who tripped all over the prizes. Geoff Edwards attempted to reveal the prize, only to be interrupted by Pieface, a stuttering nag covered with pie. Maybe the contestant would get a phone call from somebody demanding something ridiculous before the prize could be revealed. Prince Charming might show up with a tiny shoe, refusing to hand over the prize unless the shoe fit. Barris had taken this traditional game show idea and loaded it with slow-moving comedy sketches that

---

25. Personal interview. 7 May 2019.

forced the contestant to wait, and wait, and wait, for their prize, or maybe wait for the revelation that they didn't win anything at all.

Barris' continued success made critics and even his own peers pull their hair out. In a 1975 *TV Guide* profile, his smiling portrait appears alongside the words "banal, stupid, and mawkish." In the article, Chuck gleefully agreed with every one of those terms applied to his shows and chimed in

Chuck Barris' attempt to be "more traditional," Treasure Hunt *starring Geoff Edwards.* AUTHOR'S COLLECTION

that the word "exploitative" belonged there too. And then he went right on to brag to the interviewer profiling him about his lavish vacations in France and his two Mercedes in the garage. The article laments the "obscene" amount of money Barris was raking in from his shows — estimated at that point to be about $40 million.

While other game show producers frequently defended their craft and fought any perceptions from critics that game shows were harmful to society, those producers were appalled when Barris dubbed himself "the king of slob culture."

Monty Hall fumed, "When you ask two newlyweds, 'What's the first thing you do when you climb into bed?' or 'What's the first part of your body that you wash when you step into the shower?,' then you know the questions are being deliberately framed to embarrass the couple. He's fouling his own nest when he makes statements like ['king of slob culture']. I resented it because I regard a show like *Let's Make a Deal* as perfectly valid light entertainment, no better or worse than a prime-time action show like *Kojak*. And I know judges and doctors and professors who get some laughs out of my shows. Would they be considered members of the slob culture?"[26]

Chuck remained cheerfully dismissive of his own field, saying of daytime television, "It's the bargain basement of the arts. Daytime TV does not make meaningful statements. You begin and end with the banal. I'm not like some of these guys who'll tell you what they're doing is Pulitzer Prize stuff. I know what the elements are."[27]

Chuck Barris couldn't do anything normal, a problem that seeped into his home life. With the security and money that his ABC shows were providing, Chuck had purchased a fancy house with a swimming pool in an upscale neighborhood in Encino. He did it because he knew he was "supposed" to. Successful men with families lived in nice houses.

Every weekend, he dutifully mowed the lawn, assuring his wife that he enjoyed taking care of his home, even though she could see him seething. His wife welcomed the neighbors to come over and use the pool. They stayed all day, playing the music too loudly. Chuck walked back there one day and saw one woman from down the block pulling a towel out of the Barris family's laundry and using it to clean the baby while changing a diaper. Chuck tried dropping a hint to his wife, pointing out that, for a pool as small as the one they had, there were just too many deck chairs surrounding it. Their pool needed fewer chairs — fewer places for visitors to sit. But to no avail, all the deck chairs remained.

Gradually, Chuck would start each Saturday by announcing he had to pick up something at the hardware store. He stayed at the store for hours at a time, waiting patiently until he figured the neighbors had finally left. One day, as Chuck mowed the lawn, another herd of neighbors showed up with their dogs and babies to use the pool for the day. Chuck's wife entertained the guests. As the dogs yapped, the babies cried, and the radio blared, she noticed that she no longer heard the lawnmower. Chuck was gone.

The Barrises separated, and subsequently divorced, with Chuck moving into a cheap apartment on Sunset Boulevard; most of the other tenants were prostitutes. A cheap apartment in a seedy complex didn't suit a television mogul, but it made Chuck happier than "normalcy" ever did.

26. "How Well the Games Play on Television." *Broadcasting* Magazine. 9 Sep. 1974.
27. Whitney, Dwight. "His Shows are Banal, Stupid, and Mawkish." *TV Guide*. 29 Mar. 1975.

Vince Longo remembers, "I had just bought a new car, an Opel GT, which looked like a mini-Corvette. I'm at work and Chuck calls the switchboard to tell us his car died, so he needed a ride from the restaurant he was at. I went up there and I found out that it's not just Chuck, he's on a date. He didn't tell me that. My car was a two-seater.[28]

"We get out to the car and Chuck says 'Vince, you get in the back.' I was still in my 20s and I was crazy enough to do this — I say to Chuck, my boss, 'No, no, I'm the captain of my ship. I'm driving this car. You get in the back.' So, Chuck had to scrunch into the back of this car while I sat up front with this soap opera actress that he was wooing, and Chuck was still trying to look like a bon vivant for her."

Lynnette Kearns says, "Dating was difficult for Chuck. The Chuck Barris Productions staff was, if I had to estimate, probably about 75% women. And after his divorce, yes, he dated women on the staff. Because there's been so much scrutiny in recent years about the relationships that male bosses have with employees, I need to say this — women on the staff came on to Chuck far more than he came on to them. I witnessed it. I saw Chuck walking down the hallway once and a staffer just walked right up and grabbed his crotch. Chuck ended up marrying a woman on the staff, and she definitely came on to him, too. [29]

"As far as why Chuck dated women who worked for him," Kearns continues, "Honestly, it just amounted to this: Chuck was a workaholic. His life revolved around being at the office. He dated his employees because those were the only women he ever saw. How was he going to meet women?

"Chuck invited me to France once. I was so excited, I called my mother immediately to tell her, 'I'm going to France!' A little while later, Chuck comes up to me and says, 'Hey, this trip to France…I just want to make sure you understand that the idea is we're sleeping together during the trip.' And I told him, 'Oh, no, no, I'm not interested.' And Chuck said, 'It's okay, don't worry about it.' And I promise you, he never held it against me. I never feared for my job. I stayed there until 1983, and I quit because I had just given birth to my first son, and I wanted to stay home more. He was completely fine with it if his employees said no to him."

Ironically, at the same time Chuck's marriage was imploding, he was devoting his spare time to penning a love story. He didn't look far for inspiration. He authored a novel about a blue-collar guy who falls in love

---

28. Personal interview. 7 May 2019.

29. Personal interview. 4 Oct. 2019.

with a rebellious heiress. It was titled *You and Me, Babe*, and even a casual reader could deduce that it was an autobiography in disguise.

Chuck rounded up several of his staffers and dubbed them his "plumbers," in honor of the Watergate scandal that was dominating the country's attention. He gave them a list of key bookstores and dispatched them to purchase multiple copies, ask the store to order more when they were out

Chuck Barris, photographed in 1973, right before he had an idea that would end up altering his life. AUTHOR'S COLLECTION

of stock, and ask for gift wrapping on each copy, to make the store's staff spend more time looking at the book and thinking about it.

The respect that eluded him as a television producer wouldn't come forth for his efforts as a novelist, either. Sure, it made the top ten on *The New York Times* Best Seller List, alongside *Watership Down* and *Jaws*, but critics complained that Chuck had cheated by investing $100,000 of his own money into publicity, and word of the plumbers' scheme got out. The press reported that Chuck Barris had purchased about 1,200 copies of his own book to inflate the sales figures. It seemed fated that Chuck wasn't going to make friends in any of his professional pursuits.

The one thing he couldn't seem to do was adhere to what had already been done. When he tried to do something that had been done on television, something that seemed inflexible and impossible to reinvent, he put his own stamp on it. Conventionality didn't satisfy him. When he had the idea that maybe he should do a talent show, it went without saying that it wouldn't look like *Ted Mack's Original Amateur Hour*.

> **THE BEST, THE MOST UNUSUAL, THE MOST UNIQUE ACTS NEEDED FOR "THE GONG SHOW"**
> A NEW NATIONALLY TELEVISED SERIES.
> Such as: Acrobats, jugglers, tap dancers, puppeteers, mimes, stilt-walkers, dog acts, mimics, harmonica acts, washboard and saw players, impressionists, bell ringers, sword swallowers, fireeaters and WHAT HAVE YOU.
> **AMATEURS or PROFESSIONALS**
> CALL CHUCK BARRIS PRODUCTIONS
> **(213) 466-9153**

CHAPTER 4

Look To The Stars

AUTHOR'S COLLECTION

In the early 1970s, game shows on TV had become ubiquitous. During the summer of 1974, the three major broadcast networks had more than 12 hours' worth of game shows. Syndicates like Viacom and Firestone were distributing even more among local stations across the country. Another game show at this point stood a good chance of making as much impact as a single raindrop in the Mississippi River.

Chuck Barris assessed television at that moment and noticed a dearth. Ted Mack had pulled the plug on *The Original Amateur Hour* in 1970. Ed Sullivan's show had been canceled with shockingly little fanfare in 1971 after more than 20 years. Arthur Godfrey and his talent scouts were long gone. Variety shows still existed on television — big, splashy spectaculars filled with guest stars, glamourous hosts, and lavish musical numbers. But a pure variety show, where guests of varying levels of recognition came out and created a goulash from their miscellaneous performances, had disappeared into the ether. Chuck viewed variety shows as a staple of television and felt that the medium was due for another one.

Barris had taken steps into the realm of variety shows in 1974, packaging a revival of a 1950s music series, *Your Hit Parade*. A regular troupe of singers and dancers would stage musical numbers revolving around chart-topping songs of the day. Barris' revival, produced for CBS, was surprisingly not an updated show but rather a throwback. Each episode was dedicated to a specific week in the 1940s and 1950s, with all the songs coming from that week.

Chuck was also surveying the American landscape and felt that nightclub shows were on the wane. Most nightclubs wanted bands or stand-up comics. There didn't seem to be a stage that would invite any other type of act. Chuck thought that new talent needed a forum for exposure.

The Chuck Barris Productions staff prepared for a pilot to show prospective buyers at the networks and syndicates. ABC particularly had expressed interest and made it known that although Chuck Barris had originally conceived the idea for a weekly slot, the network wanted it as a five-day-a-week show. The staff held open auditions for every kind of act. Chuck envisioned this new project as the next great star-making vehicle in TV history. Arthur Godfrey and Ted Mack had launched dozens of careers. Now, so would Chuck Barris.

Or maybe they wouldn't. Chuck and his staff were horrified by the auditions, which proved to be a ceaseless parade of squawking songbirds, clumsy dancers, and mouth-flapping ventriloquists. Dozens, if not hundreds, of prospective performers had shown up for the auditions, and Chuck Barris Productions would be hard-pressed to come up with a list of five who had any discernable talent. A weekly show would be hard enough, and the five-day-a-week series that ABC asked for was impossible. Chuck called off the pilot, and his staff moved on to other projects.

A few weeks later, Chuck went to a hockey game with a friend, Chris Bearde. Bearde was a British-born comedy writer whose talents had taken him all over the world. He had hosted a popular children's show in Australia before moving to Canada to write for the comedy series *Network*. He created two series for Canadian TV before heading south and making a name for himself in American TV as a writer for *Rowan and Martin's Laugh-In* and the creator of *The Sonny and Cher Comedy Hour*.

Bearde asked Chuck what he was up to these days, and Barris brought up the attempted talent show that he had buried after the disastrous auditions. Bearde suggested that Chuck re-visit the idea. If the auditions were wave after wave of terrible performers, with only an occasional decent one showing up to provide a respite, then that should be the direction for the show: one terrible act after another, and occasionally, a good one would appear, as if by accident.

Bearde took it further. He brought up the old tradition of bringing out the hook for a bad act on amateur nights long ago, and the gong of the golden age of radio. The gong, Bearde suggested, was an effective way to keep the show moving and to dispense with the bad acts.

Albert Fisher of *Ted Mack's Original Amateur Hour* explains, "The concept of the gong is something we couldn't legally protect. A lot of local radio stations began doing their own talent shows after Major Bowes became popular, and all of them used some form of noise or another instead of the gong. There was one show in the Midwest that used a cowbell. A show in the south used an old-fashioned *aa-oooga* car horn. Again, our idea had been drawn from the old hook. It was the same idea, creating a disruption to end the act. Banging a gong wasn't anything so unique that we could make a claim for it. We never even attempted to take legal action when Chuck Barris began developing this because there wasn't really a case for us to make."[1]

One man felt he did have a case to make and filed a $450,000 against Chuck Barris. Copley News Service reported that the man was claiming that the show borrowed elements from two different ideas he had

---

1. Personal interview. 28 Nov. 2018.

proposed for shows of his own. The limited press that the lawsuit got seems to indicate that it was swiftly thrown out before it ever came to trial, for presumably the reason outlined by Albert Fisher. "Interrupting an act that performs poorly" is a difficult concept for anyone to claim as their own.

Bearde helped flesh out the idea so well that Chuck pulled him into his empire and created a second company, Chuck Barris-Chris Bearde

The other founding father of The Gong Show, *Chris Bearde.* AUTHOR'S COLLECTION

Productions, for the new enterprise. Chuck Barris' fondness for extremely literal titles, combined with what would obviously be the show's "hook" (no pun intended...maybe) led the two CBs to dub their joint venture *The Gong Show*. The concept got a lukewarm reception from the networks. The co-creators sensed dislike from across the negotiating table, but the good news was, both of them were hot properties. Chris Bearde had a solid line-up of variety shows on his resume — *The Hudson Brothers Razzle Dazzle Show*, *The Ken Berry Wow Show*, *The Andy Williams Show* — and Chuck Barris was Chuck Barris. If it had been any other two producers pitching this series, it might never have made it past a pitch meeting, but at the very least, the proposal got the major networks' attention.

With their revamped vision for the show, Chuck Barris and Chris Bearde held open auditions. Broadening the show's scope of acceptable acts was a good move, but it also turned auditions into an exhausting process. Droves of all make and model of aspiring performers turned up at the NBC offices that the men were occupying in the developmental stages.

One of the aspiring contestants was an Oklahoman by the name of

Mountain John Hilligoss, circa 1975. PHOTO PROVIDED BY MOUNTAIN JOHN HILLIGOSS

Mountain John Hilligoss. He remembers, "I had moved from Oklahoma to Los Angeles to pursue a music career. I didn't have my own apartment, so I was living in a garage that I was renting from a woman named Mary while I looked for one. To stay alive, I sang on street corners for tips. I found a manager to represent me, but even with management behind you it can be tough to become a singer. Someone once warned me that the Top 40 only has room for 40 singers. There's truth to that.[2]

"My manager was in his executive bathroom one morning with a copy of an LA theatrical magazine. Chuck Barris and Chris Bearde had taken out an ad listing the types of acts that they wanted for the show and one of them was 'authentic cowboy singers.' The manager called me

2. Personal interview. 14 Apr. 2019.

immediately and said 'You need to borrow Mary's truck and get down to NBC Studios for an audition. Bring your guitar and your best-looking cowboy hat.' I got there at 8:30 a.m. It was 5:00 p.m. when I finally auditioned. There was a line of what seemed like 500 cowboys ahead of me. There was a Japanese cowboy in that line. Everybody had come to audition for this new show.

"Finally, at 5:00 p.m. I get called in. I remember there were three people sitting there. Chuck Barris, Chris Bearde, and a fellow who looked like Dr. Zorba from *Ben Casey*. I found out he was going to be the bandleader for the show. I told them I was a country singer from Oklahoma, but that I had studied opera for five years, so I could sing in Italian and French, too. They looked like they were going to faint when I said that.

"I sang 'Cowboy Lullaby' in my big operatic voice with my Oklahoma accent. They asked me if I could sing something up-tempo. So, I did 'Okie from Muskogee' by Merle Haggard, then I sang 16 bars of an Italian aria, then I sang 'Up Against the Wall You Redneck Mothers' and I yodeled at the end of it. When I finished, Chuck Barris yelled, 'WHERE HAVE YOU BEEN ALL DAY?' I said, 'At the end of the line!'"

Despite his history with ABC, Chuck's account was he pitched the show to NBC first because at the time, he felt NBC had the most "need" for the show; a few of their daytime slots needed sprucing up and he was offering something new and different. He met with NBC Vice President of Daytime Programming Lin Bolen and laid out his idea.

"What have you got for me?" she asked.[3]

"A reverse talent show. Instead of a lot of good acts and a few bad ones, we have a lot of bad ones and a few good ones."

"Why?"

"Because when we went out looking for good acts, we only found bad ones." This pitch probably sounded better in Chuck's head than it did when he finally laid it out. To Lin Bolen, it sounded like a ghastly concept.

"So now, correct me if I'm wrong," she replied, trying to maintain her bearings. "So now you want to do a daily half-hour daytime television show that showcases a lot of bad acts?"

"Right."

"I don't believe you."

"That's not all," Chuck assured her. "We'll have…celebrities on the show who have the right to get rid of the act any time they want to."

"How?"

---

3. Barris, Chuck. *The Game Show King: A Confession*. Carroll and Graf Publishers. New York. 1993.

"By hitting a huge gong!"

"Wait! Don't tell me! Let me guess. *The Gong Game*, right?" It was an astute guess by Bolen. As unconventional as his ideas were, Chuck was, looking back, stunningly unimaginative with the names he gave them.

"Close," Chuck told her. "*The Gong Show.*"

Bolen wasn't dismissive of the idea, but she wasn't a believer quite yet. "Before I put a penny into this hare-brained idea of yours, I want to see a live run-through." (The term run-through can be used a few different ways in television, but in this case, Bolen was asking for a low-budget "episode" of the show, done with minimal staging, solely for an audience of network brass.)

Chuck assembled a run-through consisting of some of the more eccentric acts his staff had seen during their original auditions, including a one-man band, a dog act, and a trained baboon. Chuck assembled them all, explained how the show would work, and was in the middle of giving them some detailed instructions when Bolen and some other executives walked in unexpectedly early. They took their seats and carried on a conversation. Chuck ignored it for a bit, but the conversation got louder. He had to repeat himself for some of the contestants and struggled to concentrate on his own sentences. Barris calmly walked over to Bolen and the executives and asked them to keep the chatter at a low volume until he had finished working with his contestants.

Chuck resumed the rehearsal, but seconds later, he was shocked to see Lin Bolen out of her seat and standing right next to him.

As he recounted, she warned him, "Don't you ever fucking give me instructions again. Especially on an NBC stage and especially in front of my producers. Do you fucking hear what I just said?"[4]

Chuck gave back as good as he got. "I'll give you fucking instructions any time you and your goddamn producers make it impossible for me to do my job."

"You do and you'll never fucking work on the NBC lot again as long as I'm around."

Chuck's patience was gone. "Up yours, Lin."

In a matter of moments, Bolen and her producers were gone, and so were the NBC crew members operating the cameras. Chuck's employees, sensing that NBC had just been crossed off the list, walked out too. Barris dismissed his run-through contestants. The live baboon bit his owner on the neck.

---

4. Ibid.

Chuck got a warmer reception at ABC, primarily because the network's owned-and-operated stations (O&Os, local affiliates that the network itself directly controlled) were looking for new ideas for prime access shows: shows that would air on a weeknight at 7:00 pm or 7:30 pm Eastern time, the hour of prime time television which local stations had to program themselves. Per an FCC regulation, the networks couldn't air national programming during that hour.

ABC put up $150,000 to tape a pilot. The network, hampered by limited finances, told the producers that to minimize costs, the pilot had to be taped outside of Los Angeles, in cheaper studio facilities. Barris & Bearde shot their pilot in the lower-rent studios of KGO, the ABC affiliate in San Francisco.

Barris agreed to the terms, though he wasn't completely happy about having to travel to San Francisco for a few days. Barris had immersed himself in writing another novel, a curious draft called *The Game Show Man* about a producer so desperate for a hit show that he creates a game show in which some contestants will die. Shooting the pilot would pull him away from his typewriter for a few days.

Chris Bearde opened his rolodex and called three former *Laugh-In* cast members — Richard Dawson, Jo Anne Worley, and Arte Johnson — to come to the Bay Area and serve as judges. *Maude* co-star Adrienne Barbeau came along as well. Bearde told all four of the judges that he couldn't pay them, but he'd cover their round-trip plane tickets from LA to San Francisco, he'd rent limos for all of them, and he promised to treat them to dinner at the best Chinese restaurant in the city after the taping.

Bandleader Milton DeLugg (that fellow who looked like Dr. Zorba), who had been in charge of the music for the short-lived *Your Hit Parade* reboot, was charged with leading the band. Live music suited a talent show better than pre-recorded music, after all. DeLugg's resume went all the way to the beginning of television. In 1950, he had been the bandleader for the first late night TV show, NBC's *Broadway Open House*, where, in addition to supplying the music, the hammy, rubber-smiled DeLugg performed in comedy sketches. He had a brief stint as Johnny Carson's bandleader on *The Tonight Show* before being replaced by Doc Severinsen. And he had composed the theme song for one of the strangest science fiction movies of the 1960s, *Santa Claus Conquers the Martians*. His career path had been so eccentric that it seemed that all roads were leading to *The Gong Show*.

For a host, Bearde suggested another *Laugh-In* cohort, Gary Owens. Owens had been a popular disc jockey at KMPC in Los Angeles, but his voice and face became famous to the nation as the on-camera announcer for the raucous sketch comedy show. Owens would stand stiff-spined with a hand cupped to his ear for his bombastic delivery of the show's absurd introduction.

"From the back room of Benny's Beanery and Firework Factory in downtown Burbank! In defiance of thousands of requests, NBC once again presents *Rowan & Martin's Laugh-In*! Starring the former Dan Rowan and the recently-titled Dame Richard Martin! Tonight's surprise guest will not be announced until later, but he looks a lot like the actor,

Los Angeles disc jockey Gary Owens, whose off-the-wall sense of humor and deadpan delivery seemed to make him a dream host for the new talent show.
AUTHOR'S COLLECTION

singer, dancer, and almost unpronounceable Englebert Humperdink! Plus, THESE delightful doo-doos!"

Chuck Barris and Chris Bearde thought that their anti-talent show would be funnier if the acts were introduced by somebody who could come off a bit pompous and distant. With that magnificent voice, and a penchant for delivering the most absurd dialogue without a trace of humor, Gary Owens seemed to be the man for the job.

For Owens and Worley both, the concept of this new talent show sounded vaguely familiar. Worley had done a "bad puppet show" as part of her act. Her lips moved and she spat water everywhere as she bungled her attempted ventriloquism. The routine led to a recurring feature on *Laugh-In* called "New Talent Time," in which cast members and guest stars performed acts similar to the more askew segments of *The Ed Sullivan Show* or *Ted Mack's Original Amateur Hour*. Arte Johnson and Tim Conway played a pair of electricians from the Midwest who banged on their helmets with hammers, inexplicably producing the sound of handbells and playing a medley of Christmas carols. In the nascent stages of production, Owens and Worley both thought that this new creation of Barris & Bearde sounded a bit like "New Talent Time."

Worley says, "I remember the first time I met Chuck Barris. I came into his office, which was like a playpen, and we chatted for a while. I remember looking up at the acoustic ceiling tile in his office and there were dozens of pencils sticking out of it. And Chuck was an easy laugher, I remember that. It didn't take much to amuse him.[5]

"Once we got to San Francisco, the staff briefed us on our role as judges. There was a particular sentence that stands out to me. They said, 'Do not hesitate to gong.' They also made it clear what they wanted this show to be and what they didn't want it to be. We were there to entertain, not to help people with their careers, which is what reality shows today try to do. Chris and Chuck didn't want to turn people into stars. They told us just to have fun and be silly, and don't offer any kind of advice to the contestants."

Chris Bearde noticed fear setting in before the taping started. Richard Dawson told him, "I can't gong anybody! I'm a professional! I just can't gong these amateurs!"[6]

The contestants were all plucked from the auditions held at the NBC studios in Los Angeles; Chuck arranged for a flight and hotel accommodations. One of the lucky ones chosen was Mountain John Hilligoss,

---

5. Personal interview. 10 Jan. 2019.
6. "The Gong Show." *E! True Hollywood Story*. Final edit 19 Dec. 2002. Aired 2003.

who was told that his hotel and airfare were covered, and that he'd be paid $380 for his performance at the pilot taping.

Mountain John says, "The plane ride from Los Angeles to San Francisco was the funniest thing. They booked all the acts for one flight, so we all knew why we were on that plane. All of us did our acts for each other. By this point, we had learned that instead of making it a search for new stars, like we had heard at first, it was going to be done for laughs. We figured out our roles in the show from that. We knew some of us were being set up to fail. They found a comedian who didn't speak English. His whole shtick was going to be that he only told jokes in Vietnamese, so we realized, 'Okay, he's here to get gonged.'

"There was one guy there who had a marionette puppet. It was a curvy woman, and he made her strip. She started in an evening gown, and he moved the strings around and made her remove that, and she gets down to this teddy, and then down to a g-string, and he made the pasties on her tits twirl. I thought, 'There ain't no way I'm going to win! This guy's puppet is the greatest thing I've ever seen in my life!'"[7]

The marionette artist was Fred Spencer. "I was recruited through AFTRA. Chuck Barris had put out a call to agents all over Los Angeles who represented AFTRA talent for this pilot that he was putting together. The way he described it when he called my agent was 'We're looking for variety acts.' I had been doing puppetry for a long time. I joined Sid and Marty Kroft in 1964 and I had worked with them at *H.R. Pufnstuf* and *Lidsville*. I had just started working independently, and my agent knew about this puppet that I had. She was an exotic dancer puppet, and I could make her gyrate. She said, 'You should do that for the audition.' I took the puppet to the audition, but at the time, the puppet was nude. All she had was pasties and tassels and that was it.[8]

"Three weeks pass, and they suddenly called and said they would pay me to fly to San Francisco and tape this pilot. They asked me to change the act, though. Instead of nude dancing, they wanted her to do a striptease, because just the nude dancing was way too short, and they wanted the acts to take about 90 seconds each. I had a costume made, and I worked up the act and practiced making her strip. Milton DeLugg's band played 'Satin Doll' for her, which worked very nicely."

Mountain John Hilligoss picks up the story. "Chuck Barris booked all of us in the Fairmont Hotel, an enormous place. If you remember in the

---

7. Personal interview. 14 Apr. 2019.

8. Personal interview. 17 Apr. 2019.

1980s, James Brolin starred in a TV show called *Hotel*. The Fairmont was the hotel they used for that show. It had just been rebuilt by the Marriott company and it was gorgeous. And it was only three blocks away from the TV studio where we were going to tape the show.⁹

"We go to the make-up room. At this point, the studio is already packed. They had a live audience, and we could hear them out there, getting coached to cheer us, and boo us, and holler. And there were six make-up chairs with all the acts crammed into the room getting made up at once. I'm in the make-up chair, getting my face dusted. And a guy walks in with a legal document and says, 'I need you to sign this.'

Fred Spencer and his friend Trixie.
PHOTO COURTESY OF FRED SPENCER

"I was only 23 years old, but my mother taught me about this well. This was a three-page document, I said 'I'm gonna read it first.' Guy tried to tell me I didn't have to read it, and he got really frustrated because I insisted on it. It's three pages long, but the gist of it was they were paying me so much money for union wages. It mentioned AFTRA wages…well, I'm not a member of AFTRA…and then it mentions Equity, the theatrical actors' guild. The gist of the document is, if I signed all three pages, they'd take the membership fees out of my money for tonight. I was a street singer living in a garage. I said, 'I'm not signing this!' I didn't know what I was doing.

"The guy leaves the room and comes back with Chuck Barris. Chuck asked me what was wrong. I told him 'I'm broke, I'm living in a garage. I came here tonight because I need the $380 to find an apartment.' Chuck said, 'I understand…if I paid your fees to get in all of the unions, will you do the show tonight?' Well, who wouldn't trust Chuck Barris? I said

9. Personal interview. 14 Apr. 2019.

yes. He must have done it because I got my union memberships for all those groups, and I never got billed. I never owed them anything. Chuck did that for me!"

The pilot taped that evening in 1975 might have felt in some ways like *The Gong Show*, but the look and the presentation were mighty different. The show opened with a crude animation of a caveman struggling to drag a heavy rock into place, setting up some rods, and hanging the rock to build, apparently, the first gong. A sweeping shot of the camera revealed audience members holding up signs as if they were there for a political convention or *Let's Make a Deal*. Gary Owens oddly betrayed the stuffy, aloof veneer he was supposed to present by running onto stage and performing a high-stepping dance to thunderous applause. The judges sat in front of an array of brightly colored tubes adorned with ribbons and stars. Gary Owens stood center stage, the proscenium likewise painted with solid colors and festooned with chunks of material. The design gave off the feel of an ambitious high school fundraiser.

Gary Owens laid out the rules for the show to the "home audience" — the executives who'd be watching this show in their offices. Ten acts would be featured on each episode; the ones who survived their entire performance without being gonged would be rated on a scale of one to ten by each of the four judges. He also revealed that Chuck Barris & Chris Bearde were anticipating a lofty budget for this show.

"Welcome to *The Gong Show*, everybody's chance to make it big in show business! As you know, we have a great selection of talented newcomers backstage…and this may be their one and only chance at the big time. The winner gets a $5,000 check, and everybody [else] gets a $1,000 consolation prize. "

With the formal explanation of the rules out of the way, it was time to bring on the performers. Let history record that the first *Gong Show* act ever was an Elvis impersonator, naturally. Little El sang "See See Rider." Bob Bonnie, with bells attached to his head and ankles, played a song by shaking parts of his body. A singer named Terri Hyman missed her first note so badly that Arte Johnson picked up his mallet in seconds, making Hyman the show's first Gongee. Nina and Robbie Wolcott, a pair of pre-teen dancers, wowed the judges and the audience. A balloon artist annoyed Richard Dawson so much that Dawson gonged him twice and told him he gave birthday parties a bad name. Nyna Shannon silenced the audience with a haunting rendition of "On a Clear Day"; Fred Spencer's friend Trixie jiggled her wooden implants; and Mountain John strummed the guitar and sang "Okee from Muskogee."

Technical problems hampered the show somewhat; an adjustment was made to the lights halfway through the pilot, and for some reason, the audio quality suffered for the rest of the night. Everyone pressed on despite the setback because they were working on a rather tight deadline. KGO had given the orders that the studio had to be cleared out by 11 p.m. so they could use it for the late newscast. Everyone got through it, and Chuck Barris and Chris Bearde, buoyed by the sight of audience members literally falling on the floor laughing at one point in the show, were utterly certain they had a hit on their hands.

Mountain John Hilligoss was the winner of the pilot episode. The set was struck, the late local news got on the air on time, and everybody walked out of the studio into the streets of San Francisco... in the middle of a snowstorm. San Francisco experienced snow for the first time in decades, on the night that *The Gong Show* pilot was taped, a possible omen for the rare, once-in-a-lifetime storm that Barris and Bearde were ready to unleash on television. Everyone stuffed their faces at the Chinese restaurant afterward, utterly certain of their hit show.

Although Barris and Bearde were originally approached about doing the show for prime access, they discussed pitching it to the networks with a five-day-a-week daytime version. Their logic was that the daytime show could use the same set, same facilities, and same staff, all costs that the nighttime version would absorb. A daytime version would cost a fraction of any other new show the networks might pick up, and the network, Barris, and Bearde could rake in a lot of extra money that way.

ABC, which had already heard about the show anyway since it was their O&O stations that asked for it, was the first network to hear a pitch for daytime *Gong*. Barris & Bearde proudly sat in the ABC executive offices as the network brass sat down and watched the pilot. There was no anticipating the reaction it got.

An ABC executive stood up, pulled the videotape out of the machine, turned to Barris & Bearde, and said, "You guys ought to be ashamed of yourselves."[10]

---

10. *E! True Hollywood Story.*

Michael Brockman, at the time the head of daytime and children's programming for ABC, didn't abhor what he saw as intensely as his colleagues. But ultimately, he decided to pass on it.

Brockman explains, "I reported to Ed Vane, who had run daytime himself at one time. He asked me what I thought of the pilot, and I told him I thought it was funny, but that it didn't feel like a daytime show."[11]

Barris and Bearde were shaken, but undaunted. Chris Bearde even went north to the Canadian Broadcasting Corporation in search of a sale. No luck. But in a twist of fate that Chuck had been quietly anticipating, Lin Bolen was fired from her post at NBC and replaced by her more agreeable assistant, Madeline David.

Madeline David had loved the *Gong Show* concept from the moment she heard it. She had wanted to shake up the predictable blocks of talk shows, soap operas, and game shows that populated network daytime TV schedules. She had been given a greenlight for the summer of 1976 for *The Fun Factory*, a game show that incorporated sketch comedy and songs. Hearing that Chuck Barris and Chris Bearde were pitching a talent show for daytime television caught her attention. She watched the pilot and saw something that ABC didn't — she saw a worthy show.

"This is really interesting," David told the producers. "I think it has possibilities. Can I keep it for a few weeks? I'd like to do some testing on it and give it some further thought."[12]

David made a holding deal, paying Barris and Bearde a "good faith fee" in exchange for a promise that they wouldn't pitch the show elsewhere while NBC was considering whether or not to buy it. NBC then ran the pilot tape through the usual procedure for a show being considered for the networks. Focus groups of potential viewers were assembled, shown the pilot, and asked what they thought.

David claimed, "[*The Gong Show*] got probably the worst results of any show we have ever tested in daytime."[13]

That should have been a death blow, but for some reason, Madeline David wanted to ignore the overwhelming evidence in front of her and put the show on the air anyway. Network president Bob Howard stood by her. The show was just so odd that he wanted to give it a shot, too.

---

11. Personal interview. 19 Jun. 2019.

12. Carruthers, Michael. "Producing the Network/Syndicated Gong Show." *Broadcast Programming and Production.* July 1977.

13. Ibid.

Michael Brockman of ABC says, "It didn't surprise me that NBC bought the show after we passed on it. NBC was having a lot of trouble in daytime at that point, and frankly, they just needed shows."[14]

The Gong Show was getting a chance to step on NBC's stage. They just had to see if the panel of 250 million judges would pick up their mallets.

14. Personal interview. 19 Jun. 2019.

CHAPTER 5

Up To Chuck

Above: The man who would be host. ROBERT BURROUGHS COLLECTION

Despite ABC's own reservations, four of the network's owned and operated stations had signed up for the nighttime show that would premiere in the fall of 1976. By summertime, 81 other stations joined them.

Chris Bearde said, "If there wasn't a place for such a show in television, it wouldn't be on, now would it? The people who bought it — a network and station managers all over the country — are people who have their finger on the pulse of the public. Are all those people crazy? You can't force anything down the public's throat."[1]

Chuck Barris dried the celebratory beer from his hair and got to work fulfilling some requests from the network. NBC did want some changes before the show went on the air. E. Jay Krause was hired to design a better set, with Krause giving it the earthy arrangement of orange, red, gold, and white that eternally locked the show in the 1970s. In an inspired touch, he designed multiple backdrops for the stage that could be swung in and out and a second's notice, so the show could change atmosphere a little bit from act to act.

NBC requested one more change. They wanted Gary Owens to be replaced. Chuck Barris wasn't going to fire him completely; they had already sold the nighttime show to stations with Owens billed as host. But David saw the pilot tape and thought that Owens wasn't quite right.

She explained, "I felt the host should not be somebody who was basically a comedian going for a laugh, but someone who was going to be sympathetic to the contestants. Someone who wouldn't take it all too seriously but could just go with what happened."[2]

Barris and Bearde thought they had their man for the daytime show. John Barbour had made his name with a comedy album called *It's Tough to be White*...before becoming "critic-at-large" for KNBC in Los Angeles. His biting critiques had netted him three local Emmy awards, with more Emmys on his shelf for specials titled *The 19-Inch Variety Show* and *John Barbour's First Annual Telethon to Save New York*. His criticisms were fearless and humorful. He was exactly what Barris wanted.

NBC did their part, promoting their new series with press releases that, in hindsight, are charmingly bland. Madeline David, vice president of the network, was quoted in one, saying, "With this series, we are bringing back a once very successful television form — the talent show — but in a zany contemporary format. Amateur performers will get their chance to be seen by millions and perhaps make it big in show business.

1. Shull, Richard K. "The Offbeat Amateur Hour." *The Indianapolis News.* 6 Jul. 1976.
2. Carruthers. July 1977.

"Each contestant performs for a panel of celebrity judges and a studio audience and is rated on a scale from one to 10. If a judge decides the talent is below certain acceptable standards during the performance, the act gets the gong and is rejected. You can expect a lot of humor in this show."

Gosh, it sure sounds like a hoot already, doesn't it?

TV critics, who seemed to delight in targeting game shows or anything that smelled like them, sharpened their swords early. Columnist Gary Deeb, without having viewed a single episode, wrote, "Chuck Barris, the game show producer who exploits psychological morons, is readying an amateur hour series called *The Gong Show*. The idea, natch, is to get stagestruck folks to make fools of themselves. Sounds like a real scream."[3]

Noel Holston chimed in, "[Chuck Barris] is to bad taste what Sir Laurence Olivier is to acting."

Perfect hosts, perfect music, celebrity judges booked, talent ready for their moment in the spotlight, set built. Nothing left but to tape the show. Some shows hit the ground running. *The Gong Show* tripped on its own shoelaces and collapsed on the concrete.

As Chuck Barris recounted in his memoir *The Game Show King*, the first sign of trouble came during a rehearsal for the new show. To preface Chuck's account of what went wrong, it should be noted that John Barbour himself seemed to dispute it entirely when interviewed about the experience in late 1976 — as he recalled, the show began taping without a run-through at all.

Barris' account was that he had explained that *The Gong Show* was supposed to be slapstick in atmosphere, tongue firmly planted in cheek regarding the actual "talent" presented. Jaye P. Morgan, a witty singer who had been pressed into service to serve as a celebrity guest for the rehearsal, struck the gong to terminate a butchering of the song "Friendship," performed with an orangutan hidden underneath the songstress' overcoat.

John Barbour asked, "Why did you do that, Jaye? Why did you gong Mrs. Klebenoff?"[4]

Jaye fired back, "Because Mrs. Klebenoff showed her little monkey once too often!"

John Barbour indignantly replied, "What kind of reason is that, Jaye? You should be ashamed of yourself for being so flip with somebody's career!"

3. Deeb, Gary. "Will Beat Go on for Sonny and Cher?" *Chicago Tribune*. 14 Jan. 1976

4. Barris. *The Game Show King*. 1993.

Chuck was flabbergasted. He confronted Barbour after the rehearsal and asked him, "Instead of Jaye saying that the woman exposed her monkey once too often, would you rather Jaye had said she gonged Mrs. Klebenoff because she was the worst singer Jaye had ever heard in her life?"

The first five episodes of *The Gong Show* with John Barbour were taped on June 3, 1976. On the panel were Jack Cassidy, Jo Anne Worley, and Jamie Farr.

The man who was host...for the moment: John Barbour. AUTHOR'S COLLECTION

Jamie Farr says, "The first I had heard of the show was at NATPE, the annual convention where packagers sell syndicated shows to local stations. *M*A*S*H* was a hit and they sent members of the cast to NATPE to help sell the reruns. There was a lot of buzz about this pilot that had been screened called *The Gong Show* hosted by Gary Owens. Now I didn't see the pilot, but when I was a kid, I was a big fan of Major Bowes, so as soon

Judges Jack Cassidy, JoAnne Worley, and Jamie Farr at the historic first taping of The Gong Show *for NBC. The episodes never aired on the network.* PHOTO COURTESY OF JAMIE FARR

as I heard the title *The Gong Show*, I knew instantly what the show must be. I had just started doing game shows as a guest in 1975 — my first was *The Magnificent Marble Machine*, and the producer, Merrill Heatter, was so impressed with me that he said, 'I'm going to start booking you on all my shows!' And I had loved game shows since I was a kid, so that made me feel good, and I began doing a lot of game shows. The schedule for *M*A*S*H* was strictly Monday through Friday, and most game shows taped on weekends, so I was usually available. Once I heard about *The Gong Show*, I made it known that I was available, and I wanted to be a part of that."[5]

5. Personal interview. 25 Apr. 2019.

Watching the first five episodes now, something just feels…off. Barbour speaks glowingly of the contestants' prospects for stardom. The celebrity judges, all dressed in their church clothes, write down their scores thoughtfully, and then give the performers some constructive criticisms. The singer needs to find a better key, they'd say. Or they might tell the pianist that she shows promise but needs practice. It's normal. Worse than normal…it's a little boring.

The first celebrity brave enough to bang the gong on show #1 was Jamie Farr, who saw a skinny, older man in a dress singing opera in a falsetto and decided after only fifteen seconds that he had enough. He banged the gong, and in a nod to his signature attire as Klinger on *M*A*S*H*, explained, "He stole my act!"

Barbour seemed disturbed by Farr's dismissive quip. He scolded the judge. "Jamie, you didn't let him get started at all!"

During the next commercial break, Barris sprang into action, pulling Barbour aside and trying to explain what was wrong with his presentation. Yes, he was sympathetic to the contestants, like Madeline David suggested, but to an extreme that she probably hadn't envisioned.

Barbour took the note, went right back on stage, and didn't change a thing. Barbour attempted to talk off the cuff a few times, but said "Ladies and gentlemen" repeatedly, almost as a vocal tic. A comedy writer, Rick Kellard, was charged with writing jokes for Barbour to introduce each act.

"Our next guest's mother wanted her to be a tap dancer, her father wanted her to be a surgeon, and today she's going to make both of them unhappy."

An introduction like that ideally should have tipped off Barbour about what the tone of the show should have been. Not only did he look visibly confused as he recited the joke from his cue card, but he also bobbled the punch line, saying "happy" instead of "unhappy," leading the viewers to think they were about to watch a tap-dancing surgeon.

Larry Spencer, a freelance cue card man who worked on most of Chuck Barris' shows to that point, remembers, "I don't remember anything about that taping except thinking to myself, 'Wow, this is really bland.'"[6]

Susan Simons, from NBC's Compliances department (she was in charge of enforcing the rules that contestants had to adhere to; no visible logos on clothing, no talking to staff members, etc.) watched John Barbour's performance. She didn't think he was bad; just a bad fit.

Simons explains, "John performed it as a game show host. Hosting a game show is a skill and an art, and the people who do it well were a

---

6. Personal interview. 2 Feb. 2019.

significant part of my career — Tom Kennedy, Peter Tomarken, Bill Cullen. There's nothing wrong with being a game show host, but that kind of performance is just so wrong for what *The Gong Show* was supposed to be. You could look at it and tell that Chuck wanted it to be a joke, and John was doing this very earnest performance."[7]

Vince Longo, Chuck's staff photographer, was fascinated by the boss' reaction to how badly his show was going so far. In between shots of the judges, John Barbour, and the acts, Longo surreptitiously snapped pictures of Chuck, whose face was changing color, and whose forehead had slowly come alive with the throbbing of a vein that grew more prominent as the day went on.

Longo remembered, "Chuck was already annoyed when I got there. So even in preparations, he could see this wasn't going to go well. To be fair, Barbour was hired when the show was still in an embryonic stage, and nobody could quite see what it was going to be. But once we began taping, John didn't really get what the show was turning into, and he didn't suit what it became. That taping wasn't a pleasant experience. Not for us and not really for John either. Chuck yelled at him."[8]

Jamie Farr was frustrated too. He wasn't hurt about getting scolded in front of the audience, in essence, for doing his job. That, to him, was only a symptom of a larger problem. The show looked all wrong to him. Milton DeLugg and his orchestra were decked in striped suits and straw hats, looking like carnival barkers. John Barbour was attempting an earnest performance as host. The panelists had been given strange instructions about their role on the show. In stark contrast to the instructions Jo Anne Worley remembered being given before the pilot, the Barris staff was now telling the judges to offer a critique and advice to the contestants. Jamie Farr's account was that it was an order from NBC.

"The networks have departments that oversee game shows and competitions, and they have rules that everyone adheres to. In the beginning, NBC didn't quite understand what this show was supposed to be, and they were insisted that we had to give an explanation for the scores we gave."[9]

Farr thought there was a flaw there — he, Worley, and Cassidy were all actors by trade. What right did they have to tell a singer, a juggler, or a ventriloquist how to improve their acts? It was disingenuous.

After three episodes were taped, everyone took a break. Jamie Farr was relaxing in his dressing room when Chuck Barris walked in. Barris had now

7. Personal interview. 18 Apr. 2019.
8. Personal interview. 9 May 2019.
9. Personal interview. 25. Apr. 2019.

been producing television shows for a decade, so Farr was a bit stunned to hear Barris asking him for guidance.

"Jamie, what's wrong with the show?" Chuck asked.[10]

Farr laid out the problems and solutions quickly. "Chuck, if there's one thing I've learned from working in television, it's that when you have garbage, you wrap it in a nice package. You have all these bad acts on the

A lot of serious thought went into a fun show. Chuck Barris stands to the side of the stage, jotting down notes during a conference with his staff. Chuck had a vision for The Gong Show, *and the first taping wasn't it.* PHOTO BY AND COURTESY OF VINCE LONGO

show, but the show itself doesn't look great. How about giving everybody formal wear? Put the judges in nice evening gowns and tuxedos. Take the band out of the carney suits and put them in tuxedos too. It's going to look funnier if we're getting that dressed up to watch a guy crack eggs on his forehead."

Chuck, with a bit of restored hope in his eyes, said, "Yeah, that's a good idea."

Jamie also explained his objection to what was expected of the judges. "We're not producers like Abe Burrows or somebody like that. We aren't

10. Ibid.

the ones who make the decisions and hire people. We're actors. We're out there in the open market, offering ourselves as performers, and we get rejected and told 'no' when we try to find work. It's wrong for us to go out there and make serious comments about what these contestants need to do to improve their acts. We're in the same boat as them, we're trying to find work too. What advice can we seriously give?"

Besides, Farr pointed out, as much as Chuck was going to try to vary the acts seen from show to show, there was only a finite amount of advice to give. How many different ways could the judges say "Take some singing lessons"? Chuck thought back to Jaye P. Morgan's "monkey" joke at the run-through and concluded that the network's instincts about constructive criticism were wrong. Jamie was right, the judges shouldn't be doing this.

It was too late in the day to do anything about tuxedos now, though. They still had two more episodes to get through, and to the very last shot of show #5, John Barbour hadn't taken a single note to heart. Not every host is perfect out of the gate. In 1966, Chuck watched the first taping of *The Newlywed Game* and promptly alerted Bob Eubanks that he had gone the full 30 minutes without blinking. Eubanks jotted down a note on his lectern reminding himself to blink until the beginner's nerves got out of his system.

Barbour, on the other hand, was Teflon. Barris had given him instruction after instruction for those first four episodes, and Barbour delivered the same performance on episode #5. He opened the fifth episode by talking about how "terrific and wonderful" the acts were, and how they'd entertain America, and how *The Gong Show* was offering them "a shot at the big time." Even the contestants were grasping the joke by this point and going along with it. A woman who played "Blue Danube" by making flatulent sounds into the crook of her arm reacted to the sound of the gong by haughtily asking the panel, "Have you no feeling for classical music?"

Barbour sent her on her way by saying he hoped that her appearance on *The Gong Show* meant something to her and that the advice from the panel was of value to her. It was all wrong. Barris knew the first week was bad. Madeline David knew they were bad. But what to do?

They agreed that John Barbour had to go. He was given his paycheck and shown the door. NBC and Chuck Barris tried to make it as painless as possible. The network, which had already publicized the show with Barbour as host, declined to give a reason when they announced that Barbour wouldn't be there after all. One reporter called Chuck Barris

Productions and said the company officially denied the rumor that Barbour was fired because he didn't measure up as a host.

Lynnette Karnes sympathized with Barbour somewhat. "John Barbour was awful, but you can kind of understand why. He had to host that show with no frame of reference. There had never been a TV show like the one Chuck was trying to do, so how can you know the right way to host it?"[11]

Chuck Barris, where he never expected to be: onstage as the host of his own creation. AUTHOR'S COLLECTION

Barbour himself was willing to discuss what happened with the *New York Daily News*. He said, "I'm the first recipient of the Golden Gong Award...When Madeline David, NBC's daytime programming chief, first approached me to do the show, she said she wanted somebody who could be witty, low-key, and someone the audience could trust. Then, without any run-throughs, we taped five programs.[12]

"But what Chuck Barris wanted was a loud, top-40 disc jockey approach to the program. He has a knack for capturing the stupid side of television, judging from his previous shows...I didn't want to be a shouting

---

11. Personal interview. 3 Oct. 2019.

12. Maksian, George. "Emcee of The Gong Show Gets Gonged by Producers." *New York Daily News.* 14 Jun. 1976.

emcee…After all, it's not really a game show. It's a talent show. I wanted the program to be something of a cross between *Hollywood Palace* and *One Flew Over the Cuckoo's Nest*, with some good acts presented as well as some clinkers. But Chuck kept saying read the cards, read the cards."

Barris was in a quandary. Episodes #6-#10 were taping on June 9, just six days away. The show was to premiere on NBC at the end of the month. Barris was trying to figure out if he could find a suitable host in less than a week.

Madeline David suggested a solution that Barris wasn't ready for. "You know who should host the show? You should…You know *The Gong Show* better than anyone else."[13]

Chuck demurred. It sounded like a suggestion to him, and one that he didn't think was worth taking seriously. But when he resisted, David insisted.

"Either you do it or I don't put the show on the air."

Chuck remembered, "I thought that over one day at Nibbler's. It's a small breakfast restaurant. One morning I hung over a cup of coffee… and I just sat there thinking about it, thinking I'm gonna blow my cover. It's going to change my life a lot…I didn't think the hosting part would really be all that difficult. I just thought you go on, you introduce an act, you thank them for being there, you say goodbye to them, you bring on another one. That doesn't seem very complicated."[14]

Barbour told *New York Daily News*, "The next day, Barris called me and said he was taking over the reins as host himself. I felt bad that as a host, I was the last to be consulted. The problem with the show was not the host but the construction. I feel the program has the potential of being a hit."[15]

Chuck Barris looked in the mirror, shocked to see himself in a tuxedo and dusted with light powder by a make-up artist and let out a heavy cough. He began having coughing fits and wheezing from almost the moment that Madeline David told him he had to host the show himself. While it always merits mentioning that any story told by Chuck Barris deserves just a degree of suspicion, he later claimed that the coughing fits were persistent for the next four years, and that the moment the series ended, so did the coughing fits.

Taping started for what, despite being episode #6, would now be the first episode of *The Gong Show* seen on NBC. The network and Chuck

---

13. *The Game Show King*. 1993.
14. Interview with Chuck Barris. *The Mike Douglas Show*. 1978.
15. Maksian. 1976.

agreed to ignore John Barbour's five episodes and begin anew with this taping. Episode #6 would be treated as the show's debut. With the judges and the band now in Jamie Farr's recommended formal wear, Chuck Barris strolled onto the stage as a host for the first time in his life.

In any other circumstances, a producer watching Chuck Barris' performance would have had more notes than Brahms, Bach, and Beethoven

Chuck, Sivi Aberg (far left), and the contestants on episode #D6, Chuck's first episode as host and the first episode of The Gong Show *to actually make it on the air.* ROBERT BURROUGHS COLLECTION

combined. Chuck stared at the camera with a frozen grin. He read cue cards robotically. He kept his arms to his side for much of the taping. When anybody off camera gave him a signal, Barris would go silent and unhinge his jaw, his eyes darting like he was searching for someone, anyone, to help him. Genetics hadn't blessed Chuck Barris with anything that suited a master of ceremonies; he was just a bit short, with an unmanageable poof of graying hair, a perpetual squint, and a voice that seemed to go up an octave or two whenever he was in front of the camera.

And yet…that seemed to be exactly what the show called for. This was a talent show that showcased mediocrity, after all. Didn't it make sense that it would be hosted by an unkempt bundle of nerves? Besides, the most enduring variety show in television history had been hosted by Ed Sullivan, a man who became a show business legend by having no business being on camera. Sullivan leaned on words like "really big." Chuck kept uttering the word "stuff." Ed Sullivan had a perpetually dour expression locked onto his countenance for 23 years. Chuck had a mild semi-smile. For a talent show that highlighted the worst of the worst, you couldn't have a better host than a poor man's Ed Sullivan.

In a hilarious coda to the whole saga, some early advertisements for The Gong Show *used publicity stills in which Chuck's head was superimposed on John Barbour's body.* ROBERT BURROUGHS COLLECTION

Barris' first day on the job included a five-year-old tap dancer who was…well, for a five-year-old tap dancer, she was fine. But with the judges now being told to follow Jamie Farr's lead and take this whole exercise less seriously, Anson "Potsie" Williams shot right out of his seat and banged the gong on the child, who was so oblivious about what she was a part of that it didn't seem to register with her.

Barris shuffled over to the girl, got on one knee, and put an arm around her. He asked Anson why he banged the gong, and instead of the constructive feedback that bogged down John Barbour's week, Anson Williams went straight for a joke. "I gonged her because I'm a mean guy. She should be at home watching *Mickey Mouse Club* and her mother should be looking for therapists."

Barris consoled the girl (who, again, didn't even seem aware that she should be upset about something) by telling her that "all the kids at the candy store could see her on TV" and then, realizing that his knee had locked and he couldn't stand back up, he hastily threw the show to a commercial break.

There was a sweetness to the moment. Barris tried to say something off-the-cuff to relate to the child and presented a world where five-year-olds apparently went to the candy store and hung out like Norm and Cliff. And then, in a moment any parent could relate to, he accidentally hurt himself by trying to get himself down to the child's level. The creator and host of a show that put minimally-exceptional talent out there with the potential of seeing them torn down revealed in that moment that he genuinely liked the people who were brave enough to be a part of it, and that he respected them for the effort. The genuineness wrapped in a genuinely poor performance was perfect. Barris found his host.

On July 12, 1976, one month after *The Gong Show* premiered, Ted Mack died.

CHAPTER 6

Bang The Gong Quickly

Above: "What are we looking at?" wondered the critics.
BOB BODEN COLLECTION

The first critics' reviews slid off the printing presses during the summer of 1976. The earliest critics to devote some paragraphs to *The Gong Show* didn't seem to love nor hate it. They didn't seem to have clear thoughts about it at all. They seemed to view it like an abstract painting in a museum, struggling to make sense of what they were seeing and what reactions it brought out in them.

John J. O'Connor scratched his head and mused, "Barris is flirting with the germ, if you will, of a good idea, the kind of idea that might make a good sketch for *Monty Python's Flying Circus*. But *The Gong Show* seems to be playing everything strictly for smirks. The format is nervous about honest laughs."

Lee Marguiles shrugged his shoulders and typed, "*The Gong Show* had a few good moments, thanks to those performers who either were very good — or very bad…In any case, it's nice to see NBC making an effort to find something at least slightly different."[1]

Michael Bennett chimed in, "The performances are pathetic, poised, and sometimes pitiable. The reactions of the judges produced some of the best lines in months, day or prime time."[2]

Bill Granger seemingly held his nose with one hand and typed his review with the other. "It exploits greed and need; it is based on the lowest principles of public humiliation and its cynicism makes the cynicism that inspired *The Newlywed Game* seem positively shallow. *The Gong Show* is also funny."[3]

John H. Corcoran, Jr. penned perhaps the definitive early review of the series: "It has managed to be the most gawdawful show on television, to send television back to the stone age, and simultaneously, to become the most watchable daytime show in eons. It is silly, puerile, objectionable, insulting, degrading, and ridiculous. And I wouldn't miss if it my house were on fire."[4]

Tom Shales called *The Gong Show* "a merciless variation on the old *Amateur Hour* and a bedazzling fantasia in humiliation…*The Gong Show* is loud, shameless, and vulgar, but it's not like any other game show on the air."[5]

1. O'Connor, John J. "Crazy Game Shows." *Quad-City Times*. Davenport, Iowa. 9 Jul. 1976.

2. Bennett, Michael. "What a Way to Spend a Weekend!" *The Province*. Vancouver, BC. 4 Aug. 1976.

3. Granger, Bill. "Gong Show Gonged for Its Poor Taste." *The Tampa Times*. 26 Aug. 1976.

4. "Gong Show: Loud, Shameless, and Vulgar." *The Daily News-Sun*. Hobbs, NM. 19 Jun. 1977.

5. Ibid.

A handful of TV critics had a clear mind about what they had seen and how they felt. Their reactions to *The Gong Show* were about what you'd expect.

"They should be ashamed." — Orma Webb[6]

"Unless the silent majority, the greater number of people who refuse to allow themselves and their children to be desensitized by Barris' sick humor speak up, the *Gong Show* mentality of television will persist. And worse, grow."[7]

Gary Deeb beat the rush by releasing his bad review before the first episode had been taped. "NBC actually plans to revive such shenanigans on a daily basis by bringing us *The Gong Show*, a hyperkinetic update of *Ted Mack's Original Amateur Hour*. *The Gong Show*, produced by the same exploitative lout who gave us *The Dating Game* and *The Newlywed Game*...Chuck Barris, a wretched character who has amassed a spectacular fortune by providing people with new ways to make jackasses out of themselves."[8]

A watchdog group, the National Association for Better Broadcasting, brought out its firing squad: "This show, like other Chuck Barris series, is gross and ugly. It exploits and demeans anyone who is willing to perform, and anyone else who comes close enough to be contaminated. Immeasurable bad taste, and a disgrace not only to NBC, but to television itself."[9]

The Silver Throated Tenor, who donned a mask for his performance of "Yesterday." He was hardly the only contestant who wanted to hide his face.
AUTHOR'S COLLECTION

6. Webb, Orma. "Orma Webb's Electric Eye." *Richmond Review*. Richmond, BC. 30 Jun. 1976.

7. Mermigas, Diane. "Gong Show Hits a New Low." *Daily Herald*. Arlington Heights, Il. 22 Dec. 1977.

8. Deeb, Gary. "'Amateur Hour' is Updated." *Tallahassee Democrat*. 20 May 1976.

9. "Association Screens Some TV Shows." *The Mercury*. Pottstown, PA. 23 Apr. 1977.

Chuck professed, in public and private, that critical censure didn't matter to him. Television shows are free, he reasoned, and how much weight could a critic carry complaining about something that was free?

"TV critics, like the dinosaur, will someday be extinct," he liked to tell his daughter Della.[10]

From his own experiences, people who had negative things to say about

Willie the Juggling Ape, as seen on The Gong Show. *The name of the act was a bit of a misnomer; Willie also danced.* BOB BODEN COLLECTION

television shows tended to represent the worst in humanity. Chuck was having dinner at the Palm Restaurant when a woman made it a point to interrupt the meal and let Chuck know he should be ashamed of himself for making stupid shows. Another woman confronted him one day in Santa Monica to lambaste him for putting too many black contestants on his shows. If these people wanted to say that Chuck was a terrible human being, they were certainly experts on the subject.

Chris Bearde cheerfully replied to all the detractors, "This show is succeeding because it's controversial. People want to be affected. It's like

10. Barris, Chuck. *Della: A Memoir of My Daughter.* Simon & Schuster. New York. 2010.

Above: It's like looking into a mirror! Phyllis Diller stares in amazement at impersonator Ann Lapp. Below: Lucie Arnaz begs Paul Williams for mercy. Some judges were comfortable on the panel; some never showed up again.
ROBERT BURROUGHS COLLECTION, AUTHOR'S COLLECTION

going to see *Jaws* or *The Exorcist*. You don't go to be entertained. You go to be affected."[11]

Among the affected in the herky-jerky early episodes were the gongees, most of whom had auditioned not realizing what they were signing up for. Chuck shocked one wannabe song-and-dance man, a victim of the gong, by bringing out his mother to take a bow after he had lost. Barris staffers, dressed in hospital scrubs and lab coats, would occasionally walk onstage with butterfly nets to escort the losers offstage. Milton DeLugg and the Band with a Thugg accentuated the sound of the gong with some musical accompaniment, a bicycle horn followed by a brassy "Waa-waa-waa-waaaaaaaa," with the last note usually going wildly off-key.

But actually, the most affected in the beginning seemed to be the celebrity judges. Initially, *The Gong Show* seemed to use the same rolodex that *Match Game, Hollywood Squares*, and the rest of the star-studded daytime games of the 1970s relied on. The difference was *The Gong Show* would see many of those celebrities only once, and then they'd vaporize from the show forever.

Actor/comic Avery Schreiber was afflicted by an attack of sudden guilt when he banged the gong. Chuck Barris asked, "Why did you do that?" and Schreiber squirmed like he was being interrogated by Congress before blaming it on the audience, saying he felt like they wanted him to do it. Puppeteer Shari Lewis only tapped the gong lightly, not even eliciting a sound from it. Actress Joyce Bulifant recounted her experience during a later appearance on *Match Game*, telling host Gene Rayburn she was too embarrassed to do anything at all. Another *Match Game* favorite, Fannie Flagg, covered her face and turned away during the worst of the acts. Singer Sarah Vaughn sat at the panel for a five-episode taping session, with a facial expression that seemed to announce to the world that her agent was two hours away from being fired.

Wardrobe coordinator Jefferson Beeker says, "One name really stands out to me. Suzanne Somers. You could tell she just didn't have a clue what the show was even about. Pearl Bailey was a lot of fun. I had worked on Broadway with her, and it was interesting — she was fun, but as fun as she was, you could tell she didn't really get it."[12]

JoAnne Worley, who had gamely sat on the panel for the pilot and for John Barbour's ill-fated five episodes, did a couple of early tours of duty with Chuck Barris, and then politely asked never to be booked for the show again.

---

11. "Amateur Talent 'Hooked' on 'Gong Show.'" *Hartford Courant*. 18 Jul. 1976.
12. Personal interview. 10 Apr. 2019.

Worley remembers, "There were times when it was fun. There were acts on that show that were so ridiculous and over the top that you knew they were treating the show as a joke and that they really didn't care. I had no problem banging the gong on those people. For them, getting gonged was fun. It was part of the experience.[13]

"Then there were times when it would be a singer who would just sing

Some contestants handled getting gonged more gracefully than others.
ROBERT BURROUGHS COLLECTION

her heart out, and she couldn't find the right key. And you could tell, even though it was bad, that she had worked hard on it, and the audience in the studio is booing and yelling 'GONG!' at the judges. In those moments, it didn't feel fun anymore. So, I stopped appearing on the show after a few months."

Indeed, there were some contestants who were there in earnest. And Jamie Farr remembers, "In the early weeks of the show, people were auditioning without really having a chance to see the show and understand what it was. There were performers that were very serious about what they were doing. There were a few times in those early shows when Chuck would have a police escort take us to our cars after the tapings were over

---

13. Personal interview. 10 Jan. 2019.

because he got word that family members in the audience were angry that their wife or their daughter didn't win."[14]

"We had an Al Jolson impersonator on the show once," says Lynnette Karnes. "After the judges gonged him, he went backstage, and he wouldn't leave. He said he wanted to wait for the judges after the show was finished. We had to have NBC security escort him from the building. We even

Rex Reed has seen enough. The dour film critic's pointed barbs were a precursor to American Idol *judge Simon Cowell's style.* ROBERT BURROUGHS COLLECTION

sent a staffer to go down the hallway and pull the celebrity names off the dressing room doors, so he wouldn't know where the judges would go."[15]

Writer Ann Woodall was in the studio penning a story about *The Gong Show*. One of the contestants, according to her story, was "a 300-pound go-go dancer named Bubbles, decked out in a frothy, Shirley Temple-type dress, shocking pink leotards, and white ballet slippers...

"Bubbles — the overweight go-go dancer — appears in all her finery. Barris tells the audience how much he 'loves this little lady,' and she

14. Personal interview. 25 Apr. 2019.
15. Personal interview. 3 Oct. 2019.

takes over, filling much of the stage just standing still. As Bubbles heaves and twitches, the celebrity panel stares, dumbstruck. The audience boos and yells 'Gong! Gong!' One celebrity cries, 'I can't take it anymore,' and slams the deafening instrument. Bubbles has bombed. To demonstrate her disappointment, she spread-eagles herself on the stage floor. Barries tries to pull her to her feet without success. His 100 pounds or so are no match for Bubbles."[16]

Gonged contestants would look forlorn and walk offstage without sticking around for the banter in which Chuck asked the judges why they banged the gong. One contestant had a bit she wanted to do with that '70s fad, the pet rock, but she was so visibly terrified when she walked onstage that the judges ignored the 45-second minimum and banged the gong immediately to put her out of her misery.

A sixteen-year-old girl, Lynn Turner, appeared on the daytime show singing "The Morning After." Arte Johnson banged the gong. Turner wept. Openly, onstage, in front of the audience, cameras rolling, she buried her face on Chuck Barris' shoulder and sobbed. Chuck froze. Arte Johnson phumphered for a reason to give, but what could he really say at this point? Chuck hastily threw it to commercial, and the show faded to black.

Turner composed herself and when the show returned from commercial, she mustered a smile and stood side by side with Chuck as he thanked her for being on the show. After it was over, Arte Johnson handed her a scorecard with a "10" on it, plus his autograph. He gave her a kiss on the cheek and promised he would never bang a gong on her again. To her surprise, Barris' staff called her a few months later and asked if she wanted to come back and sing again on the nighttime show. They were equally surprised when she agreed.

Writer Ann Woodall asked producer Gene Banks about the emotional toll of getting gonged, and Banks was unapologetic. "They know it might happen…as a matter of fact, the studio audience is much more intolerant of the performers than the celebrity judges [are]. The audience wants the acts to get killed. They yell for the gong after 30 seconds — they're like the Romans were to the gladiators.

"Sure, the show gets hate mail…and people think it's cruel and sadistic, but just last week, we auditioned 180 acts in one day — one day — and the ratings are climbing and we're catching on with the college kids.…

---

16. Woodall, Ann. "Game Shows: The Television Network Attack on Human Dignity Continues Unabated." *Playgirl*.

[W]e are all closet gongers. Look, haven't you ever been at a party where you turn around, and 'uh-oh, here comes Charlie with that lampshade on his head again, he's gonna go into his act' — don't you just wish you could gong him?"

Jamie Farr says, "We didn't have to gong anybody. There were absolutely times when I didn't feel comfortable about doing it. I remember a

Guitarist Steve Bricker, who had a running vacuum cleaner attached to his instrument. BOB BODEN COLLECTION

day when I was a judge, and this very heavyset woman came out and did an awkward-looking dance. The audience was screaming like Romans waiting for someone to get fed to the lion. I did not have the heart to bang that gong. So, I didn't. I never gonged anybody if I felt genuinely bad for them. The ones I felt bad for, I would just let them finish their performance, and then I'd give them a low score, a one or a two, and make a joke about the score."[17]

Jamie's enthusiasm for the show and his means of dealing with his own personal reservations made him a valuable star for Chuck Barris at a time when it was becoming clear that the usual group of stars that populated '70s game show panels were staying away from *The Gong Show*.

17. Personal interview. 3 Oct. 2019.

Although he was never officially under contract as a regular, Jamie Farr would appear on over 200 episodes.

Farr says, "I won't name a name, but there was a time when somebody fairly well-known took me aside and told me I should stop doing the show. M*A*S*H was a hit and they said I was way too big a star to be on The Gong Show. First of all, I had fun doing game shows. Second, it had an impact on me. Before I started doing game shows, if people recognized me on the street, they would say, 'Hey, it's Klinger! It's Klinger!' After I began appearing on game shows, they began saying 'Hey, it's Jamie Farr!' Now after all these years, I can tell you there was one more benefit to doing that show. AFTRA determines what kind of pension you qualify for by the amount of work you do on radio and television. I did so many appearances on game shows that it pushed me over the line, and I became eligible for a huge pension. I don't regret The Gong Show at all."[18]

Mike Metzger says, "The Gong Show had an element of cruelty for sure, but I doubt that Chuck lost sleep over it. Even if you consider yourself a great singer, if you're a guy who sings opera and truly believes yourself to be the next Caruso, you still go to the audition and agree to the show knowing you could be gonged. Everybody knew that. Whether they accepted that or whether they deluded themselves into thinking it couldn't happen was out of our hands. If a contestant is a terrible singer but honestly believes himself to be something special, and he's surprised and hurt by getting gonged, that's really not our problem."[19]

John Hill notes, "Chuck liked the people who came on the show. He truly did because, let's be honest, they were his bread and butter. We don't have a show without them. He genuinely appreciated the way that they put themselves out there for ultimately our benefit. He cared about them. He didn't have a malicious spirit at all."[20]

Lynnette Karnes gets philosophical about whatever mean streak the show had. "I never had any aspirations to be a singer, but let's say I did. If I wanted to sing for a living, but I needed improvement, or if I tried to improve and just wasn't improving…I would want my friends and family to sit me down and tell me, 'You know, this just isn't working for you.' That was the thing that always got me. The people who showed up with a high opinion of themselves, who showed up with an ego, and then they went out onstage, and they would just be awful, and the audience would boo

18. Ibid.
19. Personal interview. 13 May 2019.
20. Personal interview. 14 May 2019.

until the judges banged the gong. Those contestants were heartbroken, but at the same time, you looked at them and wondered, 'How did you go this long not knowing this about yourself?' I mean really…nobody told them?"[21]

In the early weeks of *The Gong Show*, with the panel largely occupied by stars who popped in, appeared for five episodes, and never set foot

Jamie Farr couldn't contain his joy. He loved being a judge. AUTHOR'S COLLECTION

near the show again, Chuck Barris managed to book the woman who quickly established herself as the anchor of Barris' ship, an alluring face with come-hither eyes and a go-away smirk: Jaye P. Morgan.

She was born Mary Margaret Morgan. She started performing with her family in the later days of vaudeville. Her family settled down in California, where an appointment to class treasurer inspired schoolmates to refer to her with a punny nickname inspired by the famed financier J.P. Morgan, and it stuck.

She released a steady stream of albums over the next 20 years, while becoming a television mainstay, appearing frequently with Robert Q. Lewis, Perry Como, Merv Griffin, and Mike Douglas. Her blonde hair

21. Personal interview. 3 Oct. 2019.

and fresh face were fitting when she came into her own in the 1950s — it was the preferred look at the time. But the 1970s arrived, Morgan entered her 40s, and she tired of her own image.

"When you start out, you're a different person," she told reporter Bill O'Connor in 1982. "You're trying to build some sort of career or reputation, so you follow the advice of people you're involved with. After I turned 40, I said, 'That's it, folks, no more cutie-utums.' It doesn't work anymore. There's nothing worse than seeing a 40-year-old Baby Jane. It isn't even interesting."[22]

She appeared somewhat frequently with Johnny Carson in the 1970s, but now sporting mid-length brown hair, glasses, and blue jeans, and updating her repertoire to include Simon and Garfunkel's songs. In her TV appearances in the 1970s, she was more laid-back, at ease with herself, and as a result, more prone to fire off a snappy line, something she turned out to be quite adept at while giving her score.

"No matter what you may achieve, no matter how far you go, no matter how famous you become…who cares?"

(To a contestant named Buck) "Are you and Chuck related? You must be brothers. Chuck, Buck, and…Fargo."

"I'm a little tight…wad."

(To a juggler) "You got a lot of balls."

Early on, Chuck Barris had touted *The Gong Show* as offering its contestants "a shot at the big time." The winning acts would return after several weeks to compete against each other in a play-off, with the winner of the play-off getting a professional engagement at a nightclub. The show had one playoff week and then never offered a nightclub engagement as a prize again, because Chuck had concluded that the prize was redundant. The weird acts were the show's appeal, not the chance at the big time. Besides, the nightclub engagement seemed to directly contradict Chuck's stance that the show wasn't really intended to create new stars.

The problem, if you can call it that, was that even though Chuck Barris insisted on treating the show as a lark and saying that it was all in playful fun, it was showing potential for being exactly the star-making vehicle that he was trying to avoid. *The Gong Show* was less than a month old when NBC joyfully sent out a press release touting the careers that had already been launched. Fire baton twirler Wanda Ward got booked for a show at Knotts Berry Farm. Michael Sherman, who donned a Viking helmet and Groucho glasses, then lip-synced to a song, was hired to

---

22. O'Connor, Bill. "…Ms. Morgan is Made for Role." *Akron Beacon Journal.* 7 Feb. 1982.

open for Phyllis Diller. Singer Nina Shannon sang "On a Clear Day" and got a recording company meeting the same day that the episode aired. Al Jolson impersonator Adrena Jenson and elderly singer Penny Rupert both got signed by talent agencies. Margee McGlory did some impressions on a day when Redd Foxx happened to be watching, and the *Sanford and Son* star was so dazzled, he signed her to a three-year

Jaye P. Morgan became known largely as a judge on The Gong Show *despite a 20-year singing career that preceded it.* ROBERT BURROUGHS COLLECTION

management contract. Singer Darvy Taylor landed a booking on NBC's late-night music showcase *The Midnight Special*. A dance team that did the cha-cha found themselves on a cruise ship tour. Even an act that got gonged, a comic who called himself Lenny Tunes, got a nightclub gig in New York. No matter how much Chuck Barris fought it, his creation was making people famous.

If you think The Gong Show *is bad, you ought to see the auditions. Not that the talent is any worse... Without the bright lights, the costumes, the band, and all the hoopla that surrounds the show, you see the acts for what they are. The effect is not unlike watching your first autopsy.*[23]

The Los Angeles Times curiously sent reporter Ursula Vils to Old World Restaurant, where *The Gong Show* held regular auditions. The Chuck Barris Productions staff referred to the employees at the Old World auditions as "The Shock Troops" because they saw everything. Yes, the *Gong Show* did reject acts, but those acts all had to come in for the auditions, and the shock troops saw an unfiltered version of the show. They saw the 60-year-old lady in a tutu who stood on her head while playing the mandolin; the man reciting poetry while crouched inside a barrel; the 60-year-old fire eater in a bikini.

The first auditioner that the *Times* reporter met was an exuberant 22-year-old named Merry Kay Cote from Seattle. Just a month earlier, she had finished college, packed up her car, and moved to Los Angeles seeking a career in show business. Decked in a form-fitting blue dress and a blonde wig, she assumed the identity of "Roxie Paramour" and did some dumb blonde shtick before singing a song. She told the reporter that if she made it onto the show, she was planning on taking out an ad in *Variety* the day that the episode aired. An unemployed actor named Ron Wilson became "Orson Bells" and performed a trained dog act with a clearly-untrained dog. He needed exposure, and the $516.32 would help him with Screen Actors Guild union dues, he explained.

Everybody wanted that shot at stardom. But little did performers like Cote and Wilson realize that *The Gong Show* already had a cautionary tale. Martin von Haselberg was a commodities broker who created the alias "Harry Kipper" to scratch his performer's itch. He appeared as a contestant on *The Gong Show*, wearing only face paint and polka dot boxers. He took to the stage, smashed an egg on his face, poured flour over his head, then covered himself with blueberries, chocolate syrup, spinach, baked beans,

---

23. Cavagnaro, Ted. "Outlet for Talented and Untalented: Gong Show." *St. Louis Post-Dispatch.* 12 Mar. 1978.

toothpaste, and to top it all off, glitter. It didn't matter that he was using an alias or wearing face paint. People recognized him. He lost two clients.

Much as JoAnne Worley had discerned, a number of contestants didn't have aspirations for anything. *The Los Angeles Times* reporter spoke to a woman named Tina, who cracked up Barris and his staff during her audition, strumming "Listen to the Mockingbird" on an autoharp and doing

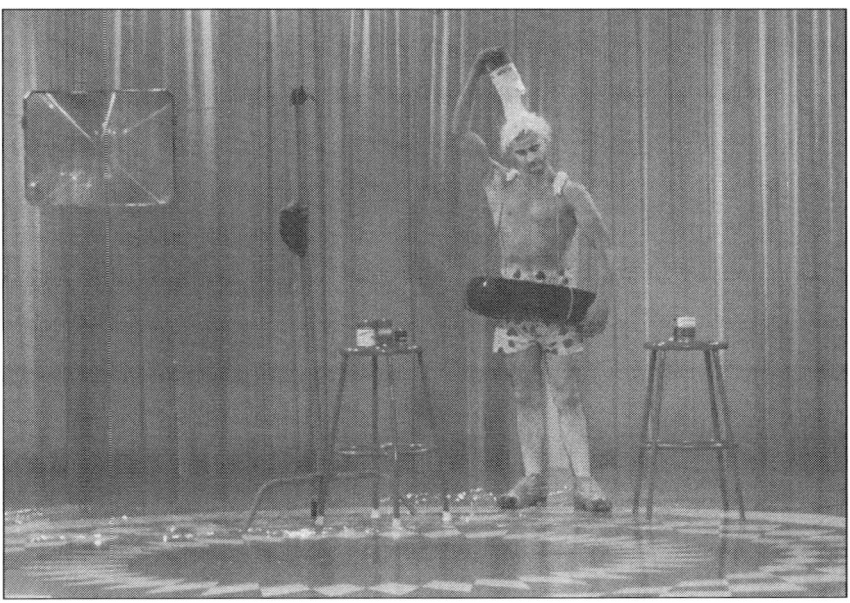

Harry Kipper, a/k/a Martin von Haselberg, whose career as a commodities broker was affected by his appearance on The Gong Show. ROBERT BURROUGHS COLLECTION

duck calls in rhythm with it. It was an idea she had solely so she could be a contestant on *The Gong Show*. Tina made it onto the show. The woman who showed up for her audition with 45 live snakes wrapped around her body plus two live tarantulas covering her eyes was told "No, thanks."

Looking at *The Gong Show*, you could be forgiven for expressing surprise that there was an audition process. The contestants came from all walks of life — some were professionals who had already made a living with the talent they were highlighting. Some were amateurs who had cut their teeth on their high school talent shows or open mic nights. Some weren't even that experienced. A handful of people concluded that being on *The Gong Show* looked fun and brainstormed their acts specifically for the show. Eliot Corey, for example, had been considering assembling a group of friends for a "helium balloon choir" before safety concerns crossed his mind and he discarded the idea. He gradually realized that a trick he had been doing to amuse his friends at parties was a viable act. He could place his guitar on his shoulders, strings facing out, and play it competently.

The contestants who arrived at Old World Restaurant had their pictures taken by Barris staffers as soon as they walked in. They were given "a biography sheet" to fill out and then ushered in to perform. Everybody was given a chance to perform to the best of their abilities. Bands were told to take as much time as they needed to set up their equipment and make sure everything was perfect before they started their performance. Every act was videotaped, every act was timed with a stopwatch.

After the acts left, the Barris staffers would make notes on the auditioner's biography sheet for later review. It only took a few weeks and a few hundred auditions for the staff to get so accustomed to what they were seeing that most of the notes were just sets of initials:

> GN — *No good (the abbreviation was backward just in case the contestant happened to see it being written down)*
> B — *Book (getting on the show)*
> AB — *Almost book (maybe, leaning toward yes)*
> BAS — *Beats A Singer (so many singers auditioned that there was no middle ground allowed; singers didn't get on The Gong Show unless they were magnificent or magnificently awful, and the show preferred interesting acts that weren't singers)*
> PIA — *Pain In the Ass (you might have talent, but if the staff found you personally irritating they may just decide they could do without you)*
> SS — *Scared Shitless (nobody wants to watch an act who has visible stage fright)*
> OMG — *Oh My God (the highest possible score, in a matter of speaking; an OMG was a sure thing to get on the show)*[24]
> YBMINAD — *Your Basic Man in a Dress*
> SG — *Singer/guitarists, who comprised, by one estimate, 80 percent of the auditions*
> SLA — *Sleazy Lounge Act*
> NBD — *No big deal*
> DAD — *Dime a dozen*

---

24. Shock Troop Vince Longo mentions that he was not aware that "OMG" had become a common abbreviation in the era of emails and texting until his son graduated from college. He would like history to record that he was using the abbreviation daily, decades before anyone else.

Vince Longo, who operated the camera for the auditions, remembers, "We once had a mother come in with her 12-year-old son, who was dressed and made-up like Liza Minelli. The boy begins singing a Liza Minelli song, and I look up from the lens and I see his mother standing to the side, lip-syncing all the words, and moving her arms, the same way that he was moving them. It was so sad but so funny. You could tell that this

Ron Wilson, a/k/a Orson Bells, auditioning for The Gong Show *along with his untrained dog.* AUTHOR'S COLLECTION

woman really wanted a girl, and that she had really wanted to be in show business. After a few seconds of recording the son, I panned over to the mother and just recorded her for the rest of the audition. On the boy's info sheet, the note that I wrote was 'The mother is the more interesting act.'"[25]

The show's time limit was 90 seconds, so if an act exceeded that in auditions — and most did — they might get notes on what to eliminate. Roxie Paramour, for example, had a whole comedy routine that led into her song, but after her audition, she was told to cut it down to just one quick joke and then go straight to the song. The show was also mindful that the network censors had to approve the acts, so they'd voice those potential concerns too — one auditionee sang an original song called "I Just Want to be a Pimp," a heartfelt devotional about his fondness for

25. Personal interview. 7 May 2019.

prostitutes and cocaine. He was politely told to re-write some key lyrics in the song and return for a future audition. As a rule, acts were only adjusted for the purposes of time and questionable content. No other changes were suggested. Singers would try out for the show that the staff deduced were extremely talented, but they were rejected because their song choices were too dreary.

Chuck's shock troops rated the act an OMG*...but how do the judges feel?*
AUTHOR'S COLLECTION

Some auditionees would try to win over the Shock Troops with sob stories or fanciful tales. The Shock Troops did believe most of what they were hearing, according to Vince Longo, and they never got over the number of people who drove across the country and slept in their backseats for a chance to be seen at a *Gong Show* audition.

Little did anybody realize that the Shock Troops were as eccentric a group as the people trying to get on the show. During a lunch break in the middle of a long day of auditions, they went to a western-themed store and bought a set of guns with CO_2 pellets. The Shock Troops were so enchanted by the pattern that one of the gunshots left on a mylar sheet that once auditions were done for the day, they stuck around and fired off their guns around the restaurant to see what kind of patterns they could make. They also shot at each other because they were curious to see if the pellets actually hurt. (Conclusion: Yes they did.)

Everybody got 90 seconds for their audition, though that certainly didn't mean the Shock Troops videotaped the full 90 seconds for Chuck's benefit. Videotape was precious and expensive, and when the Shock Troops saw an act that they just knew wasn't going to hold the boss' attention, the camera would be gently shut off after about 30 seconds or so, without the act realizing that they had just been subjected to a much quieter gong.

Connor and Dalton, who played a single guitar together, while dancing the Hula with their free arms. BOB BODEN COLLECTION

Vince Longo says, "There came a point where all of us had gotten addicted to a board game called Conquest. It's played on a map, and your game pieces are horses, elephants, war ships, and soldiers. Really fun game with a lot of different strategies. I mean we were hooked. Well, gradually, we realized something about the set-up we had for the auditions. We were seated at a table, and in front of us were these two big bright lights shining on the performers, so they showed up better on the tapes. That meant that nobody could see us while they were auditioning, so sometimes we would just let the camera run while we played the game. We got caught once. A guy was moving all over the room as part of his act, and he got just close enough to us. 'You're playing a game?!'"[26]

26. Personal interview. 7 May 2019.

In the office, the crew weeded out the duller auditions and showed Chuck the ones that they felt were worth a look. Chuck would watch them with producer Gene Banks and Linda Howard. Together, they decided which ones they wanted to bring back for a second round of auditions, and those people had to be contacted. This was, surprisingly, a difficult job.

Lynnette Karnes explains, "I once worked for 36 straight hours, just

Contortionist Christa McKenna, a/k/a The Spider Lady. PHOTO BY AND COURTESY OF VINCE LONGO

doing call-backs for the second auditions. Chuck didn't want you to give up on people, if he wanted somebody to get a second audition, they had to get that second audition. We had people fill out forms with their contact information before their first audition, but we had a lot of people audition who had just moved to Los Angeles and were looking for a place to stay. We had people who were homeless. We had mentally ill people audition. So, their forms would have unusable information, which meant contacting people for the second audition involved tracking down addresses. Sometimes you had to track down their family and have them relay the message. Sometimes we had to write letters and send telegrams, because there was just no way to call these people on the phone."[27]

---

27. Personal interview. 3 Oct. 2019.

For the second audition, the contestants now performed for Chuck himself.

Mike Metzger remembers, "Once *The Gong Show* became popular, Chuck was doing auditions and interviews constantly. The elevators at our offices were packed once that show took off. I got on an elevator once with two men in diapers. Between them was a coat rack with an assort-

Uncle Chuck wants YOU! *If Chuck wanted you to be a contestant, his staff would come and find you, and it wasn't always an easy job.* AUTHOR'S COLLECTION

ment of animal carcasses hanging from it. I asked them what their act was. They said, 'We play the meat.' So that became every day at Chuck Barris Productions, whether you worked on that particular show or not."[28]

Tom Shales of *The Washington Post* went in to watch the second-round auditions with Chuck and observed with fascination the different interactions that aspirants had with the boss. Some tried sucking up ("I'll be seeing you on TV every day this week!"), and some tried wowing him with a verbal resume shoehorned into their conversation. Chuck really didn't care what other experience you had in the performing arts, because that was hardly the point of his own show.

28. Personal interview. 13 May 2019.

By Shales' account, the contestant that Chuck truly adored that day was a 65-year-old named Dora with an Italian accent that could be cut with a knife.

"I'm a-gonna sing 'Butcher Boy,'" she told Chuck. "I don't know one note of music. I been singing all my life by ear. I even dance by ear."[29]

She belted out the number. Her enthusiasm was contagious. Everyone in the room got up and danced. Chuck shouted "Bravo! Fortissimo!" when

Some acts were hard to find — but not hard enough for the judges' tastes sometimes. AUTHOR'S COLLECTION

it was over. Except he decided it wasn't over yet. He asked Dora if she knew "That's Amore."

Dora stretched her arms out. "Wheeeeeennnnn the moon…"

Dora didn't need to wait for a phone call. Chuck told her on the spot that she was going to be on *The Gong Show*. The audition that had made the strongest impact on Chuck was the one who wasn't trying to look like a big deal. Dora got picked because she presented herself as exactly what she was, and Chuck loved her for it.

For the ones that Chuck hadn't quite made up his mind up about yet, that discussion would happen back at the office. Each week, the staff watched 400 auditions. Of those 400, only 45 would get the call to be

---

29. Shales, Tom. "Chuckling at the Talentless." *The Record*. Hackensack, NJ. 14 Jan. 1977.

contestants. Chuck whittled it down to the final choices with the aid of a small but trusted few of his staffers — particularly Linda "Hives" Howard, who cue card man Larry Spencer referred to as Chuck's right hand.

"He really trusted her," Spencer recalls. "Chuck could find himself on the fence a lot about whether a certain act should make it on the show or not. Linda was great at judging which acts would get the audience's attention more."[30]

Dora Romani gets her moment in the Gong Show spotlight. That's bandleader Milton DeLugg at the piano. AUTHOR'S COLLECTION

Chuck clarified, "When we're picking acts, we're looking for the best and the worst. It's sort of like a 'U.' Anyone down in the valley is out."[31]

Vince Longo remembers, "Here's what I learned from conducting those auditions. Contrary to what you'd think, most people are actually good. A person who showed up with a guitar could play it well and carry a tune along with it. They got rejected because they weren't exceptional. When we were seeing so many auditions, being good just wasn't enough for us to give you a look."[32]

30. Personal interview. 2 Feb. 2019.
31. Peterson, Bettelou. "'Gong Show' Acts Can't Be Half Bad." *Detroit Free Press*. 24 Apr. 1977.
32. Personal interview. 9 May 2019.

Although each *Gong Show* included Johnny Jacobs' announcement of a phone number to call to book an audition for the show, Chuck also assigned a few staffers to go hunting for potential acts.

One was talent coordinator Danny Lies, who had been an audience member before he ever did anything else for the show. A Wichita native, Lies attending a *Gong Show* taping as a tourist while visiting Los Angeles, could see that something exceptional had emerged on television.

"I attended Wichita State, where I majored in radio and television, with a minor in journalism. I got a job at an ad agency, and I played semi-pro baseball," Lies explains. "In December 1976, the winter baseball meetings were going to be held in Los Angeles, so I made plans to go there. In the meantime, a friend had told me, 'Hey, Danny, you have to watch channel 3 at Noon, there's this crazy show on.' I was just immediately a fan of *The Gong Show*, so I decided I'd see a taping while I was in LA.

"At the end of the tapings, the pages at NBC ushered everyone out of the audience seats. I was

Elvis impersonators? Seen it. But The Gong Show *welcomed Moms Mabley impersonator Gertie King.* AUTHOR'S COLLECTION

kind of a straggler, and I just timed it perfectly. Chuck Barris walked out from backstage and came to a table nearby to look at something, and he was completely alone. I introduced myself. Chuck looked tired because he had just finished the fifth episode of the day, but he gave me the courtesy. I really was in the right place at the right time. It just happened that *The Gong Show* needed somebody, so Chuck calls for his secretary, tells her to set up an appointment for me, and walks away. Well, big decision. Stay in Wichita at the ad agency, or take a job in Hollywood at the hottest show on TV? I took the job at *The Gong Show*."[33]

Danny got settled in LA and started his new job, scouring clubs for potential acts. "I was an eligible bachelor from Wichita, so I was a lot more

---

33. Personal interview. 22 May 2019.

enthusiastic about being assigned to go to clubs at night than some of Chuck's other staffers. We would go to places that had amateur nights and talent nights, looking for good acts. We'd try to talk them into auditioning. It was harder than it sounds. A lot of performers declined because they wanted to be considered serious artists, and they thought that being on *The Gong Show* would reflect poorly on them."[34]

This act called themselves Vegas a Go-Go. Fittingly, they wore banana hammocks. BOB BODEN COLLECTION

The other staffer was Larry Gotterer, who had been such a devoted viewer of *The Gong Show* in college that it altered his career plans. "The closer I got to the end of college, the more concerned I was with my skills as an accountant. My father was a tax attorney, and studying for a career in accounting convinced me that either I was going to end up in prison without understanding what I had done wrong, or that I was going to destroy my dad's business.[35]

"*The Gong Show* was the hottest thing on TV. In the early afternoon, you could see people on campus running back to their dorms, so they'd be on time to watch that show. And I loved it too. I saw all these ridiculous people goofing around, and I thought, 'I bet working on that show

34. Personal interview. 22 May 2019.
35. Personal interview. 24 Apr. 2019.

would be a fun job.' I finished college, and instead of going to work as an accountant, I loaded up my car, drove to California, and showed up at Chuck Barris Productions to ask for a job.

"Well, *The Gong Show* was all staffed up, but Chuck told me he was starting an updated version of *The Newlywed Game* for syndication and offered me a job answering the phone for people who wanted to audition to be contestants. After I did that for a while, Chuck asked me to

This cameraman has seen it all. PHOTO BY AND COURTESY OF VINCE LONGO

write some sample questions for the show. So, I typed up a sample and Chuck comes in the next morning and says, 'Don't make any plans about moving back home, you stay right here. We're going to find something for you to do.' Eventually, he makes me a writer. Then he gives me producer duties. I ended up with duties on five different shows for Chuck at the same time. I got twenty years' worth of television production experience in less than two years."

In time, Gotterer would have duties on *The Gong Show*, joining Lies for his talent hunting excursions throughout Los Angeles. "We weren't looking for what you would think of as *Gong Show* acts. We never walked into a nightclub hoping that we would find Dr. Flame-O, who set his hands on fire and screamed the melody of 'Smoke Gets in Your Eyes.' The weird, wacky acts called the number for auditions. They always came to us.

We were looking for raw talent that wasn't professional yet — we scoured LA looking for bands and singers that we thought had potential. And when we found one, we'd give our phone numbers and encourage them to audition. Chuck had the final word, though. Even if we liked what we saw in that club, they still had to audition for Chuck."[36]

With the show's popularity booming, even professional talents and their representation threw themselves at the bandits and the Shock Troops.

Working on The Gong Show *was as much fun as it looked. Chuck and a cameraman share a laugh during a break in rehearsal.* PHOTO BY AND COURTESY OF VINCE LONGO

Danny Lies says, "We got piles of mail from managers and agents with info about when their bands would be performing. Nightclubs all over the country began calling us too. 'Gong Show Nights' became a popular thing at nightclubs, and they would call us asking to arrange an audition for whoever won their next Gong Show Night, so they could promote that as a prize in their advertising."[37]

Once the acts were booked for the taping, it was time to think about how to present them. Larry Spencer himself eventually wound up with

36. Ibid.
37. Personal interview. 22 May 2019.

duties that had expanded beyond cue cards. Writer Rick Kellard departed for a job with Bill Cosby, so Larry Spencer submitted a packet of 100 joke introductions for acts and got hired. Once an act got the nod to appear on the show, Spencer sat down and wrote the joke that Chuck would use to introduce the act.

"Coming up, we have five energetic young men who are gonna come

Two Left Feet, a mysterious woman with three legs who wowed The Gong Show *with her dance act.* AUTHOR'S COLLECTION

out here and perform a traditional African tribal dance in honor of *Roots*. I wonder if they realize that research has discovered that the name Kunta Kinte, when translated into English, means 'Larry Rabinowitz'?

"Our next act isn't having any trouble making ends meet. She's a contortionist! Get it?"

"Our next act are a musician and a dog who are going to make it big in the newspapers. But from what we saw backstage, it looks like the dog already made it big in the newspaper."

"Out next act is the only person I've ever seen play the ukulele against its will."

"The next group of guys call themselves a jug band. I don't know what that means, exactly, but one thing is for sure: I don't care what that means, exactly."

Spencer remembers, "The amount of info that Chuck's staff gave me to work with varied a lot. Sometimes, I'd get these really detailed descriptions, and I had a lot to work with. Sometimes, I got only the name, in which case I'd write a really generic introduction."[38]

"Our next performer said his hobby is glass blowing. He doesn't make little trinkets; he just likes to fog up windows with his breath."

Mr. Bell Jazzy, who played an array of bicycle horns like they were a keyboard.
AUTHOR'S COLLECTION

"This next man said he inherited his father's nose. He's pretty steamed because his sister got a tin mine in Bolivia."

"Our next act is getting a lot of exposure lately. Unfortunately, it's mostly from a weirdo wearing a raincoat."

"This next contestant is about to hit the big time, but tonight on *The Gong Show*, it's going to hit her back."

"This next act is about to prove that even the blandest act can be really boring."

Then taping day rolled around. The acts were sent to wait in NBC Rehearsal Room #3 to wait their turns. Barris staff photographer Vince Longo says, "If you can imagine what that looked like — to walk into that rehearsal hall on tape day and see all these people dressed as dinosaurs and scuba divers and everything else. It looked like a Fellini movie backstage every time we taped."[39]

The day started with a rehearsal for all five episodes, minus the judges of course. A number of the acts that spoke about their experiences afterward expressed surprise at how involved Chuck actually was in the process. Video survives from some of these rehearsals, revealing the fascinating dual role that he assumed for show preparation. A pair of apparently

38. Personal interview. 2 Feb. 2019.

39. Ibid.

high school-aged kids, dressed in costumes as an elderly couple, act out a skit while lip-syncing to a record. Director John "The Fox" Dorsey — Chuck's go-to director, who sported a "Just call me Bob" t-shirt because he believed himself to look just like Robert Redford — misses a few key shots during the act, which is reasonable because he's seeing it for the first time.

Prince Kenaga wore this outfit for his act, which consisted largely of "Guy walks into a bar" jokes. AUTHOR'S COLLECTION

    Chuck walks onstage after the kids are finished and asks, "John, do you want another shot at that?"
    Dorsey replies over the loudspeaker that he wants a do-over. Chuck turns to the kids and heaps praise all over them, telling them that they had nothing to worry about. He tells them to perform the act a second time, taking a moment to assure them that they had done everything right the first time. The second rehearsal was just to make sure the cameras were ready for them. The kids do the act the second time. Chuck, watching on the monitor, is satisfied with the shots the second time around, so he returns to the stage, showering praise on them for what a fantastic job they did.
    Next up for the rehearsal is a band. Chuck voices concerns about the audio quality and makes it known to the audio crew that he's not pleased. He keeps encouraging the band to give it another shot until the audio is

exactly right. Ultimately, he has them perform the song four times before the audio crew finally has everything set to his satisfaction. Yes, it's *The Gong Show*. But Chuck still wanted it perfect.

While ruling over the rehearsal crew with an iron fist, he would endear himself to the acts, letting them know they were there because, good or bad, the show wanted them there, and he was happy to have them. They took it to heart. The kids lip-syncing to the record got gonged that day. They reacted to the sound of the gong by breaking out in laughter and embracing Chuck before they left the stage. They had fun that day, and that little hug at the end was a thank-you to the host/producer who helped them get through it.

Chuck said, "I really feel for those people. I feel for them greatly. These are strange people. Some of them are borderline nuts. But they're not phony. They're putting it on the line. I admire their guts because I could never do what they do myself. It's Iwo Jima out there, and they're stark naked."[40]

At 4:30 pm, 30 minutes before the start of taping, producer Gene Banks would come into the rehearsal room to give all the contestants a pep talk and keep them calm, while making sure they kept their energy high. He concluded with one key detail: "Remember, if you get gonged, just take it in the spirit that it's given."

The average viewer never witnessed the empathy, the hand-holding through rehearsals, the easing of jitters, the encouragement, the meticulous management of the lighting and audio. All they saw was the finished product — a man in a safari outfit sitting at the piano and singing "Old MacDonald Had a Jungle"; two college girls in engineer caps shuffling their feet as the audience hollered over their performance of "Chattanooga Choo-Choo"; a woman who tried to sing "Come On, Get Happy" until her false teeth shot out onto the floor; the two-headed harmonica player; the circus acrobat who called his feats "the sit and spin" and "flipping me off."

That arduous work kept inspiring viewers who wanted to make career changes. Yvonne Tolbert had a path to *Gong* employment similar to Larry Gotterer. She was a fan before she was ever anything else. "I was selling shoes. My co-worker Eddie was a nephew of one of Chuck's employees. I hated my job. I was miserable. Eddie just announces one day, 'I'm sick of this place. I'm going to go work for my aunt.' A while later, I watched TV. *The Gong Show* was on. I said to myself, 'I'm going to work there.'"[41]

40. Shales. 1977.
41. Personal interview. 7 May 2019.

"I went in for a job interview, and it was strange, Chuck treated job interviews the same way that he treated auditions. I had to fill out the form and get photographed like a contestant, and I passed the first audition, so to speak, and got called in to meet Chuck. He hired me as a bandit, so I dealt with contestants for a while."

Tolbert got the attention, and then the affection, of photographer Vince Longo, and soon they were dating.

The noted tap dancer Katy the Caterpillar. BOB BODEN COLLECTION

Longo remembers, "There was a day in the studio where we had a very odd singer on the show. He had been on once before and we found out he had bicycled from Pasadena to the NBC studios in Burbank for the taping. He begins singing very poorly, and very off-key, and I'm not really listening to the lyrics, I'm just snapping photos. I'm wearing a headset so I can communicate with the control room, and John Dorsey says, 'Vince, this song is about Yvonne.' I began listening to the lyrics more closely after that. This guy had appeared on the show, been handled by Yvonne, fallen for her, gone home, written a song, and came back for an audition. Nobody realized until John Dorsey noticed it that the song he had written was about her."[42]

42. Personal interview. 7 May 2019.

Even from the earliest days of the show, the staff could tell that the show they were working on was something extraordinary. It inspired loyalty and optimism that compelled wardrobe coordinator Jefferson Beeker to take a gamble early on in his career. "I didn't work for Chuck directly, I worked for the NBC Studios as what was called a 'daily hire.' I was called in when a show needed me, I was technically employed for just that one day, and then the next time the studios needed me to do wardrobe, I'd be hired for another day. So, I might work for *Sanford and Son* on Thursday, and then on Friday I'd be brought in to work on *Chico and the Man*. On weekends, NBC taped all their game shows. I was assigned to *The Gong Show* and *The Fun Factory*.[43]

"For some reason they decided that since I worked on Broadway, I should dress the stars. I didn't have to do anything for the contestants, which was actually a rule that the network imposed on *The Gong Show*. A contestant's costume was considered part of their performance, and the contestants were being scored based on their performance, so any help from wardrobe would have been considered unfair.

"I worked for Dick Van Dyke briefly when he had a variety show around the same time that *The Gong Show* started. It was called *Van Dyke and Company*. Dick Van Dyke really liked me, and when that show ended production, he went on tour with a production of a musical, and he wanted to take me with him. I thought about *The Gong Show* for a bit, and something told me I needed to stay right where I was."

---

43. Personal interview. 10 Apr. 2019.

CHAPTER 7

Gary Gets Gonged

Above: Gary Owens and Sivi Aberg, as seen on the nighttime Gong Show *in 1976.* ROBERT BURROUGHS COLLECTION

The nighttime *Gong Show* with Gary Owens started taping in July, only a month after Chuck Barris assumed the helm in the daytime. The daytime version had a few more tapings in that time, so the show seemed to be finding some semblance of a groove. Milton DeLugg and his orchestra had a cheerful theme that blended brass horns and an old-fashioned organ, and sounded something like the theme music that an old-time radio talent show might have used decades earlier. Everyone in front of the camera wore formal wear. Johnny Jacobs, the golden-throated announcer who worked on all of Chuck Barris' shows, opened with a booming "From Hollywood — it's *The Gong Show!*" (In time, it would be modified to "From Hollywood...almost live! It's *The Gong Show!*") A lovely model — usually Sivi Aberg, actress and former Miss Sweden — introduces "the host and star of the show, Mr. Chuck Barris!" The show's "Little Man," Jerry Marin (one of the Munchkins from *The Wizard Of Oz*), dashed onstage to throw confetti from a basket at the end of each show as Chuck Barris announced the winning act and presented the grand prize — the Golden Gong trophy, which, from a distance, actually bore a striking resemblance to a Tony Award. There was also a check for "the almost-unusable sum of $516.32."[1]

All these elements had been established by the time the nighttime show with Gary Owens began taping on July 2, 1976. Yet, watching the first nighttime shows, it's almost as if an entirely different series was sneaking in to borrow the studio.

Episode #N2, the earliest episode available to research, opens with Larry Storch and Marion Ross, both judges tonight, attempting to perform a comedy sketch that was seemingly dropped in their laps right before they walked on stage. The gist of it was that Larry was giving a highfalutin, stuffy reading of a disclaimer for the program as it scrolled across the screen — not so far removed from something Gary Owens may have done for *Laugh-In*, which is why it's strange that Gary isn't the one doing it.

"Not all television programs are suitable for the entire family. The following program should not be viewed by anyone in your family under the age of ten, or over the age of ten, or who can count to ten, or not. Or who

---

1. For years, it's been rumored that the reason that Chuck picked that specific sum as the grand prize was an inside joke for anyone familiar with the business side of television; allegedly, $516.32 was the Screen Actors Guild's minimum daily wage for a television performance. Nobody interviewed for this book who worked for Chuck Barris seemed to know if that was true or not. The consensus seems to be that Chuck just wanted a funny-sounding, cumbersome number for the grand prize.

speaks English or has more than three of the five senses but not less than two, dum-de-waddy-waddy, or is known to be living at the present time."

Take one: Larry Storch, apparently trying to add his own touch to the show, grabs Marion Ross' hand and kisses it lasciviously until Buddy Hackett, sitting on the sidelines, prompts him. Larry does a double-take at the camera and starts reading the disclaimer. The problem is the scroll

Gary Owens was thought to be an ideal host for The Gong Show. *One staffer called him "a fish out of water."* AUTHOR'S COLLECTION

began as soon as the director faded in on him and it's already halfway over by the time he starts. Director John "The Fox" Dorsey jumps in and stops Larry, asking for a second take.

Take two: Larry Storch's delivery is a little on point, but the punch line — Marion Ross clonks him over the head with her gong mallet — bombs with the live audience.

Take three: Larry delivers it once more. His reading still can't keep up with the speed of the on-screen scroll, and Marion Ross' blow to the head still gets utter silence from the audience. But John Dorsey, Chuck Barris, or perhaps both were apparently losing patience and they go straight from the third take to the show's elaborate animated opening.

The caveman seen in the pilot bangs a gong, transforming the solid circle into the letters of the show's logo. Next, an animated montage of acts: A violinist's bow accidentally saws his instrument in half, a little girl conducts a choir of chickens, a circus ringmaster tries to put a leash on King Kong. A cartoon Gary Owens opens his mouth wide to reveal the little man playing Owens' teeth like a xylophone. Gary, in a plain gray business suit, walks onstage to an unfamiliar, generic theme performed by Milton DeLugg, himself in a plain button-down shirt, with his band decked out in t-shirts and ball caps. Over at the judges' dais, Marion Ross is wearing a tasteful dress, while Larry Storch and Buddy Hackett are wearing the worst leisure suits that the 1970s vomited up. Gary introduces Hackett as a "dirty" comic, and Hackett, apparently not appreciating the adjective, sticks his middle finger in the air, rendering the introduction unusable for broadcast.

Some of those acts on the nighttime Gong Show could be real hockey pucks.
AUTHOR'S COLLECTION

Gary Owens moves on with the show, explaining the rules with the help of "Gong Girl" — a lovely assistant inexplicably wearing a Zorro costume and holding the golden gong trophy. Also assisting Gary on the show, in place of "Little Man" Jerry Marin, is elderly former vaudeville comic Paul "Mousie" Garner.

Gary introduces tonight's first act: Mountain John Hilligoss, who sings a rousing version of "Okie from Muskogee" — until he's stopped in midsong by the clang of the gong, courtesy of Larry Storch. But when Gary Owens asks Storch why he sounded the gong, Storch is covering his eyes, but a pained expression is still discernible on his face. He apparently feels a twinge of guilt and tells Hilligoss, "My shoes are too tight, keep on going."

Owens, confused by the remark, asks Storch to clarify. Storch says he banged the gong "by accident." Hilligoss is allowed to continue, receives his scores from the judge — a grand total of 18 points — and is ushered offstage.

Eight minutes later on the master tape, the show starts all over again. The animated opening, Gary's introduction of himself, and the introduction of the judges, which is abruptly cut off when Buddy Hackett picks this moment to complain that he didn't like the introduction he initially got (just in case his middle finger wasn't clear enough). The show is stopped cold, so everyone regroups...and then the show is re-

Gary and the panel. On the far right tonight is the ham that made West Virginia famous, Soupy Sales. AUTHOR'S COLLECTION

started yet again. Roll open. Cue the band. Here's Gary. Here's the panel. And here's our first contestant — disco roller skater Maurice Cook. Mountain John Hilligoss is never seen, heard, nor spoken of again, an ironic fate considering he was the only part of the taping that had gone well so far.

The rest of the taping went fairly smoothly. But Chuck was so thoroughly dissatisfied with the first two nighttime episodes taped that he took the keys away from Chris Bearde, who had been primarily in charge of the nighttime show. The next taping of the nighttime show was telling: Milton DeLugg and The Band with a Thugg (as Chuck had christened them) was now playing the more familiar daytime theme music. The cartoon introduction was discarded. Gary Owens and the rest were in formal wear. And the next episode taped was numbered #1. The nighttime episodes produced by Chris Bearde were ditched, and Barris, seizing control, took over.

Nighttime *Gong* found its footing almost immediately by just copying the daytime template as much as possible with music, wardrobe, aesthetics, and even contestants. The nighttime show never featured new acts, it was exclusively acts that had already appeared on the daytime show; acts that

Nobody could wear a tuxedo and pith helmet ensemble like Chuck Barris.
ROBERT BURROUGHS COLLECTION

had done well and acts that had been gonged. Basically, acts that left a particularly memorable dint, good or bad, got invited back for a second shot on the nighttime version.

The only puzzle piece that changed between daytime and nighttime was the host. Nobody could remember Chuck Barris ever voicing any objection to the way that Gary Owens hosted the show, but watching his episodes all these years later, it feels strange trying to explain how competence proved to be detrimental to his performance. Barris and Bearde had envisioned a grandiose, borderline pompous performance from Owens — almost as if Owens would be playing the role of a host who thought his show was beneath him. Gary Owens never really assumed that role, or any other. He played it mostly straight. He read his joke introductions off the cue cards, but when an act was gonged, Owens would ask the judge why they had ended the act, thanked the contestant for coming, then got into position to introduce the next act. He was smooth, he was polished. He was an island of tranquility in a sea of roller-skating fiddlers and overweight belching women in bikinis.

Jefferson Beeker says, "I remember watching the tapings from backstage and thinking Gary Owens came off as a fish out of water."[2]

Compare it to the daytime version. Chuck Barris tugged at his hair and shuffled his feet while laughing at his own jokes, then stared at the ceiling and let out a long, drawn-out "Awwwwwwww" while grasping for something off-script to add about the next act, usually settling for "This act is so good." He used the word "stuff" over and over. He struggled with his hands so much that it became a running joke on the show. He'd clap his hands, pump his fists, then stick his index fingers in the air, then clap his hands again, then pump his fists again, then stick his index fingers in the air again, then clap etc. In time, the studio audiences were clapping along with him. Chuck, rather than being put off by having his own jangled nerves being mocked by the audience, added a new layer to it. Every now and then, he'd start to clap his hands, then stop short. The audience would clap without him, and Chuck would smile proudly and declare, "I gotcha!"

The only thing that truly made Chuck self-conscious was his eyes. They were the clearest indicator of how inelegant he felt onstage, and besides that, the bright stage lights made him squint. One day, the show returned from commercial, and there was Chuck, wearing his custom-fitted tuxedo along with a checked bucket hat, about two sizes two big, that came down to his nose. Chuck tilted his head back whenever he had to read the

---

2. Personal interview. 10 Apr. 2019.

cue cards, but otherwise did the rest of the show with his eyes covered. Eventually, the collection of funny hats that Chuck had stashed in his office made his way to the stage. The set now included a hat rack for Chuck, complete with top hat, cowboy hat, yachting cap, army helmet, and pith helmet.

Chuck even started resisting the formality of a tuxedo. On one early episode, he walked onstage wearing an ordinary gray sweater. Arte

Chuck, seen here with Gloria Hunter and her chicken marionette puppet, had used Jamie Farr's idea of dressing in formal wear as salvation for his show. But once it became a hit, Chuck began resisting tuxedos, mixing blue jeans and leather with fancy threads. BOB BODEN COLLECTION

Johnson asked why he wasn't wearing his tuxedo and Chuck just replied that he didn't feel like wearing it that day. He was the boss, who was going to tell him he had to? Another day, the tuxedo was on, but not the bowtie. He walked out with the knot unfinished and hosted a few segments with what just looked like a silky blob hanging from his collar, before getting rid of it altogether and hosting the rest of the show with his shirt half-open.

Occasionally, Chuck started mixing and matching the elements of the outfit. He'd wear an off-the-rack pinstriped shirt, one you'd wear in a casual office environment, with the bowtie and jacket. Occasionally, he'd walk out in ordinary slacks or even blue jeans instead of the tailor-made pants that were intended for the ensemble.

Susan Simons remembers, "What Chuck brought to that show, that the other hosts weren't able to, was a complete lack of decorum. Granted, that show was always going to end up saddled with people who actually thought they had talent and were surprised by the gong. But when Chuck began wearing those ridiculous hats, and wearing blue jeans with his tuxedo jacket, it made it so much clearer what this show was. This was not to be taken seriously, this was not a search for America's newest talents. This was just harmless fun."[3]

A strange scene took place on episode #N115 of the nighttime version — "strange" being a relative term in the case of this show, of course.

Gary Owens introduced the next act. "Now stepping into the *Gong Show* spotlight is a singing housewife. As of today, she has sung to 40 houses in the neighborhood…here is Evelyn Houston."

A matronly woman strolled onstage and sang, "Embrace me…my sweet embraceable you…"

Producer Gene Banks walked onstage and wrapped his arms around her to make this a very literal interpretation of the song. Writer Larry Spencer walked out next and hugged her. Sivi Aberg walked away from her post at the scoreboard and found some room to clasp her arms around the songstress. Jaye P. Morgan, Jamie Farr, and even Rex Reed at the judges' table got into the spirit and walked over for a cuddle. With so many bodies piled onto her at this point, it was hard to identify the next set of arms that emerged from behind Mrs. Houston and wrapped her Heimlich-style.

The song ended and everyone broke away from Mrs. Houston. The mystery pair of arms stepped out from behind her. It was a gum-chewing Chuck Barris, in blue jeans, a tailed tuxedo jacket, and bowtie ensemble. Gary Owens walked onstage without a look or acknowledgment of Chuck, who stood behind the nighttime host and the contestant in silence as they collected the scores from the judges. When it was all over, Chuck walked off without saying a word. He had haunted the segment like a specter and then faded away when the gag was done.

Two episodes later, Gary Owens introduced another act, identified only as "The Magical, Mystical Guitarist." It was Chuck, guitar in hand, strumming and singing the theme to *The Gong Show*.[4] Chuck got one verse out before the curtain slooooooowly lowered, and his microphone cut off.

---

3. Personal interview. 18 Apr. 2019.

4. Yes, the theme did have lyrics. Penned by Chuck Barris, the actual name of the song was "Lovee's Come Back." It was a peppy tune about a man who's excited because his girlfriend is returning after a long out-of-town trip.

Gary Owens walked onstage, looking disturbed, and said, "Ladies and gentlemen, we apologize. We really had no idea how much our standards had depreciated."

It's hard to know exactly what Chuck's frame of mind was when he devised these two gag cameos. He probably just thought it was funny. But then, he probably also recognized that he was enjoying being a famous daytime TV star, and that the bigger audiences were at night.

The man with the net comes out to remove another contestant on the nighttime Gong Show. ROBERT BURROUGHS COLLECTION

In February 1977, Chuck Barris, NBC, and Firestone took stock of the show's success. Madeline David at NBC dubbed the daytime version "the show that people love to hate." The angry letters that *The Gong Show* triggered were ceaseless, and yet the ratings reports showed NBC repeatedly that even people who hated it seemingly couldn't stop watching it. *The Gong Show* was doing nearly double the rating that *Search for Tomorrow* had been pulling in that slot before it was moved in June. Meanwhile, Nielsen was gathering ratings data for the syndicated prime access time shows. Among that specific batch of programs, nighttime *Gong* had ranked 13th in October. By February, it had jumped up to 4th. 32 stations had already signed their contracts with Firestone to renew the nighttime show for 1977-78. In advance of NATPE, the annual convention where syndicators and station managers hobnobbed and made deals, Firestone took out ads in trade magazines encouraging stations to sign up for the next season. None of the ads, however, made any mention of a host for the nighttime show.

Behind the scenes, Chuck made it clear who the nighttime host would

Gary Owens really tried to make The Gong Show *his own, but a shadow was cast over him with surprising speed.* AUTHOR'S COLLECTION

be. The ABC O&Os, the stations that had signed up first for season one and got the gong rolling, were told in no uncertain terms that Chuck Barris would be the host of the nighttime show starting in the fall of 1977, and if the O&Os objected, *The Gong Show* would leave all of the ABC O&Os and begin airing on NBC O&Os instead.

Gary Owens was notified of his dismissal via a letter from Chuck: *I feel there is a certain chemistry with me, the celebrities, and the acts that works best. You were working at a disadvantage, doing a show the producer wanted, from the beginning, to do himself.*[5]

---

5. Whitney, Dwight. "Chuckie Baby Reigns as King Gong." *TV Guide.* 15 Apr. 1978.

Chuck told the Archive of American Television, "[Gary Owens] was a good host. But I was auditioning the acts, and they would get to know me. And I thought that was a good thing, to be on the show with them."[6]

"Now let me ask you something...do you honestly believe that?" asks Joanne Worley. "You want to know why I think Chuck took over the nighttime show? Because it was fun. He got famous, he was getting

Gary has a word during the break with judges Rex Reed, Ruth Buzzi, and Allen Ludden. FRED WOSTBROCK COLLECTION

attention from the press, and hosting a TV show is a fun job. Hey, he's the boss, so if he decides he wants more episodes of the show to host, he can do that! I don't think it had anything to do with chemistry or making the acts comfortable, I just think he liked doing it."[7]

Chuck seemed to admit as much some time later. When he appeared as a guest on *The Mike Douglas Show*, Douglas asked him why he ended up hosting one of his own productions. Chuck gave him the most honest answer possible.

"I think it was basically greed."[8]

6. Archive of American Television. 2010.
7. Personal interview. 10 Jan. 2019.
8. Interview with Chuck Barris. *The Mike Douglas Show*. 1978.

Shortly after word of the dismissal reached the press, Gary Owens spoke to *New York Daily News* and didn't hold back. His feelings were hurt. "I'm not angry, just a little disappointed. I was the host of the original pilot film that was offered to stations at a convention in January 1976. It was my show that sold the series to more than 50 stations at that time. I built the program to become the number-four highest rated series in syndica-

Another losing act gets escorted off the Gong Show *stage. The man with the net seems to be looking at Gary and thinking "He's next."* AUTHOR'S COLLECTION

tion. The only shows that are ahead of us are Lawrence Welk, *Hee-Haw*, and *Hollywood Squares*.[9]

Chuck gave a blunt account. "He just didn't seem to know what we were trying to do. And besides, I thought I could do it better."[10]

While Chuck Barris himself may have been too modest to say it in public, there was another logical reason for him to take over the nighttime show. He and Gary Owens were hardly competing against each other, but

---

9. Maksian, George. "Chuck Takes His Gong, and It Tolls for Gary." *New York Daily News*. 3 Sep. 1977.

10. O'Brien, Jim. "Gong." *Philadelphia Daily News*. 14 Sep. 1977.

in a matter of months, it was clear that the public associated Chuck with the show more than Owens. In December 1976, *Sanford and Son* did an episode in which Fred Sanford and his friend Bubba were contestants, and Chuck, not Gary Owens, was tapped to guest-star as himself, hosting the show. The following month, Chuck was co-hosting the Rose Parade with Anita Bryant and Big Bird.

The one and only host of The Gong Show...*because he wanted it that way.*
AUTHOR'S COLLECTION

The most surprising example of Chuck's emergence as a star came in January 1977, when ABC attempted to poach him from his own series. The network made Chuck a lucrative offer to jump ship to host a daily one-hour variety show. Maybe you can make a case that Chuck had better chemistry, or that his presence made the acts more relaxed, or that he was the boss, and he could do whatever he wanted. But by 1977, "the star of *The Gong Show*" was much more than a scripted introduction for Sivi Aberg. It was a plain fact.

Chris Bearde was the next one through the exit. In time, the closing credits were modified from "A Chuck Barris/Chris Bearde Production" to "A Chuck Barris Production."

Vince Longo says, "In the beginning, Chris Bearde was there. He was there for a while. He had an office. Somewhere along the line, he disappeared. There were certain things that were never talked about in the office. Chuck Barris never really announced to us that Chris left."[11]

While there was never really a formal announcement or explanation made, Chuck Barris' employees tended to reach the same conclusion about Bearde's departure. Chuck liked being in control, and being in control was more difficult when he had to share that power with somebody.

The original agreement between Chuck Barris and Chris Bearde was that Bearde would own 35 percent of the show. Barris wanted him out, at one point offering him a cool million for his 35 percent. Bearde balked.

"We had harrowing battles," Chuck admitted to *TV Guide*. "Chris didn't understand the ramifications of long-term success."[12]

Chris told the publication, "Bad things were happening to the show. First I lost a little control, then a lot. Then one day, Budd Granoff, Chuck's executive vice president, came around and said, 'Hey Chris, we'll make it easy for you. Chuck will take over both shows. You continue to collect your bread.'"

The final details of the agreement were never made public, but whatever happened, Chris Bearde just quietly disappeared from *The Gong Show* one day and never returned to the office.

---

11. Personal interview. 9 May 2019.

12. Whitney. 1978.

CHAPTER 8

The Family That Gongs Together

Above: Chuck introduces "the women of NBC." Page Shelley Herman is shaking hands with him here. PHOTO COURTESY OF SHELLEY HERMAN

Susan Simons` remembers, "*The Gong Show* was really *The Chuck Barris Show*. The audience loved him. We had the craziest audiences in the studios every taping day. When Chuck walked onstage they'd scream. When Chuck would take his hat off, they'd scream again. Just every little thing he did, the audience would go wild for him. The show was really rooted in his own sensibilities, which was 'Have fun with it.' Chuck really didn't like people who took it seriously. He'd rather showcase people who were just there to have a good time."[1]

One day, Chuck Barris had an idea. Actually, on many days, Chuck Barris had ideas. That was part of the fun of working in his general proximity.

Shelley Herman was a page at NBC in 1976, where, among her duties, she gave guided tours of the Burbank studio complex where the network taped much of its programming.

"I was giving a guided tour one day, and a member of Chuck's staff comes running down the hall and says 'Shelley, Chuck needs you!' and pulls me away from my tour group. He's pulling me into the studio…[2]

"I said, 'What does Chuck need?' And Chuck runs out at that point and takes me by the arm and pulls me to the stage.

"He says, 'Don't worry, when the curtain comes up, you'll know what to do.' And he dashes offstage and just leaves me there."

A group of assorted staffers, all women, gathered around Shelley onstage and waited for their cue. Sivi Aberg introduced "The host and star of the show, Chuck Barris," who had abruptly returned to stage, joining the women right as the curtain rose and walking to his mark with them. Chuck announced that today, viewers across America would have a chance to meet the staffers he had dubbed The Women of NBC. With that, he asked the women to "introduce yourselves." They turned, shook hands with each other, and walked offstage without saying a word to the audience.

Shelley went back to her tour group and finished her job for the day. "But to just be thrust out there with no warning and get a laugh, how great is that?"

Wardrobe coordinator Jefferson Beeker recalls, "Somehow, Chuck found out I was a member of AFTRA. Chuck comes to me as taping is about to start and says 'Jefferson, you're introducing me today.' I said, 'Excuse me?' And he said, 'Think of a line and go out there.' I came up with

---

1. Personal interview. 18 Apr. 2019.
2. Personal interview. 6 Jan. 2017.

Wardrobe coordinator Jefferson Beeker is ready for the big time, performing in one of Chuckie's Fables. PHOTO BY VINCE LONGO, COURTESY OF JEFFERSON BEEKER

some line to introduce him, walked out there, grabbed the microphone, and introduced Chuck at the start of the show. And when it was over, I filled out some paperwork and got the mandatory fee since I was a union member and I had performed on the show."[3]

"Another day, he comes to me and says, 'Can you dance up a flight of steps like Bojangles?' I said yes. I didn't think anything about it. Then he suddenly says to me as we're getting ready to tape, 'Put on a tux and some tap shoes. You're going to tap dance up a flight of steps, fall into a tank of water, and then we're going to throw confetti on you.' We had next to no time to rehearse it. I told Milton DeLugg to just play 'Sweet Georgia Brown' because we didn't have time for the band to work on anything else and I knew they had an arrangement for that."

Howard Nugent was a per diem worker for IATSE, the stagehand union in Los Angeles. Although he didn't work directly for Chuck Barris Productions, his work brought him into the studio quite often for tapings, often as a carpenter or electrician. It varied from day to day and show to show, depending on what they needed.

He showed up for the February 20, 1977, taping and saw that the set was bedecked with shamrocks. Today's taping would include an episode for March 17, St. Patrick's Day. Howard didn't give any thought to that and took his spot at the ropes. Today his job was to open and shut the curtain for each act.

Howard remembers, "The gag was that Chuck would announce that they were going to do something special for St. Patrick's Day, and they were going to bring out this little old Jewish lady who was going to dance to 'Hava Nagila.' Well, they saw this act when she auditioned and there was just nothing there. The song would play, she danced like a little old lady would dance, and that was it.[4]

"Before taping starts, Chuck Barris, in his usual way of thinking, walks up to me before the taping and says, 'Howard, can you dance?' I had done *Fiddler on the Roof* in college as a papa, so I had my L'Chaim dance. So, I said yes. Chuck is going from crew member to crew member asking, 'Can you dance?'

"So once the show starts, they bring this woman out to do her dance. They didn't tell her what we were going to do."

After a few quiet moments of the bubbeh shuffling her feet to a quiet rendition of "Hava Nagila" driven by Milton DeLugg's piano, the band

3. Personal interview. 10 Apr. 2019.
4. Personal interview. 19 Jan. 2019.

abruptly switched to a louder, livelier, brassier rendition. Members of IATSE and Chuck Barris' staff swarmed the stage and danced circles around her. Completely unfazed, the woman smiled and kept dancing.

Larry Spencer remembers, "I was backstage one day and Chuck points to me and he points to a woman who worked in the studio, and he says, 'When I introduce the next act, we'll open the curtain, and I want you two

Was it still The Gong Show, *or was it* The Chuck Barris Show? *Sometimes it was hard to tell.* ROBERT BURROUGHS COLLECTION

to be making out.' Okay, well, it was a little embarrassing but…I wasn't going to question it if Chuck wanted that, you know?"[5]

Slowly but surely these gags crept into the show. *The Gong Show* started as a simple talent show, but comedy sketches, running gags, and recurring characters popped up. And as usual, necessity was the mother.

From a logistical standpoint, the problem with *The Gong Show* was

Director John "The Fox" Dorsey watches the clock. Chuck once had him sing a number from the control room to fill some time on an episode. PHOTO BY AND COURTESY OF VINCE LONGO

that trying to make the show run on time was tricky. Contestants had 90 seconds to perform their acts, with the judges forced to wait 45 seconds before they could bang the gong. If the first two acts on the show that day got gonged, suddenly, the show had a minute and a half to fill. It was obvious that ad-libbing wasn't Chuck's strong suit, so how can you fill that time now?

Chuck initially decided to fill the extra time with a series of gags he named "Curtain Closers." Chuck would introduce an act, but then stop the act with no conclusion, not even the bang of the gong. As a running

5. Personal interview. 2 Feb. 2019.

gag, he subjected a man named Cassius Sargent to multiple interruptions. Sargent would start reciting a poem with the opening line "Dear friends, a loose screw is not modern or new…" only for Chuck to apologetically announce that they had to move on. An organist named Greg Barnes would play an agonizingly slow and mournful melody until the curtain just shut on him and the show went to commercial.

Barris staffer Ellen Metzger as a "Curtain Closer," portraying the Cowardly Lion from The Wizard of Oz. PHOTO BY VINCE LONGO, COURTESY OF ELLEN METZGER

As *The Gong Show* became increasingly "the in thing" on television, celebrities agreed to show up as curtain closers, performing *Gong Show*-style acts until Chuck, looking annoyed, would close the curtain on them without acknowledging that the person we just saw was anybody famous. Lyle Waggoner played a leaf. Pat Paulsen performed a bizarre version of "Tequila" in which he mooed instead of saying "Tequila."

The one who proved to be the greatest curtain closer of all was an out-of-work actor named Murray Langston. Langston, a Nova Scotia transplant, had enjoyed a decent few years as a repertory actor on variety shows. He had spent three seasons on *The Sonny and Cher Comedy Hour* and a single season on *The Hudson Brothers Razzle Dazzle Show*. He had performed his stand-up act on NBC's *Midnight Special* too. But by 1976, he was living every actor's worst nightmare: the dry spell. He needed work, and he needed money.

A friend who had just appeared as a contestant told Murray about *The Gong Show* and suggested he audition to be a contestant. The $516.32 would be nice, sure, but there was something even better. Chuck was courting members of AFTRA for *The Gong Show* the same way that he

Barris staffers Gene Banks, Danny Lies, and Larry Spencer get ready to fill a little more time for the boss. PHOTO BY AND COURTESY OF VINCE LONGO

had for *The Dating Game*. Just for appearing on the show, a union member in good standing would be paid $250.[6] Murray Langston didn't care about winning a gong trophy, but a $250 gig was a nice thought.

The only drawback that Murray Langston could see was that people watched *The Gong Show*. He was an established television performer by 1976, and if his family and friends saw him appearing as a common contestant on an amateur talent show, he was worried that they would take it to mean he was totally broke. He needed to come up with an act that would allow him to conceal his identity.

---

6. In 1977, *Gong Show* producer Gene Banks said that due to a union rule, union members weren't allowed to perform in competition with non-union members. Because of this, some episodes of *The Gong Show* were designated "Union Shows," in which all the contestants were members of AFTRA or SAG (Screen Actors Guild).

Langston called Ruth Goldberg, the staffer in charge of talent booking, and pitched an idea. He'd wear a paper bag over his head and call himself "The Unknown Comic." Goldberg loved the idea. In fact, she loved it more than Langston hoped she would. Goldberg explained the concept of the Curtain Closers that had been added to the show and suggested that The Unknown Comic might be good for that. Langston would still get the $250 union fee; he just wouldn't be a contestant.

Murray Langston in the role that made him famous, as The Unknown Comic. AUTHOR'S COLLECTION

Langston picked his wardrobe carefully: beige and brown, a jacket that was too tight even on his slender frame, and pants that didn't reach his ankles. Every comedy club in America had seen a bad comic who looked like him. Atop his shoulders, a paper bag with three holes cut out for the eyes and mouth. And then he'd fire off a mix of some of the worst jokes ever told on television and occasionally a so-bad-it's-good one. The capper each time was an insult that would offend Chuck so much that he would stop the segment.

"Thank you! Thank you! Boy, what a crowd! You people really look like a peachy audience. I say that because somebody should call the fuzz! HEY! "All right, but I wanna tell you, this *Gong Show* is really selling a lot of TVs. I sold mine yesterday! HEY! Rimshot!

"Hey, look at this panel. Jamie Farr may not be tall, dark, and handsome, but he's handsome in the dark.

"Jaye P. Morgan, a beautiful girl with lips like petals…bicycle pedals! Hey! Ha!

"Allen Ludden! What a great guy! Just last week, he stopped a rape. He changed his mind!"

"Time now for a joke. How do you make gold soup? Put in fourteen carrots!

"Hey, Chucky Baby, wanna help me do an impression? We'll doing an impression of a horse. I'll be the front end, and Chuck, you just be yourself!"

Chuck, looking disgusted, would say "That's enough" and shut the curtain while the Unknown Comic protested. Eventually, the Unknown Comic became such a popular fixture that Chuck began playing his introduction to the hilt with a long, drawn-out build. "Ladies and gentlemen, here coooooomes the prince of puns! Here coooooomes the wizarrrrrrd of WHOOPEEEEEEE! The Unknowwwwwwwn Comiiiiiiic!"

John Hill says, "Chuck really began working up the audience for The Unknown Comic's appearance. He gave a long introduction, and he would drag out the word 'Unknown.' 'Here comes the Unknoooooooown…' Well, Chuck began playing with that with a series of running gags involving me. He would do the same drawn-out introduction and then announce The Unknown Crockpot, and it would be me wearing a full body costume. I was the Unknown Crocodile and the Unknown Pussy. Chuck would get indignant because it was the wrong act and he'd close the curtain on me after I had only been out there for a few seconds."[7]

One of the reasons the Unknown Comic appealed to Chuck's sensibilities so strongly was because it always involved jokes at his expense. Langston says, "Chuck came running to me after the show ended and said 'You gotta do another one!' Chuck was a smart guy. He could see a value to what I was doing. It gave him vulnerability. Chuck introduced every act on the show by making a joke about them. Well, some people might see that and feel like Chuck was treating the contestants as if they were beneath him. When I came out and made fun of him, it knocked him down so that he and the contestants were on the same level. It made him part of the joke, and that helped the show."[8]

---

7. Personal interview. 14 May 2019.

8. Personal interview. 4 May 2019.

It was this logic that led to two other recurring gags on the show: The Whispers, a trio of women who swayed back and forth to music but never quite started their song, and when Chuck complained that they hadn't sung anything yet, they would spit mouthfuls of water in his face; and Dr. Jerry the Singing Chef, who would describe a recipe as he was preparing it in a bowl.

Make-up artist Verne Langdon transformed himself into Johann Sebastian Bork for some segments of The Gong Show. *Langdon's alter ego released three LPs.* PHOTO BY AND COURTESY OF VINCE LONGO

"First you put your eggies right inside," Dr. Jerry would sing while cracking two eggs into a bowl. "You beat 'em to the left and you beat him to the right."

"And you add some milk and some flour," he'd add while dumping about a quart of milk and half a bag of flour into the bowl. "And you stir it up for under an hour…"

As Dr. Jerry poured the whole mixture into a blender, Chuck would wave off Dr. Jerry and apologize. "We've run out of time."

Dr. Jerry, hurt, would protest, "What do you mean we're out of time? I've come here from Passaic, New Jersey. You think it's a commute?"

Chuck would try to smooth things over, only to get the entire contents of the blender splashed in his face. Fade to black.

Many of the scripted character pieces on the show were concocted as a way of rewarding the staff that Chuck adored. He was obligated to pay extra, but NBC had given him a big enough budget for *The Gong Show* that it wasn't really coming out of his own pocket. When the spoon players and hula dancers weren't enough to fill 30 minutes, Chuck gave his faithful employees their own moments in the spotlight and a few

Billy Carroll, who sang "The Man I Love" without her false teeth.
AUTHOR'S COLLECTION

extra dollars for the effort. Danny Lies was Vladimir Voinivich, a stoic concert pianist who would walk onstage, take a stiff bow, and sit on the bench. He'd crack his knuckles, let out an agonized wail, and walk offstage without playing a note.

A priest, Father Ed, would present Chuck with some kind of gift and then offer a pithy thought.

>   FATHER ED: We have a plaque here to give to you.
>   CHUCK: Aww, thank you, Father Ed. What's it for?
>   FATHER ED: I don't know.
>   CHUCK: Oh...Okay. It's a nice plaque. Anyway, Father Ed, I understand you run some kind of a Boys' Town here in California. What do you have to tell us?

FATHER ED: I've never met a kid I liked.
CHUCK: Thank you, Father Ed...a lot of sensitivity.

Howard Nugent says, "Father Ed was Ed Holland. He was a carpenter at NBC. It was easy to work him into the show because once the set has been put up for the day, there's nothing else for him to do. Chuck had

NBC carpenters Jocko Kerns and Ed Holland, earning a nice bonus in their paychecks. PHOTO BY AND COURTESY OF VINCE LONGO

this idea and he decided he wanted Ed to play a priest for this running gag. A lot of the people from the crew ended up on the show. I looked at a list of crew members just to jog my memory and realized how many of these guys appeared on the show. *The Gong Show* was utterly spontaneous, which was why the show was what it was."[9]

A significant source of inspiration for the extracurricular bits was the exploratory work of wardrobe designer Peter Mins (who designed the formal wear that the judges wore for each show — the judges were typically color-coordinated on each program) and Jefferson Beeker. One of the first time-filling ideas the staff came up with was a segment called "Chuckie's Fables." Chuck would sit in a big rocking chair and read a fairy

9. Personal interview. 19 Jan. 2019.

THE UNCENSORED HISTORY OF TELEVISION'S WILDEST TALENT SHOW   149

Jefferson Beeker and Peter Mins with another find from NBC's costume department. PHOTOS BY VINCE LONGO, COURTESY OF JEFFERSON BEEKER

tale from a large prop book, while members of the Barris staff and the NBC crew acted out the tale on the stage. The "fable" was usually a shaggy dog story with a ridiculous or anticlimactic ending, and Chuck would announce the moral of the story, which was always a total non-sequitur.

Beeker recalls the somewhat backward approach of the inspiration for the Fables. "NBC saved all their costumes from everything the network had ever done, so all their variety shows, all their specials, everything, and the basement was just rows and rows and rows of racks of costumes. Very often, we would just go down there and make note of what was down there and report back to Chuck. 'Hey Chuck, downstairs, we found a lobster costume and a chicken costume.' Chuck would write a Fable that involved a lobster and a chicken."[10]

Chuck operated on whims so much that Mins and Beeker gradually hoarded NBC's supply of costumes, to the point that they had five full racks of assorted outfits. NBC eventually complained, but Mins and Beeker leveled with them about the way *The Gong Show* worked. Chuck Barris would have an idea, and as soon as he had it, he wanted it carried out. They wanted all the costumes there because they wanted to be ready for whatever idea Chuck suddenly had. NBC was satisfied with that explanation, although they now charged Chuck Barris Productions for extra studio space because of all the costumes that they were long-term borrowing.

Beeker says, "Even though I was a daily hire, Chuck really favored bringing in the same people repeatedly as much as he could for each taping. Chuck made it known that he wanted to begin doing things other than just the contestants' acts on each episode, just as a way of breaking things up. He called everyone into a meeting as his company offices and said he needed ideas."[11]

When Chuck asked the staff for a new idea, Beeker spoke up. A search of the basement had recently turned up costumes like what Clark Gable and Vivien Leigh wore in *Gone with the Wind*. Beeker suggested a gag where Scarlett said a line, Rhett replied, "Frankly my dear, I don't give a damn," and Scarlett would take offense, which would lead to a whole run of dialogue about things that you can't say on TV. Beeker pitched himself as Scarlett and Peter Mins as Rhett.

The following Saturday, Beeker arrived at the studio for rehearsal and found his entire idea, fully written and prepared on cue cards for the taping, but Chuck warned that depending how the acts played out, they

---

10. Ibid.
11. Personal interview. 10 Apr. 2019.

may not have time for the Rhett and Scarlett bit. Five episodes came and five episodes went, but during the last segment of the fifth episode of that day's taping session, Chuck abruptly stopped tape and asked Beeker, "How fast can you guys be in costume?"[12]

Beeker told him, "Getting into the Scarlett costume will take some doing, but I think I can do it in five minutes."

The NBC censor's least favorite act, Rhett and Scarlett. PHOTO COURTESY OF JEFFERSON BEEKER

Chuck replied, "Split that in half if you can, and you're on."
Beeker ran to wardrobe and told Mins, "Get dressed! We're on!"

SCARLETT: (gesturing to her dress) Rhett, look what I did with the living room drapes!
RHETT: Frankly, Scarlett, I don't give a damn!
SCARLETT: Oh, Rhett, you can't say that, fiddley dee! You can't say that on television!
RHETT: Tell me if I can say this, Scarlett. I wrote a poem for you.
SCARLETT: You did? How nice!

12. Ibid.

RHETT: Tell me if I can say this: Dingleberries and tulips. Dingleberries and rain. I see dingleberries and I feel pain.
SCARLETT: That's lovely, Rhett, but what are dingleberries?
RHETT: *(audio muted)*
SCARLETT: Rhett Butler! You can't say *(audio muted)!* That's terrible!
RHETT: Scarlett, I've got another little poem for you.
SCARLETT: You do, Rhett? How nice.
RHETT: Listen…I love your eyes, I love your nose, I love your thighs, I love your toes.
SCARLETT: Well, that's pretty, Rhett.
RHETT: And I love your *(audio muted).*
SCARLETT: That's terrible, Rhett!
RHETT: I have a riddle, Scarlett. "What looks like a basset and is long and flaccid?"
SCARLETT: I don't know, Rhett, what looks like a basset and is long and flaccid?
RHETT: My rama-lama-*(audio muted).*
CHUCK: Okay, that's it! Off! Off! I've never heard anything like that in my life! That's disgusting.

Beeker remembers, "Nobody — not the NBC crew, not Chuck's staff, nobody had seen us in the costumes. I remember particularly Jamie Farr was one of the judges that day, and he was just doubled over laughing at the bit. I saw something in his eye, and I could see what he was thinking — he's going to dress as Scarlett O'Hara on *M*A*S*H*. I knew he was thinking it. Eva Gabor loved the bit too. She had a line of wigs at that time, and she found out that the wig I wore for Scarlett was an Eva Gabor wig."[13]

Chuck loved the bit so much that he kept writing more Rhett and Scarlett gags. There was almost no variation in formula — in fact, it was such a set routine that Chuck didn't even bother typing either character's first line of dialogue. He just typed "Scarlett says something, and Rhett says the usual" at the beginning of each script. Beeker would make up a new opening line for Scarlett on the spot, and "the usual," of course, was the line "Frankly my dear, I don't give a damn."

The Chinese philosopher Confusion would offer words of wisdom. He was portrayed by joke writer Jaime Klein. "…[A]ll of my words of

13. Ibid.

wisdom were silly jokes. What I remember about Chuck was the way he screwed with you with absolutely no warning. One of my jokes was supposed to be that I'd say, 'In the words of my brother, How-Long — ' and then Chuck would interrupt me and say, 'Your brother was How-Long?' and I'd say, 'About six feet.' That was the gag we rehearsed. On the air, I said, 'In the words of my brother, How-Long,' and Chuck grins at me

Producer Gene Banks gets into the spirit of February 14 with a special introduction. PHOTO BY AND COURTESY OF VINCE LONGO

and says, 'Your brother was named How-Long?' What am I supposed to do with that line?"[14]

Milton DeLugg portrayed an old comic, Nazo Literatus, who recited riddles and rhymes, like this flatulent diddy: "Eep, ipe! Eat a piece of pie! Blackbird flew into a country store! He *(raspberry)* on the counter and he *(raspberry)* on the floor and he *(raspberry)* on the coffee and he *(raspberry)* on the tea and if I hadn't moved, he'd have *(raspberry)* on me."

Fillipe De Fox, the great pianist, would injure his fingers before he played a single note. The Brothers Vert would play music with the zippers on their pants, and Ruthie the Stripper would attempt to disrobe until a security guard halted the act.

14. Personal interview. 8 Dec. 2016.

Larry Spencer says, "Chuck was the greatest boss I've ever had. As long as you knew you had to be loyal to him, he would give you the shirt off his back. Every week, he'd give out awards to the crew. He had these statuettes made. 'Best crew member of the week.' Every week, he'd come in with a design for a new jacket, we'd all get staff jackets that Chuck designed."[15]

Larry Spencer had several characters on the show. He was one of the

A curtain closer called Sweetness and Light; Three sisters sang "Feelings" until a fist fight broke out among them, and Chuck got caught in the middle trying to break it up. ROBERT BURROUGHS COLLECTION

Brothers Vert — the act always ended when Larry's zipper got caught and he collapsed in agony. He was also the mean and dastardly Villain, a silent movie archetype in top hat and cape who stalked across the stage as the audience booed and hissed. But perhaps his best-known role on the show was "Larry and His Magic _____." Chuck would introduce him as if he was a real act, and Larry would bring out a musical instrument, a different one each time, and sing a repetitive tune.

"I'm gonna play my tuba!"

The audience, in rhythm, would shout back *"What are you gonna do?"*

"I'm gonna play my tuba!"

15. Personal interview. 2 Feb. 2019.

"What are you gonna do?!"
I'm gonna play my tuba!"
"What are you gonna do?!"
"I'm gonna play my tuba nooooowwwww..."

After repeating it through several iterations and even a key change, Larry would finally attempt to play the instrument, but something would go wrong; the tuba would be too heavy for him to lift; his timpani was filled with milk and the mallets would disappear into the liquid; the slats flew off his xylophone; his accordion cracked in half at the first pull; a balloon inflated from the bell of his trumpet.

Because Larry Spencer was the sole credited writer for much of the show's run, you could guess that he was writing himself into much of the show to get himself some of those juicy extra paydays. You'd be wrong.

Spencer remembers, "That was all Chuck. Chuck would walk in on the morning of a taping and announce, 'Larry, you're going to do this during show #1. During show #2, we'll have Ruthie come out and do her bit...' Chuck would come in with all of these ideas for what everybody was going to do, and he had written them all out as scripts. It seemed like all he did in his spare time was think of ways to get everybody on the staff onto the show."[16]

Larry Spencer, as Larry and His Magic Trumpet. "What are you gonna do?"
PHOTO COURTESY OF LARRY SPENCER

John Hill remembers, "Chuck was walking through the office with a bullhorn one day. He stuck his head in the door and announced, 'On

16. Ibid.

tomorrow's show, you're going to be a Curtain Closer. Sing a song. Audition for me in ten minutes.' I said, 'But I don't sing.' Chuck said, 'Doesn't matter. My office. Ten minutes.' Ten minutes later, I walk into his office and Milton DeLugg is sitting at the piano waiting for me. 'What's your song?' I said, 'I don't sing! This isn't fair!'"[17]

But Chuck worked his magic with his go-fer. John Hill finally sang

The one, the only Gene-Gene the Dancing Machine. PHOTO BY AND COURTESY OF VINCE LONGO

a passable rendition of "Yellow Rose of Texas," and did fine as a Curtain Closer the next day.

But of all the heretofore-anonymous toilers that abruptly, briefly became stars on *The Gong Show,* none shone more brightly than a burly, broadly-smiling janitor named Gene Patton.

Electrician Howard Nugent remembers, "I had been a student at John Muir High School in Pasadena. I did stage crew there, and a lot of stage crew people in the business came out of John Muir High School. Our stage teacher was a man named Bob Carroll. Gene was a custodian. There were night classes for stage crew too, and I took those classes because I was overwhelmed by the whole thing. I loved stage crew. I was fascinated

17. Personal interview. 14 May 2019.

by it. I remember Gene standing in the back, leaning his chin against his broom, and listening attentively for the whole hour. He didn't do that every day, but he did it often enough that all of the students noticed Gene the custodian standing in the back and listening to the teacher's lectures.[18]

"In the early 1970s, Affirmative Action became more enforced. Local 33, the stagehands' union, had basically been a white group. It was un-

An overnight sensation. ROBERT BURROUGHS COLLECTION

diverse, as was Hollywood in general. So Local 33 began creating openings for black stagehands. Gene was a personality unto himself and left an impression on everybody he crossed paths with, so when Bob Carroll found out that local 33 was recruiting new black members, he personally recommended Gene and got him into that union. I have no idea what work Gene did as a stagehand before he arrived, but he got hired very quickly by NBC, because they wanted to be able to say 'Look, we have diverse stagehands.'"

Milton DeLugg and the Band with a Thugg entertained the audience during a taping break one day by playing a rousing mash-up of two Count Basie hits, "One O'Clock Jump" and "Jump at the Woodside." Chuck was standing backstage and glanced at Gene, wiggling his hips and shuffling

---

18. Personal interview. 19 Jan. 2019.

his feet, all while holding onto his pushbroom. It was time for another crew member to become a star.

For the next taping, Chuck introduced the audience to "Gene and His Magic Feet" and Gene came out all smiles, wearing a floppy newsboy hat that became his trademark. He shuffled his feet and boogied to "Jump at the Woodside" until the show broke for commercial. No explanation

A staff photo, sort of. Gene-Gene dances while Barris staffer Yvonne Longo (the brunette) dances behind him. Barely visible in the background are Peter Mins and Jefferson Beeker as Rhett & Scarlett. PHOTO BY AND COURTESY OF VINCE LONGO

was given to the studio audience or the viewers for Gene's presence, or his true role on the show. None was needed. They loved him. "Gene and His Magic Feet" was quickly rechristened, and Patton became known to viewers as Gene-Gene the Dancing Machine.

Larry Spencer says, "I take credit for the name change with some reservation. I truly don't remember coming up with his name, but when Chuck was asked about it years later, he gave me the credit."[19]

As months went on, the presentation became more electrifying. Initially, Chuck just gave him a cheerful introduction, walked offstage, and let Gene do his thing. Eventually, they opted to play up Gene's appearances

---

19. Personal interview. 2 Feb. 2019.

as a surprise. The band would start playing their combination of "One O'Clock Jump" and "Jump at the Woodside" out of nowhere. Chuck's eyes would pop out and he'd break into a broad smile.

"Do you know what that music means? That must be...GENE...GENE... THE DANCING MACHIIIIIIIINE!"

Gene boogied onstage, with members of the Barris staff now pelting him with trash and props, trying to trip him up. Gene never missed a step. One day, a staffer lobbed a basketball at him. Gene caught the ball, dribbled it while spinning in place, and tossed it aside, all in perfect beat. The hat might have been knocked ajar once or twice, but none of the flying objects ever took Gene down.

Chuck, meanwhile, stood at the edge of the stage, in full view of the camera, performing such a ridiculous dance that he got as much camera time as Gene during the music. Chuck thrust his entire body about, striking a balance somewhere between a seizure and rapture at a tent revival. As the music reached its brassy crescendo, Chuck and Gene would both fling their arms out and freeze into place for a fraction of a second, striking various joyful poses in time to the music. The judges got into the act. The audience danced too. Time stood still when Gene-Gene the Dancing Machine performed. He appeared on the show so frequently, and grew so popular, that in an apropos display of navel gazing, Chuck had Gene fitted for a tuxedo one week and booked him as a celebrity judge.

Everybody showed up for a *Gong Show* taping on standby, knowing that at any moment, Chuck might press them into service to throw on a costume and do whatever he had daydreamed for them. On a good day, it was to fill time because the acts got gonged too quickly. Sometimes, it was to fill time because of a more significant issue.

Spencer says, "We had a woman die backstage. I don't remember what her act was specifically, but it involved food. She was backstage, not in the bullpen, where all the acts gathered to wait for their call to come to stage, but in a corner just offstage doing some sort of preparation with the food in her act. We found her back there, we called a paramedic, and the paramedic pronounced her dead. She had choked to death."[20]

Yvonne Longo says, "Her husband was out waiting in the audience, wearing a big button with his wife's photo on it. They wanted me to go out there and notify him that his wife was dead. I said that was outside of my pay grade."[21]

20. Ibid.
21. Personal interview. 7 May 2019.

Her name was Esther Wolf. A Brooklyn native, she had been married to a pharmacist until he was shot and killed in a hold-up. She moved across the country to an apartment in Los Angeles, where she fell in love with a Russian immigrant who had just retired after 50 years of running a dry goods store. Enamored with show business, Esther applied for, and received, membership in AFTRA, the American Federation of Television and Radio Artists. Armed with her union card, she spent her golden years pursuing whatever work she could find, mostly teeny-tiny extra roles or one-line parts on TV shows.

The Gong Show was just one more chance at being in show business as far as she was concerned. On episode N314, she strolled onstage, smiling and giggling slightly before she even managed to get one word out. She was just purely overjoyed at being on the stage of a TV show, even as an audience hooted and catcalled her. She finally composed herself enough to announce that she was about to perform a song that she wrote herself.

"It's a song about a boy in love with a girl, but they had a terrible fight, but they're all right now, and the boy's jumping for joy. So…here goes!"

With that, she marched around the stage, belting out the lyrics "Oh my baby! Oh my darling!" in a monotonous staccato. And while some scattered heckling is audible during her performance, the audience couldn't bring themselves to boo her. Judge Michele Lee shot the hecklers in the audience a dirty look. Next to her, Pat McCormick smiled pleasantly at Esther's performance. And on the other side of Pat, Jaye P. Morgan was absolutely beaming. Esther's song wasn't great, but her enthusiasm was so infectious, and so fitting the spirit of the show, that the judges cheerfully let her survive the attempt and gave her a mediocre score of 21. She didn't win, but for 90 seconds, she had the spotlight all to herself.

As they had with other performers, *The Gong Show* told her that the door was open if she ever wanted to be a contestant again. On the day she died, she was preparing to sing "Happy Days are Here Again."

Chuck became fond of using his introduction to showcase people he took a liking to. He became fond of a Chinese restaurant and asked them to send over an order right before a taping started. Once the food arrived, Chuck had the delivery man stick around for a few minutes to open the show. "Ladies and gentlemen, the host and star of the show, and our best customer, Chuck Barris!" A karate instructor, the waitresses from Nate 'N Al's Deli in Beverly Hills, and a few more members of the Barris staff did the honors too. So did a game show question researcher who had been looking for work in front of the camera as a model and actress; her name was Markie Post.

Aside from Sivi Aberg, the duty of introducing Chuck most frequently went to Della Barris, Chuck's daughter, only 13 years old when *The Gong Show* premiered. Her over-the-top, arm-swinging and pointing introduction of "Myyyyyyyyyyy DADDY!!!" revealed a stage presence and comfort in front of the camera that clearly wasn't genetically inherited, and bellied how unnerved she genuinely was doing it. She became a semi-regular on

Della Barris in the NBC parking lot. PHOTO COURTESY OF SHELLEY HERMAN

the show despite — or maybe because of — her fractious and unusual relationship with Chuck.

After the divorce was finalized in 1972, Lyn and Della moved to Switzerland; as long as Richard Nixon was President, Lyn wanted to be out of America. Lyn blamed Chuck for the demise of the marriage and Chuck was certain that she had presented it that way to Della, but he

Phyllis Diller has had enough. AUTHOR'S COLLECTION

dutifully made international phone calls as often as he could to keep tabs on his daughter and stay in her life. She was miserable in Switzerland and most of the phone calls consisted of complaining — it rained all the time, she said. Everyone in Switzerland smoked and she couldn't stand the smell. She missed her friends, and she referred to her school as "the penitentiary."

Chuck and Lyn agreed that during the summer months, Della could live with her father. The problem was that Chuck had readjusted to the single life by that point and was accustomed to leaving the apartment on whims to go to a movie or a nightclub. One night, Della, who had gone to bed at 9 p.m., woke up and walked into the living room to find her father drunk. Chuck confessed that he was bored when she stayed with him and that he hated being in the apartment while his daughter slept. From that point forward, Della tagged along for Chuck's late-night ventures to jazz clubs.

It was a bonding experience for them. They grew closer after that summer. When Della was 12, Chuck spoke about his relationship with her in *TV Guide,* although his choice of words was frankly bizarre. He called Della "one of the few things I own that I can really relate to."[22]

"Della is very possessive. She demands a lot. She gets upset if I get too serious about a woman."

Maribelle Scott, the dancing flea. ROBERT BURROUGHS COLLECTION

For *The Gong Show,* Della, usually decked out in a tuxedo matching her father's outfit that day, would introduce Chuck, who would usually hand her a rose and take a playful swinging kick at her as she strolled offstage, jokingly calling her "my rotten kid." There was more truth to that than either one could admit. Since the divorce, Chuck had listened in horror to countless phone calls from Della, detailing how terrible her mother is and how miserable she was underneath that awful woman's thumb. One night, Chuck took Della to dinner and joyfully broke the news that he had obtained sole custody of Della. Della's face fell and she went silent, a reaction Chuck wasn't expecting. In an instant, he realized that Della had been playing one parent against the other, and that Lyn was a good mother after all. But there was no going back now, and Della, suddenly

22. Whitney. 1975.

realizing that she would miss her mother, reluctantly moved into Chuck's new home in the Hollywood Hills.

Chuck and Della's relationship was almost nothing but tension. Her grades took a precipitous fall as soon as they began living together, and Chuck had to leave the office increasingly often for parent-teacher conferences. Chuck, who had maintained a steadily active dating life since the divorce, couldn't bring dates home for dinner; one encounter with Della tended to repel every girlfriend.

The tension finally spilled over one day during a *Gong Show* taping. Even though the audience didn't know anything was amiss, Chuck addressed it with cameras rolling. On episode #N205, the show returned from commercial with Chuck standing center stage with Della, dressed in a hoodie and jeans, clearly not expecting to be on camera. Chuck told viewers, "This is my rotten kid. I yelled at her before the show because I was nervous…and you always hurt the ones you love. I just wanted to make it up to her."

Susan Simons remembers, "Della became the show's mascot in a way. I don't mean that in a demeaning way. We all loved Della. She was such a sweet girl. Liked to laugh, liked to talk. Chuck began putting her on the show, either introducing him at the opening or sometimes using her in comedy bits. Della liked it, but at the same time, you could tell it wasn't important to her."[23]

It really wasn't. In fact, the first time her father suggested that she be on the show, Della asked him if he was sure that was a good idea. After appearing on the show semi-regularly, after about a year, she told Chuck she wanted out.

In his book *Della,* Chuck recalled her saying, "I don't know why you make me introduce you. If I didn't tell you before, I'll tell you now. It isn't a good idea. It just isn't. Maybe it's what I'm told to say. Maybe it's the way I say it. Maybe it's the makeup and the hairdos that make me look special, or different, or spoiled, or something. Maybe these days kids my age are jealous of sons and daughters of stars parading around like big shots."[24]

Della stopped appearing on the show after that. But she was still a part of the show off-camera.

John Hill says, "I was Chuck's go-fer, so I spent a lot of time with Della. She was just a kid when I started working there so I would have to pick her up from places and take her to places. I had never been around

---

23. Personal interview. 18 Apr. 2019.
24. *Della: A Memoir of My Daughter.* 2010.

someone who was tapped into that kind of money, who could just do what she wanted to do. Chuck would ask me to take her clothes shopping, and she would be there for hours. There were two issues with Della that I saw. First, Chuck did not seem to give her very much responsibility. And second, she completely lived in an adult world. She spent all her time with her dad and her dad's staff. She was never around people her own age."[25]

The Vatican Four, who danced to a record of Tom Lehrer's "Vatican Rag."
ROBERT BURROUGHS COLLECTION

Susan Simons says, "Della spent most of her time with her dad. She glommed into me a bit and called me 'Mom' in kind of a pretending way. For the dinner breaks at NBC, I'd usually go home because I lived very, very close to the studio, and I had some cats. Della would come home with me during the dinner breaks. I think she longed for somebody who really cared about her and would pay attention.[26]

"Della, I think, was broken by her parents' divorce. She was a bright kid. Smart beyond her years, really. At the same time, she was still a little girl. She was 13 when that show started. Age 13 is the point where you

25. Personal interview. 14 May 2019.
26. Personal interview. 18 Apr. 2019.

begin really getting interested in make-up, you know? Della still played with stuffed animals. She was younger than her age, in a way."

Lynnette Karnes says, "Chuck just felt overwhelmed by Della. He really tried with her. A lot of men at that time weren't very involved with their children, but Chuck really did what he thought was right for her. She was 13 at the time. Chuck hired a driver named Joe, who was only 18 at the time. He learned Joe was going to a party. Chuck asked Joe to bring Della along because he just wanted her to be around people that weren't from Beverly Hills. Chuck wanted her to have a normal life, but he didn't know how to go about giving her that. I think she was just kind of a lost little person. He loved her, but he didn't know what to do."

"I don't think Della ever had a chance," says Ellen Metzger. "There are people in the world who need love presented to them in the form of material things, because the authentic way of loving them isn't working. Della was like that. Chuck constantly had to give her jewelry and clothing and it wasn't enough. There wasn't enough of anything for her to understand that she was loved. She was a sweet kid."[27]

---

27. Personal interview. 15 May 2019.

CHAPTER 9

Gong Bananas!

Above: Tap dancers Manette and Steve LaChance. Sometimes, truly gifted performers accidentally got on the show. ROBERT BURROUGHS COLLECTION

John Hill recalls, "Chuck had custom jackets made for everybody who worked on the show, with GONG SHOW STAFF embroidered across the back. I made the mistake of wearing mine to a Dodger game one night. I went to the concession stand to get a hot dog, and people mobbed me. I swear, at least 60 people surrounded me. They were cheering. Some started singing and dancing like they were trying to audition for me. I had to yell back 'I don't work on that part of the staff!' I wasn't a celebrity. But when people found out what show I worked on, I got treated like one."[1]

Vince Longo remembers, "The first sign we had that the show was something special was the way people reacted when they saw my equipment. I'd be wheeling things in and out as we were getting ready for a day of auditions, and people knew what show we were working on in there. The way people looked at me on the sidewalk changed."[2]

Rex Reed, the notoriously bitchy and blunt film critic who often sat on the *Gong Show* panel with a dour expression and a snide remark ready to fire after every act, spoke of the show's booming popularity in 1977.

"*The Gong Show* has gone totally bananas in New York. Everyone from Barbara Walters to Joshua Logan to Lotte Lenya to Walter Cronkite's wife Betsy has called me to tell me they are totally hooked on the show. I have developed new legions of fans who never knew I was alive, renewed old fans who always thought I was just an intellectual critic, and received literally scores of letters from people who are seeing me in a brand-new light. The show has been a whopping success."[3]

For NBC, success could be measured with simple arithmetic. At the end of 1976, *The Gong Show* brought in five million viewers per day — a remarkable number for 12:30 p.m. Each of those episodes cost the network about $16,000 in production expenses. Each of those episodes, in turn, would generate about $45,000 worth of advertising revenue.

The math was even more enticing for the nighttime syndicated version. For the second season, when Barris replaced Gary Owens as host, the number of stations carrying the nighttime show ticked up from 90 to 130. By one estimate, the nighttime show was generating about $70,000 a day for Chuck Barris Productions.

More money talk: In the 1970s, Chuck Barris Productions became a publicly traded company, making Chuck even richer. The stock tended

1. Personal interview. 14 May 2019.
2. Personal interview. 9 May 2019.
3. Bowles, Jerry, *The Gong Show Book*. Ace Books. New York, NY. 1977.

to hover around 2⅛ a share, which financial reporter Robert Metz at the time attributed to how little Barris publicized that aspect of his company; potential buyers flat-out didn't know they could invest in Chuck Barris. Despite the lack of promotion, during the summer of 1977 the value shot up to 3¼. The curious thing, Metz reported, was that an investigation of Barris' books indicated that the company was seriously undervaluing itself.

String Bean, who sang "Look for the Silver Lining." ROBERT BURROUGHS COLLECTION

Metz determined that the stock was logically worth more than $4 a share, but the stock remained a real bargain at 3¼.

Chuck Barris' next move was taking a page from Major Bowes' book — another page, that is — by taking *The Gong Show* on tour. Bob Eubanks, the host of Barris' *Newlywed Game*, was actually a full-time concert promoter. He had overseen acts like Dolly Parton, Merle Haggard, Willie Nelson, and most famously, the Beatles' concerts at the Hollywood Bowl. In 1977, Chuck Barris and Bob Eubanks introduced *The Gong Roadshow*, a touring production. Unlike Major Bowes' road show, which featured winning acts from the *Amateur Hour*, *The Gong Roadshow* staged live versions of *The Gong Show* all over the country, with a touring master of ceremonies, Richard Clark, and local celebrities, like the morning drive disc jockeys and wacky weathermen, acting as judges. The contestants made the cut from local auditions. The winning acts on the road received $102.62 apiece (a figure chosen because it was the exact amount of money Bob Eubanks had in his pocket the first time that prize money for the touring show was discussed) and a chance to audition for the actual series in Hollywood. *The Gong Roadshow* had extracted yet another egg from the golden goose.

Three favorites at the judges' desk tonight: Rex Reed, Jaye P. Morgan, and Jamie Farr. AUTHOR'S COLLECTION

Vince Longo talks about one business venture that fell through. "One day, these three guys who look like mobsters come in. We were afraid of them immediately. They went in to talk to Chuck and we were all wondering what about. After they leave, Chuck calls in the Shock Troops for a meeting. We found out they were from a hotel/casino complex in Las Vegas. They have a talent show every Saturday night, and they want us to feature their winners on *The Gong Show*. Well, Chuck told them no, he said everybody had to audition. But he had us, the Shock Troops, go to Las Vegas, to videotape the show."[4]

The plan was that Chuck would view the show along with the usual stack of videotapes from Old World Restaurant to determine who he

---

4. Personal interview. 7 May 2019.

wanted for the program. Vince Longo, Johnny Michel, and Jimmy Commore went to Las Vegas together for a working weekend at the casino.

Longo continues, "We walked into this casino, and we could do nothing wrong. 'Oh my god, it's the guys from *The Gong Show!*' We were treated like gods. We check into our rooms, and a guy from the hotel tells us,

Renee Brecker, a 76-year-old who sang "Joseph Make Your Mind Up."
BOB BODEN COLLECTION

'You can have whatever you want, just let us know.' We had an extended conversation afterward where we tried to figure out if he meant drugs or women.[5]

"I set up my camera, and some members of the local union want to know what we're doing in their building with camera equipment. I showed them my IATSE card, and they said, 'Okay, you can do whatever you need to, but the other two can't.' Johnny and Jimmy didn't have union cards. Basically, this union guy just told them that they weren't allowed to do any work while they were in Las Vegas, which they were more than happy to hear.

5. Ibid.

"At showtime, I had a machine gun nest set up with my camera surrounded by all my equipment. The first woman comes onstage, and she begins singing 'Feelings.' Suddenly there's a tapping on my shoulder. More insistent tapping. But I'm working, so I just ignore it. Then this hand grabs me by the scruff of my neck and drags me out to the hallway. I turn around to see who grabbed me and it's the largest man I have ever seen wearing a tuxedo. He tells me the musicians want to be paid extra since you're videotaping. I said, 'These are audition tapes, this is never going to air anywhere!' He said, 'Doesn't matter, you need to get out.' He was nice enough to help me pack up and carry my equipment out.

Violinist Florence Cato, who played "Raindrops Keep Falling on My Head" while roller skating. AUTHOR'S COLLECTION

"The next day, we got yelled at in the casino manager's office for causing trouble with the unions. We were invited! We were told to come here and do what we were doing. In a very threatening tone, he says, 'I want that tape.' I said, 'There's maybe four minutes' worth of footage and one song on it.' He says, 'I don't care, give me that tape.' I looked around his office and I noticed he doesn't have a videotape player anywhere in there, so I gave him a blank tape and walked out. We went up to our rooms, and all our belongings were in the hallway."

The seemingly obvious merger of Las Vegas and *The Gong Show* was not meant to be. But *The Gong Show* had achieved fad status and Chuck was able to cash in on ways that other producers might not even have fathomed. There was a *Gong Show* board game, *Gong Show* trading cards, an official *Gong Show* book, and even an official kid-sized Chuck Barris Halloween costume, complete with bucket hat.

Jefferson Beeker remembers a trip home to Washington, DC to visit his family. "NBC had forced Chuck to take a hiatus. NBC did not like their daytime programming to tape particularly far in advance. Chuck taped so many episodes of *The Gong Show* that NBC made him shut down production for a while until they had aired most of the episodes that they had in the can. I flew east to visit my family, and I went with two of my aunts to a restaurant called Anton's Loyal Opposition. The walls were lined with pictures of Congressmen. Like Sardi's in New York, except with politicians instead of actors. It was absolutely the last place I would have expected this to happen…[6]

"We're sitting there, and a woman came up to me and said, 'You're on *The Gong Show!*' I said, 'Well, yes.' She said, 'Oh, my son is right over there, I want him to meet you.' And they pull up two chairs and eat with my family. My aunts just looked at me and said 'Wow.'

"When it was time to go back to LA, I flew out of Dulles International Airport. Dulles used to have these chairs that had TVs attached to them, and you'd feed coins into them to watch TV while you were sitting and waiting. I'm waiting for my flight, and I see two kids watching *The Gong Show*. And I happened to be on. They looked over at me and blurted out, 'That's you!' I said, 'Don't be ridiculous, that's in California!' The kids said, 'They tape TV shows, that's you!' I said, 'Okay, yeah, it's me.'"

For as many celebrity judges who had skittered away from the early weeks of the show, vowing never to be a part of it again, and for as many stars like Bob Barker and Gene Rayburn who vowed that they would never have anything to do with *The Gong Show*, there were just as many who openly professed their love of it. Carol Burnett, who had already achieved legend status even then on the strength of her weekly variety show, did a long sketch one night featuring her recurring characters, The Family, in which Eunice appeared as a contestant on *The Gong Show*, with Chuck Barris, Jamie Farr, Jaye P. Morgan, and Allen Ludden appearing as themselves. Eunice's act: she sang "Feelings," naturally. The sketch was taped as part of a five-episode taping session for *The Gong Show* that day, and as a show of appreciation, Carol returned the guest-starring favor and opened one episode by introducing Chuck.

Pop artist Andy Warhol called it his favorite television show. Singer Linda Hopkins would call the staff regularly to ask about the show; she wanted to know everything about it. Dick Van Dyke and John Davidson popped in as guest announcers to open the show. So did Chevy Chase,

---

6. Personal interview. 10 Apr. 2019.

who had departed *Saturday Night Live* after a stellar freshman season, and Robert Goulet, a singer whose talent negated any need to set foot anywhere near the stage of *The Gong Show*.

Mike Metzger says, "Chevy Chase's appearance is an interesting story. I did not work much on *The Gong Show*. Chuck had one writer, Larry Spencer, who really got that show and was in tune with it. Chuck loved

Hooray! We're going to be stars! PHOTO BY AND COURTESY OF VINCE LONGO

him. I didn't have the same feel for it that Larry had. Every time I tried to pitch in and write content for *The Gong Show* it felt wrong. But for some reason, Chuck liked having me in the studio for the tapings. He would always say 'I need you.'[7]

"I was in the hallway at NBC before the shows started taping that day and I bumped into Chevy Chase. I introduced myself and told him we were taping the show, and it would be a big kick if he would just come in for one minute to open the show and introduce Chuck. Chevy agreed right away and followed me in. I thought, 'Wow, Chuck is really going to be surprised by this!'

"Chevy steps out to start the show and it's the first time Chuck has seen him. Chevy gives a good introduction and announces Chuck. I was

7. Personal interview. 13 May 2019.

surprised by the look on Chuck's face as he walked out. He looked like he had been violated. Chuck knew this was a cool moment, but in an instant, I realized there were two problems here: *The Gong Show* was a hit and turned Chuck into a big star in his own right, and now we had someone on the show who was clearly a bigger star than him. Chuck felt it reduced him a little. I also realized, Chuck is the boss, and he's in

George Beagle and Twilight: The women's high notes would prompt the dog to yowl. ROBERT BURROUGHS COLLECTION

charge of the whole company, and by doing this, I had just demonstrated that something could be orchestrated behind his back, and that really disturbed him."

Gradually, *The Gong Show* penetrated the English language in surprising ways. A particularly disastrous showing by the home team would inspire sportswriters to gripe "It looked like *The Gong Show* on the court last night." In conference rooms all over America, brainstorming sessions took on a new moniker. Corporate offices held meetings in which employees were invited to pitch whatever ideas they had for their departments to a group of executives, who would decide instantly whether to implement the proposals or reject them. These kinds of meetings came to be known as "gong shows."

Then there was the effect that it had on Chuck. By emerging from his office, he had become first the host of *The Gong Show*, then unquestionably the star. In a matter of months, he was arguably a bigger star than some of the judges on the panel.

Chuck soaked in adulation, even though he never got completely accustomed to it. When he appeared on *The Mike Douglas Show*, he was

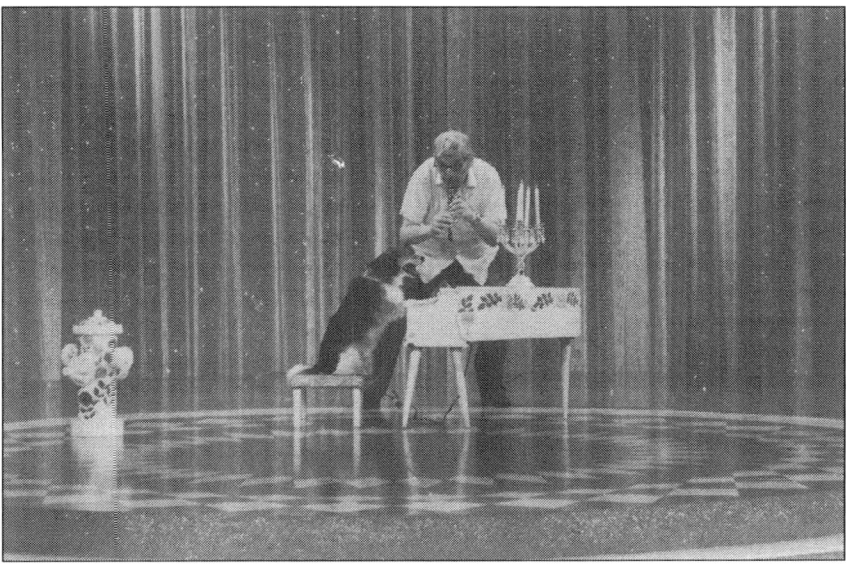

Oscar and Poncho play a duet. ROBERT BURROUGHS COLLECTION

greeted with a thunderous ovation. But when Mike Douglas referred to Chuck as a "matinee idol" and asked him what he thought of that reception, Chuck could only muster a shy mumble.

"Those are very weird kids," he said of the audience. "They're my friends."[8]

Ticket requests for tapings were overwhelming. At one point, the show deviated from the usual protocol, in which the network oversaw rounding up audiences for each taping. Chuck insisted on "the right type of audience," so his staff gave preference to ticket requests from the specific fans they were looking for. Even with that kind of process guiding them, the tapings were still so full that NBC pages occasionally had to seat people on the aisle floors. And they roared when Chuck walked onstage at the start of the program.

8. Interview with Chuck Barris. *The Mike Douglas Show.* 1978.

Chuck loved having a live band onstage for his show. All the musicians remained onstage so Chuck could unwind by bringing out his own guitar and having a jam session after the taping. Common sense would indicate you'd wait for the audience to leave first, but Chuck was so eager to get started that he often went straight from the main stage to the bandstand after signing off on the last show of the day. The audience, realizing what

Penny Rupert, who sang "Alley Cat." ROBERT BURROUGHS COLLECTION

was happening, wouldn't budge. They stuck around to watch Chuck play. Chuck's relaxation had turned into a bonus show.

Vince Longo says, "We had a phenomenal guitarist in the band, Bill Neale. Somebody pointed out something strange about Chuck during the jam sessions. I don't know if it's true that this was Chuck's thinking, but this co-worker noticed that during the jam sessions, Chuck sat with his back to the audience so they couldn't actually see his fingers on his guitar. The theory was he wanted the audience to think he was the one doing those incredible things that Neale was doing on the guitar."[9]

Even though a taping day could be a long one — including the five rehearsals and five-episode tapings, it took a bit over twelve hours — a

---

9. Personal interview. 9 May 2019.

post-taping dinner became a ritual among *The Gong Show* staff. Chuck would treat everyone to a lavish meal, followed by the presentation of some awards to the employees. Not the handwritten certificates that he doled out at The Closet. Chuck was now handing out Lemmy Awards — short for lemming, because he felt his employees would follow him anywhere. The Lemmy Award trophies weren't the kinds of statuettes you'd find at a gift shop on Hollywood Boulevard. They were solid, heavy, brass awards, about the size of an Oscar, all with customized inscriptions.

The Lemmy Awards, another of many tokens of appreciation from Chuck to his staff. COURTESY OF ELLEN METZGER

"Chuck had high expectations of all of us," remembers Lynnette Karnes. "I had my wisdom teeth taken out and I was at my desk the next day, making phone calls with my mouth totally swollen, because I had to book acts. I had to be there. But Chuck knew that if your staff feels appreciated, they'll work themselves to death for you. And Chuck worked just as hard as us. It wasn't like Chuck was watching over us. He was in there doing all the work with us."[10]

Although Chuck tried to remain the same mild-mannered, if quirky, production empresario that he had always been, he found it understandably difficult to live the same life. He told Mike Douglas how much things had changed since he became the host.

"There's no question that I'm enjoying [fame]. There's certain things that I really like about it. Obviously, it would be hypocritical if I said that I didn't. It seems to me that there are nice things about it. It's nice to be liked. If you come out here and eight or nine people clap or yell, that's nice, to think that somebody likes you. Most people like to be liked."[11]

10. Personal interview. 3 Oct. 2019.
11. Mike Douglas. 1978.

Chuck still had the same eccentricities that he had before. Being in the public eye didn't change that. During a dark week when *Gong* wasn't taping, Chuck called John Hill on the phone. "I'm coming back to the U.S. in three days. I'm flying into San Francisco. Now the last time I was in San Francisco, I was out taking a walk and I came across a car dealership. There was a car in the window that I just loved. I want you to buy it for me."[12]

Professor Kaka Churian, who played the trombone with his feet. BOB BODEN COLLECTION

Hill asked, "What was the name of the dealership?"

"I don't know."

Hill thought for a moment. "What kind of car was it."

"I don't know. Some European car. Never saw one like it."

Hill worked with the boss a little more. "Do you remember the name of the hotel you were in?"

Chuck at least remembered that. Gofer-turned-sleuth John Hill called the hotel in San Francisco and asked if any of the employees remembered seeing Chuck Barris leaving the hotel to go for a walk the last time he had stayed there. The concierge asked around and found one employee who remembered seeing him and handed off the phone.

12. Personal interview. 14 May 2019.

"I remember seeing Chuck go through the exit. He made a left turn and walked downhill."

Hill said, "I promise there's going to be a nice tip if you do this. Can you go through the exit, walk down that hill, and see if there's a car dealership at the bottom of the hill with a European car on display in a window?"

There was! The employee gave him the name of the dealership. Hill

Marcene Lewis, who sang "Oh Johnny, Oh Johnny" to her teddy bear.
AUTHOR'S COLLECTION

made another phone call, explained who his boss was, and the dealership prepared the car for Chuck to pick it up.

The next day, a memo went out. Chuck gave John Hill a nice fee, a couple hundred dollars. And then…

"Chuck calls me on the phone. He says the car is a piece of shit. He just abandoned it in Monterey because he hated it so much and he told me to sell it off for whatever price I could get for it. Then he fined me for getting him a crappy car!"

In 1977, *The Newlywed Game*, which signed off from ABC for the last time three years earlier, came back to life. Chuck Barris Productions sold the show into syndication, with five new episodes per week hosted once again by Bob Eubanks. Behind the scenes, it brought to light a change in priorities for the boss.

An autographed photo of Chuck Barris. He was a star now. AUTHOR'S COLLECTION

Mike Metzger says, "I'm not sure what fame did to his brain, but once Chuck became the star of *The Gong Show*, something went screwy. What he did on the air became his whole persona, and he just became totally consumed by that show. He lived and breathed *The Gong Show*. When it was confirmed that *Newlywed* was going back into production, Chuck pretty much dropped it in my lap. He declared that this was my show, I was in charge, and he was trusting me to run it. It wouldn't be accurate to say he neglected the new version, but *The Gong Show* was his whole life."[13]

13. Personal interview. 13 May 2019.

CHAPTER 10

More Stuff

Above: Chuck and Tony Randall on The All-Star Gong Show, *a prime time spectacular.* ROBERT BURROUGHS COLLECTION

On April 26, 1977, NBC, the network where 99.99% of the corporate brass didn't want *The Gong Show*, with Madeline David seemingly the sole holdout a year earlier, turned 180 degrees with a vengeance. The network set aside one hour of prime time to present *The All-Star Gong Show Special #1*. It was a showcase of some of the best acts from the past year — a pair of young boys recited suggestive poems about women's bodies; a teen trio costumed as elderly people lip-synced a Barry White song; a Martian ate his lunch in time to Billy Joel's "Root Beer Rag": the UCLA marching band disrupted some unsuspecting contestants with their fight song. Among the other surprises during the hour: Tony Randall showed up in a Curtain Closer gag, rocker Alice Cooper sang "I'm Going Out of My Head" while perched in a guillotine, and legendary bandleader Harry James and his orchestra played Gene-Gene's theme music.

John Dorsey closed the show with a wide shot of the set as the credits rolled, with everyone involved in the show savoring their shared moment in the spotlight. Harry James and his orchestra continued playing while elderly women danced the hula and the Charleston; the faux-elderly teens tore up the floor next to them; the Martian spun in circles; the two-headed harmonica player marched forth with the trophy and the check in the air; Gene-Gene boogied to his own beat; the porn star whose act was edited out of the final cut was lifted onto the shoulders of some other contestants so she could have a fleeting moment of prime time network fame. The UCLA marching band members, who had done their routine in the tiny studio with such precision earlier in the night, let their guard down; two draped their arms around each other and raised their arms triumphantly for the cheers of the audience. This wasn't a freak show. This wasn't degradation. This wasn't Chuck Barris mocking mentally-defective people who would do anything to get on TV. It was unrestrained, heartfelt joy. For those final two minutes, viewers saw a full-blown party erupt on stage. Maximum Gong had been achieved.

In the never-ending hunt for not just a big audience, but the right audience, NBC was shocked to see that an overwhelming 78% of *Gong Show* viewers were in the desirable 18-49 age range. They plugged it into a one-hour slot on that Tuesday evening to see if *The Gong Show* might just be the thing to take a bite out of ABC's blockbuster hour of *Happy Days* and *Laverne and Shirley*. Ultimately it wasn't; despite the "#1" in the show's title and the fact that NBC signed up for four specials, it would be the only *All-Star Gong Show*.

Chuck was unswayed by the disappointment. If anything, he dug into his work harder. As far as his staff could see, *The Gong Show* was swallowing him completely.

Howard Nugent remembers, "Chuck's personality was so big. That was him; even off-camera. He was extremely focused, and very intense. But that intensity turned into intense enthusiasm on camera. He was a man of just unquenchable passion for that show."[1]

Being on The Gong Show *was a barrel of fun.* ROBERT BURROUGHS COLLECTION

Chuck Barris felt a pressure that he had never experienced with any of his other shows. Game shows are usually more of the same day in and day out. The contestants might change, but bachelors and bachelorettes were always going to flirt, and newlyweds were always going to bicker.

But *The Gong Show* was different in that it was…well, different. That's what viewers liked. Ask a *Gong Show* fan at the time why they liked it so much and they were apt to say, "There's always something different." They certainly wouldn't say it if anything happened that was the same as yesterday. Staffers noticed that Chuck felt tremendous pressure to prevent a rut from setting in.

1. Personal interview. 19 Jan. 2019.

The staffers in charge of the auditions got notes from Chuck about imposing moratoriums on certain types of acts that he was plain getting sick of seeing. These folks wouldn't even get auditions. For example, there was a period when, if a musician called the show wanting to do an instrumental piece, they were flatly told not to show up, but to call back in six weeks. Six weeks was enough time, the staff determined, for Chuck

Arte Johnson, Jaye P. Morgan, and Rip Taylor are almost too scared to look. What act will the show subject them to next? AUTHOR'S COLLECTION

to eventually regain interest in what had worn him out. After so many weeks of singers, the instrumentals eventually returned to *The Gong Show*. The urban dance craze of the late 1970s, pop-locking, was frozen out for a while. So were child acts.

Danny Lies says, "The ban on children wasn't entirely because Chuck was sick of them. All of us became very aware of the amount of pressure.

The Clonettes — Nan & Fran Clark and Karen & Kim Halliday danced to disco arrangements of the themes from Star Wars *and* Close Encounters of the Third Kind. ROBERT BURROUGHS COLLECTION

Even if it's just *The Gong Show*, where we treated everything as a total joke and just had fun with the contestants, putting a kid onstage with cameras rolling and a national audience looking in is just a lot of pressure on a kid and some of us felt uncomfortable putting them through that. I watch modern reality shows and competition shows and I'm always shocked when I see kids as contestants. That is so much to subject a kid to."[2]

Chuck also seemed bothered by a fear that the outrageous acts that had given the show its identity might just stop showing up for the auditions. When Chuck would tell the origin story of *The Gong Show*, how it was

---

2. Personal interview. 22 May 2019.

originally supposed to be a straightforward talent show, but then they repurposed it, Chuck would emphasize that it was a good move to make because surely, they would never run out of terrible acts!

But what if they did?

Danny Lies says, "After I had worked there a few months, we realized that we didn't give the bad acts — the novelty acts — enough of an

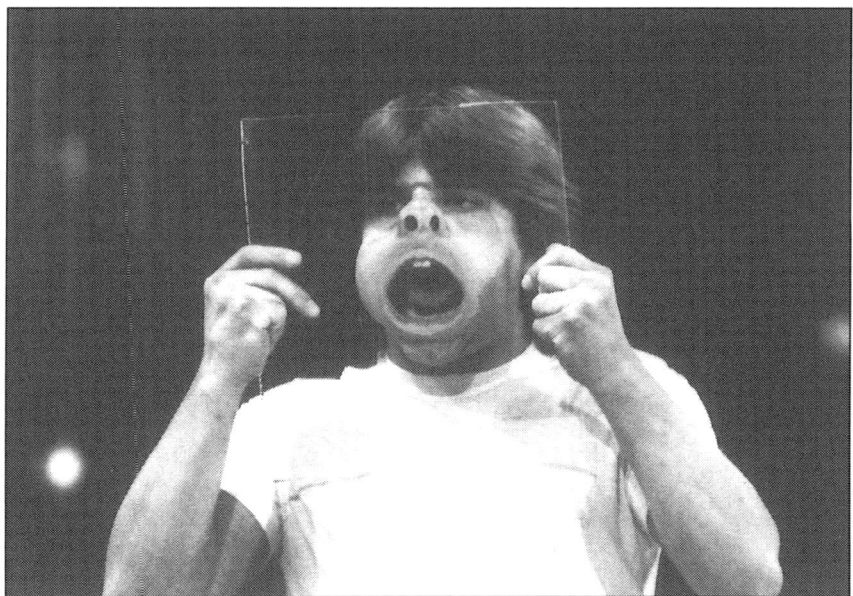

Tony Van Doren...this was his entire act. AUTHOR'S COLLECTION

incentive to be on the show. If you weren't already a union member, and you got on the show, and got gonged, then you didn't get any money at all. We came up with the idea of Most Outrageous Act of the Week, where at the end of the fifth episode of a taping session, the celebrity judges would vote for the worst act that they had gonged among all of the acts in those five episodes, and that act got a dirty sock, plus a check for $516.32. So now there was an incentive for people to keep coming up with bizarre acts. You could be gonged and still win the grand prize."[3]

Chuck was still worried because sheer numbers could lead to a short supply of zany performances. Taping six episodes a week — five for NBC and one for the nighttime show — meant seeing one horrific act after another come and go after only a minute or so onstage.

3. Ibid.

Chuck handled this by incorporating "ringers" onto the show, as he had done with *The Dating Game*. Danny Lies had described an idea for a *Gong Show* act that a friend in his hometown in Wichita had shared with him. Chuck liked it and put Lies on the show, without explicitly revealing to the audience that Lies was an employee of the show.

Lies, in a tuxedo, walked onstage with a violin case. A woman set up

Yakov Noy, one man who disguised himself as two and danced with himself.
BOB BODEN COLLECTION

a music stand with some sheet music as Lies opened his case and pulled out a dead, plucked chicken. Lies "played" the chicken by hitting it repeatedly. Meanwhile, the woman turned the pages on the sheet music that he was supposedly reading. The act delighted Chuck so much that he asked Danny to do the bit again and again. Sometimes it would be a chicken, sometimes it would be a giant sausage, sometimes it would be a ham, etc.

The purpose of the act was to keep the weirdos with odd ideas calling for auditions. If the show's line-up of acts for an episode threatened to be just too far on the side of "normal," Chuck sent a ringer act out there to do a bizarre act like the ones that he wanted to keep coming in. An alert viewer could have figured out that something was askew — ringer acts would leave the stage, without the judges giving them a score. At the end of the show, a disclaimer would flash on the screen stating that any act that didn't get scored by the judges featured "non-contestant talent."

Ringer acts came from outside the company too. One such act was Mark Sweet, a show business jack-of-all-trades — comedian, magician, hypnotist, actor, audience warm-up man, and he was even Willy Wonka in commercials for Wonka candies for many years. His spot as a ringer came from having the right connections.

Sweet explains, "At the time, I traveled around doing GM's auto shows.

No eating in the studio, please. PHOTO BY AND COURTESY OF VINCE LONGO

I worked for them for 25 years. If you've been to an auto show, you know how they have the turntables with the cars on them? I'd go on the turntables, and I'd do a ten or fifteen-minute set, and I'd work information about the cars into my act.

"I was booked for the GM auto show in Los Angeles in 1978. A friend of mine, a comedian named Harry Jarkey, knew Milton DeLugg. Harry asked if I wanted to be on *The Gong Show*. Initially I said no because I thought it was too high a risk. I was building a good career for myself as a professional entertainer, so if I go onstage as an experienced pro, and I get gonged, that's a bad look. Harry said, 'You won't get gonged,' and he explained this to me…

"When Chuck Barris made his deal with AFTRA to use AFTRA talent for acts on *The Gong Show*, they made this deal that Chuck had to feature a specific number of acts per taping that would be AFTRA talent and that would be guaranteed they wouldn't get gonged. I was a member of AFTRA, so if I went on the show, I'd fulfill this deal Chuck made with AFTRA — I'd be the act that didn't get gonged at his taping session. At the same time, *The Gong Show* was also a competition, and it had a winning act that got prize money, so part of the deal was that the act that didn't get gonged also would not win. So that was my deal — I was guaranteed a booking on the show, knowing I would neither win nor get gonged, and I was paid AFTRA scale. I didn't even have to audition. I did a joke, I did a magic trick that I could do in my sleep — I only had ninety seconds, so I needed to perform as fluidly as possible. And then I did a big gag at the end where the stool collapsed. It came off wonderfully."

Chuck's need for a different show from day to day manifested itself in his wardrobe. Wardrobe coordinator Jefferson Beeker remembers how Chuck's urgent need to be different came to the surface.

"My main priority as wardrobe coordinator was dressing Chuck. I would prep everything for a five-episode taping. I would arrange five tuxedos for Chuck as if he'd be dressed properly for the full show, and Chuck would take it from there. I wasn't going to dictate what Chuck had to wear, because he was the boss. Besides Chuck was fun, and the show was like nothing else on TV, so I was willing to be flexible with what Chuck wanted with his wardrobe."[4]

"In the beginning of the series, Chuck's wardrobe was all velvet tuxedos and silk shirts, and Chuck felt uncomfortable wearing it because he felt that he was a man's man. That's how he saw himself. We changed the materials used for his tuxedos."

Vince Longo says, "Rick Kates, the show's head of syndication, asked me to take photos of Chuck standing next to the gong in his tuxedo. He really wanted that for press kits and sales pitches. During the taping day, I asked Chuck to stick around and pose for photos standing at the gong. I wish I had more photos than I was able to take, but I snapped about a dozen of them, and then Chuck just draws the line across his neck and walks off."[5]

Beeker adds, "Gradually Chuck began asking us to make costumes that he could wear other than tuxedos for the show, and he brought in other clothes he owned. He'd switch from one outfit to another in mid-show. It didn't really bother us at all. We knew that his discomfort with wearing tuxedos was nothing personal against us, and he was very respectful of

---

4. Personal interview. 10 Apr. 2019.

5. Personal interview. 9 May 2019.

us. Whenever he went off-stage to do these mid-show costume changes, he'd hang up his tuxedo jacket."⁶

In addition to the hat rack that had been added to the set, Chuck now kept a trunk just off-stage with different outfits. As the acts performed, Chuck would change layers. He might start the show in a tuxedo, introduce the first act, walk off-stage, and re-emerge 90 seconds later wearing

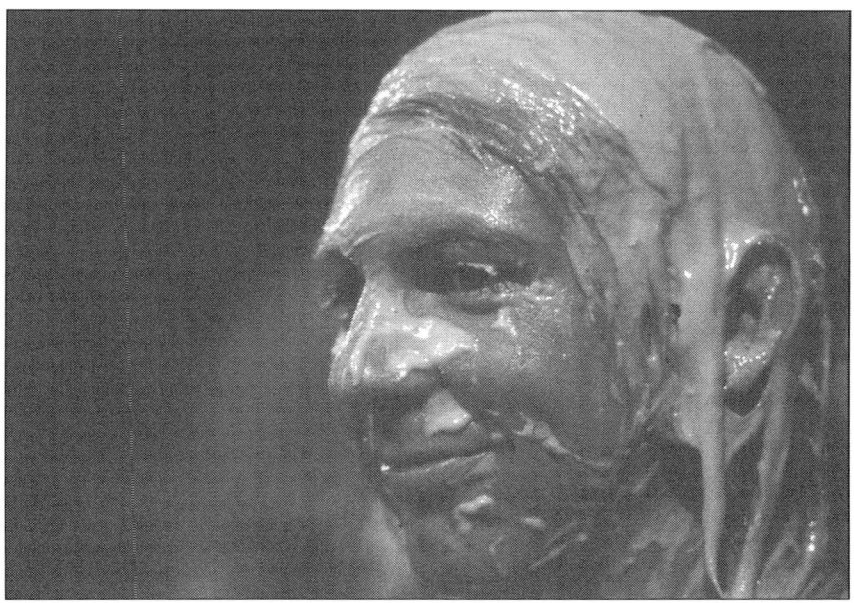

And this contestant got the food everywhere except her mouth. PHOTO BY AND COURTESY OF VINCE LONGO

a rumpled military uniform and a bandana. When the show would return from commercial, he'd be decked out in a boxer's robe and a yachting cap. Later, in the same episode, he'd switch to a vest and a cowboy hat. He was the world's largest paper doll.

Vince Longo says, "Chuck had to get rid of some of the hats. He had hats from the military, and suddenly, he stopped wearing them. I noticed it during the taping, so I asked him about it. He said the US Navy complained."⁷

Chuck and his staff became quite fond of interrupting acts. A creature called "The Thing" would snarl and snort off camera as a contestant did

6. Personal interview. 10 Apr. 2019.

7. Personal interview. 7 May 2019.

their song and dance, and suddenly a large claw whisked onstage and yanked the contestant off-stage, never to be seen again. It was a kooky twist on the old hook from years past, and the contestants never saw it coming.

Larry Spencer remembers, "We never told contestants what we were going to do. Any time we interrupted an act, it was a surprise to them."[8]

The Graveyard Grease; they sang doowop music. ROBERT BURROUGHS COLLECTION

A mannequin dropped from the ceiling while a contestant sang. As a classical pianist toiled away, Chuck and some of his staffers fenced. A pair of pianists was put through the ringer by judges Jamie Farr, Patty Andrews, and Willie Bobo, who walked over and took turns jumping on the piano. When that didn't faze them, the judges knocked their sheet music off the stand and pushed the piano away. During the holiday season, when a Christmas tree adorned the set, the judges removed the ornaments, walked over to a contestant, and hung them from her sweater as she struggled to maintain her composure and finish her performance. The staff had a hoedown while a fiddler scratched out a square dance. During

8. Personal interview. 2 Feb. 2019.

a spiritual number, Chuck hobbled onstage with a set of crutches, triumphantly threw them away, and then collapsed face-first.

The biggest surprise *The Gong Show* ever unleashed on its hapless hopefuls came when Shock Troop Johnny Michel decided he had had enough of "Feelings." He was so sick of singer after singer coming in for auditions and singing the schmaltzy ditty that he suggested booking seven of the

The Bait Brothers, who played their harmonicas and danced in a single plus-sized pair of pants. AUTHOR'S COLLECTION

songsters for the same episode. None of the contestants were told that this was the plan, though. The judges didn't know either.

Singer Andy Jackson was caught off-guard as a mannequin dropped from the ceiling, but shook it off, let himself laugh, and sang "Feelings." Scott Charles Hensel came out and sang the first word "Feelings" with so much emotion and extra body language that one gets the sense that he was all too happy to let himself be part of the joke, rather than be the butt of it. Mitzi McCall banged the gong with her head to stop him. A woman identified as Chris looked first flustered, and then resigned, as she sang the first lyric and the judges erupted with laughter. Ron Devo sang the song until the crew stunned him by just shutting the curtain on him and shutting the microphone off. Emmanuel sang "Feelings" and the judges walked off the set in mock-exasperation. He turned and looked to writer Jaime Klein, who was standing just out of view of camera, and asked if he should even finish the song. Jerry Flanders was surprised by the Woo-Woo Chorus' presence onstage as they backed up his performance. Sue Williams grinned and rolled her eyes as she began the chorus. To close the show, Chuck assembled all the contestants onstage for a spectacular

Susan George doesn't know what to make of this. AUTHOR'S COLLECTION

encore, forgoing the usual theme music in favor of seven contestants, the judges, and Chuck singing "Feelings" together.

Jamie Farr remembers, "The judges were never told anything in advance about the acts we'd be seeing that day, and they certainly didn't tell us they were going to do that. I was really, really sick of that song by the time the taping was over."[9]

The Shock Troops got their next order from Chuck Barris after the show. The song "Feelings" was banned forever.

The judges could deliver surprises too. One day as Jamie sat on the panel with Arte Johnson and Jaye P. Morgan, they joked off-microphone about Chuck's nervous habit of clapping his hands. A twinge of inspiration hit all of them.

9. Personal interview. 25 Apr. 2019.

Jamie Farr remembers, "We didn't tell Chuck our idea, we didn't tell John Dorsey, the director our idea. We told nobody. We were taping five episodes that day. During one break, we walked over to the guys in the prop department and asked them if they had some rope and some duct tape, and they said yes, and they gave it to us. They didn't even ask why.[10]

"During the show, we just ran from our seats over to Chuck and we tied him up, and we took over the show. Arte and Jay would read the cue cards, and I'd stand there silently and clap my hands and point at the camera like Chuck. John Dorsey was on top of it, he kept one camera on Chuck and for the rest of the show, he'd cut back to Chuck to get shots of him trying to free himself. But that was how Chuck ran things. Think about that — he was the boss, the guy running the show. When three people grab him and tie him up and steal the show from him, he doesn't even consider stopping tape. His reaction was to just go with it and see what would happen."

Though Jamie was never officially a regular on the show — he never had a contract with Chuck Barris and was only committed for one taping at a time, like a guest performer on any other show — he was on often enough that Chuck dubbed him "a member of the family." Chuck even had the judges' panel adorned with a giant photo of Jamie Farr, so that he was constantly on the show, whether he was booked or not. On the opposite side of the stage, where Chuck usually stood while acts were performing, there were two dolls hanging over him. Those were gifts from Jamie's wife.

---

10. Ibid.

CHAPTER 11

The Horror... The Horror

Above: In the face of overwhelming critical disdain, sometimes, all Chuck Barris could do was smile. ROBERT BURROUGHS COLLECTION

> *The only thing more pitiful than* The Gong Show *is its emcee, Chuck Barris.*[1]
>
> *...[M]isuse of television is typical of Chuck Barris, whose insensitivities and snickering sense of humor make him a cross between Caligula and Soupy Sales.*
>
> FRANK SWERTLOW, *Chicago Daily News*[2]

> *[Chuck Barris' shows] make me ashamed of the medium. Some of Barris' shows...make me ashamed to admit I'm in television. They make me understand why people look down on television and sneer at it.*
>
> HOWARD FELSHER, producer of *Family Feud*[3]

Every kid that ever dealt with a bully heard the same well-meaning advice from some adult. "Just act like it doesn't bother you."

At the beginning of *The Gong Show*, Chuck Barris seemed to heed that advice when dealing with denouncements. In its sixth month on NBC, Chuck, smiling from ear to ear, devoted part of a few episodes to reading his hate mail.

> *Dear Mister,*
> *Your emcee on the morning* Bong Show [sic] *talks too much. He sure has the gift of gab, and when he steps down from the short platform, he walks as if he had to (audio muted).*
> *Signed,*
> *A disgusted viewer.*

> *Dear Mister Chuck Barris,*
> *Just in case you were considering why all the* Gong Show *acts are in a rush to get off the stage, it's because no one wants to be seen with you.*

The hate mail could honestly amuse Chuck at times. It was hard to take someone's intense dislike of him seriously when they kept addressing their letters to "Chuck Berry." He even brought his barber onstage to take a bow after reading a nasty letter from a viewer who called his hair "absurd."

1. Ettinger, Stewart. "Sure Beats the Breaks on 'The Gong Show.'" *Courier-Post*. Camden, NJ. 3 Mar. 1978.

2. Swertlow, Frank. "Chuck Barris Perfect as Producer of Live Execution Show." *The Vancouver Sun*. Vancouver, BC. 1 Mar. 1978.

3. Young, Mort. "Though Others Might Gong Him, Barris is Daytime King." *The News-Press*. Fort Myers, FL. 10 May 1979.

Chuck convinced himself that the bad publicity from critics was a plus. The reviews were so vituperative that viewers may have been tuning in to see if the show was as bad as it sounded. Then they'd be amazed to find that they enjoyed themselves and the show had a new regular viewer.

And besides, Chuck recognized that despite their high profile, critics had truly insignificant impact on his business.

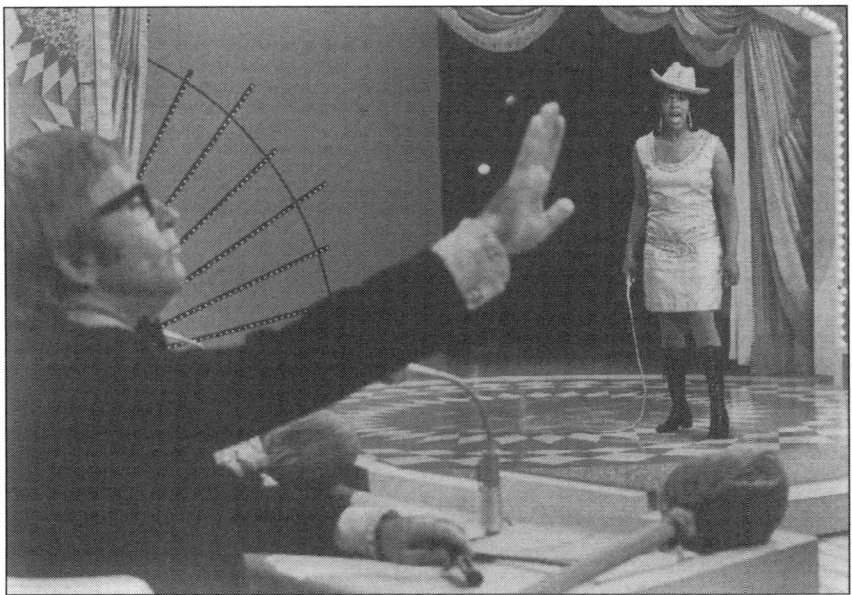

Texas Lil, who cracked her whip while singing. ROBERT BURROUGHS COLLECTION

"If you're doing your job well, your responsibility first and foremost is to your audience," says network executive Michael Brockman. "You do not take influence from a critic's opinion. That's not a lack of respect for them. That's recognizing that a critic is one voice of many that happens to have a much louder microphone than the others. The ratings tell you much more about a show's value."[4]

Chuck happily made himself available for interviews in those early months too, all too eager to address the condemnations of the show and give his side of it. When *Washington Post* columnist Tom Shales asked him about the criticism leveled against the show for its cruelty, Chuck presented a rebuttal: "People call it sadistic. But what it's basically doing

4. Personal interview. 19 Jun. 2019.

is fulfilling some kind of fantasy that these people can live on for a long time. They are going to be seen coast-to-coast. Why look upon these things as sad? Most of them know they're never going to be anything in show business. So what? Even a good person...so he's good, but what's he gonna do next week? What fascinates me is the mentality of these

Miss Gigi, the six-foot-tall drag queen. AUTHOR'S COLLECTION

people, what makes them think they're good. And besides, what was so great about their lives before?"

John Hill says, "Outwardly, Chuck would react to criticism with a 'Who cares?' attitude. But Chuck had a serious side to him. He had written novels and he was proud of that work. He was genuinely surprised at how popular *The Gong Show* became. He was proud of *The Gong Show*.

Chucky in the sky with diamonds…A lot of viewers thought the same thing about Chuck, but his staff was adamant that Chuck was always clean and sober, onstage and off. PHOTO BY AND COURTESY OF VINCE LONGO

He loved doing it. But I don't think he expected it to be his legacy. If he had his druthers, he would have wanted the world to remember him as a great author. I've read his novels. He was right to feel proud of them."[5]

Whatever they had to say about the show, the knocks on Chuck himself began to leave their mark. He became a favorite target of Johnny Carson, who one night donned his turban for his signature bit, Carnac the Magnificent, in which he divined the answer to a question sealed in an envelope, then tore the envelope open and read the question.

"Paul…Lifebuoy…Chuck Barris" was the answer that Carnac announced for one gag. He tore the envelope open and read, "Name a Pope, a soap, and a dope."

---

5. Personal interview. 14 May 2019.

Despite having plenty of episodes under his belt after a year or so, he showed no discernible improvement. He still bungled jokes. He still needed hats to cover his squinting eyes. He still shuffled his feet and clapped his hands. He would pause and say "Ooooooooh..." while grasping to articulate whatever just popped into his mind. This was the 1970s after all, so audiences could be forgiven for never considering the possi-

The country sounds of Mama Hooch and Her Maid June. AUTHOR'S COLLECTION

bility that Chuck just wasn't cut out for the job. There had to be a reason that Chuck was acting that way.

Larry Spencer says, "Everybody thought Chuck was on drugs. He wasn't. Everyone thought he was an alcoholic. I never even saw him take a drink. Off-stage, I wouldn't call Chuck introverted, but he could be a very quiet person away from the show."[6]

"Unknown Comic" Murray Langston says, "I didn't really get to know Chuck all that well during the time I was doing the show. I had heard the same rumors as everyone else, that Chuck was drugged out and drunk when he did the show, and that's why he was acting that way.

6. Personal interview. 2 Feb. 2019.

"I asked Gene-Gene the Dancing Machine about the rumors one day and if he thought Chuck was on anything. Gene says, 'No friggin' way!' Gene told me there were guys on the crew who smoked weed, but they had to hide it from Chuck. He didn't like drugs and didn't want to be around people who were using. The way Chuck acted on the show was just the way he was."[7]

This act was a real charmer. PHOTO BY AND COURTESY OF VINCE LONGO

Vince Longo adds, "Two people at *The Dating Game* got fired for bringing marijuana to work, because one of the bandits snitched on them for it. I leapt over the guy's desk and choked him. I screamed 'SNITCH!' The entire office saw me do it. I stormed into Chuck's office. He's in the middle of a meeting with Loretta and with Walt Case, the producer of *The Dating Game*. I said, 'I just want to let you know that I smacked around the guy who ratted, and I probably spoke out of turn. I'm packing up my desk, but I want to tell you, it's bullshit to hang a rap on somebody for having marijuana when everybody here is using something!' I stormed out.[8]

"Chuck said, 'Listen, I like having a rat in the organization.' He didn't fire me and wouldn't allow me to quit. Chuck was very worried that if word got out that we had a lot of drug use in the organization, it would scare off the networks, or the local stations, or the shareholders. Or

---

7. Personal interview. 4 May 2019
8. Personal interview. 7 May 2019.

maybe the FCC would start viewing the shows more closely. One of the two people who got fired was brought back, but Chuck made an announcement to the staff. He called this one guy 'our hostage.' The policy was laid down that if somebody else got caught using, that person would be fired, and so would the hostage. Chuck really, really hated drug use."

Moore's Mongrel Review. BOB BODEN COLLECTION

Mike Metzger says, "Chuck sent out anti-drug memos to the staff. There were to be no drugs on the premises, and he would fire anybody who had them. We absolutely used marijuana, but we went to each other's houses. Sometimes, if we needed to brainstorm *Dating* or *Newlywed* questions, we would leave the office, go to someone's apartment, smoke, and then come back and write. It's so funny because our entire company image was that Chuck's office was run by dope-smoking hippies, but that was just the atmosphere. Chuck himself pulled that off without drugs. It's kind of like that phrase people used to say, 'high on life.' But Chuck really was."[9]

Ellen Metzger says, "To some extent, he looked the other way. Yes, we had potheads at Chuck Barris Productions, but nobody would sit around

9. Personal interview. 13 May 2019.

smoking so much grass that it left a cloud in the hallway. If you were functional and you were good at your job, Chuck tolerated it, but he really, really did not want to know for sure that you were doing it."[10]

John Hill adds, "Chuck hated it so much, especially after he took the company public. Because a publicly traded company is going to have extra scrutiny. Considering that, it made sense. But I remember Chuck warned that if he even found out you spent your weekends hanging out with somebody who had a reputation for using illicit substances, he'd fire you just for hanging out with them."[11]

Lynnette Karnes says, "Chuck told us a story once about Mama Cass Elliott. Mama Cass had invited him to her house once and gave him brownies. She didn't tell Chuck that she put marijuana in the brownies, and he told us that made him absolutely furious. He didn't like the way it made him feel, and he didn't like the idea that he didn't have control over his own body. And that experience really left a mark on him.

"We had a woman on our staff — I won't name a name — but you could tell what she was doing because she was sniffing all the time and you could see rings around her nose. California law requires work permits to be filled out if you're going to have children performing on television. One of this woman's duties on the show was to get work permits whenever we booked children to be contestants. She told us she had the permits, we taped the episode, and we found out after the fact that she didn't have the permits done. She lied about it. We taped the episode, but we had to can it because we really couldn't legally air it — we had children performing without permits. Chuck fired her.

"After he fired her, Chuck had a staff meeting, and he said to all of us, 'Going forward, I'm not even going to demand proof. If anybody even says you're using drugs, you're fired. I don't need people hearing about this stuff happening.'"

The criticisms extended to something deeper than any one show. Critics hated all these shows produced by the same man, who was now also putting himself out there as the sweetly inelegant host of one of his own creations. Chuck Barris was the root of society's ills, it would seem. He was dubbed "the king of video schlock,"[12] his name in the credits serving as a critical Seal of Disapproval, a mark of television programming to be deemed beyond reproach.

10. Personal interview. 15 May 2019.
11. Personal interview. 14 May 2019.
12. Beck, Marilyn. "Mork and Mindy Star Nervous." *Pensacola News Journal.* 15 Sep. 1978.

Danny Lies says, "The 'king of schlock' name really got to Chuck. At one point we had six shows on the air. We were getting great ratings. It just irked Chuck to no end that a person could have that kind of success and that nobody would publicly give him any kind of credit for achieving that."[13]

And just putting down the newspaper and walking away wasn't enough to stop the onslaught. Once, Chuck was in his car, sitting at a red light,

The Disco Lizards, who flicked their tongues in rhythm to "A Fifth of Beethoven." ROBERT BURROUGHS COLLECTION

when a car pulled up in the next lane. The passenger stuck her head out of the window and yelled, "You're the dumbest thing that ever walked! Your show stinks!"[14]

As the scolding and scorning from the outside world took its toll, Chuck tried to isolate himself more. He wore a fake mustache when he went out in public, only to pitch it in the trash when he was recognized immediately. But the man who had so gregariously welcomed TV critics to sit in on auditions now became increasingly wary of outsiders, and more protective of the people who were loyal to him.

13. Personal interview. 22 May 2019.
14. Breznican, Anthony. "Chuck Barris." *The Evening Sun.* Hanover, PA. 10 Jan. 2003.

Larry Spencer says, "Chuck Barris was the best boss in the world. He'd give you the shirt off his back. When I decided I wanted to move into writing for television full-time, he paid my fee so I could get into the union."[15]

This wasn't unique to Spencer. When Chuck featured other members of his staff or the NBC crew on the show, he frequently encouraged them

Employees of Chuck Barris remembered him as a boss who would give the shirt off his back. And it's a good thing, because this contestant needs it.
ROBERT BURROUGHS COLLECTION

to join a performers' union, SAG or AFTRA, to make sure they'd receive the proper fees for their appearances, and, if the show ever went into reruns, residuals.

John Hill remembers, "Chuck was not afraid to speak up. Neither was I. We had a lot of squabbles. I was 'let go' several times, never for more than a few hours. Chuck and I had a huge blow-out one day. A while later, Chuck hands me an envelope without saying a word and he walks off. I figured it was discharge papers. I got up from my desk and walked away without saying a word.[16]

15. Personal interview. 2 Feb. 2019.
16. Personal interview. 14 May 2019.

"Chuck chases me down the hall and says, 'Aren't you going to open it up?' I told him 'I know what it is.' Chuck says, 'I bet you don't.' It was a letter of introduction to the Directors' Guild with a note saying that Chuck had paid my dues. It came with a guarantee for 13 weeks of work."

Chuck's embrace of unions, and his encouragement to his staff to connect themselves as much as possible, didn't particularly endear him to

Daniel Schock, who moved around like a robot and flung spaghetti on himself. ROBERT BURROUGHS COLLECTION

NBC. Chuck was confronted one day by a network lawyer. He recounted the conversation in his memoir *The Game Show King*. He was told to stop using NBC crew members as performers.

"Why?" he asked.

"Because you've now forced them to join two unions: the stagehands' union and the actors' union. It's against our corporate policy to allow employees to join more than one union."

"Why?" Chuck repeated.

"We now become vulnerable to strikes from not just one union, but two. We want you to cease and desist using network employees as actors right now."

That Chuck might refuse to budge apparently hadn't occurred to NBC's legal department, because they didn't seem to know what to do when he kept right on using his stagehands to perform sketch comedy. To Chuck's delight, the network buckled and changed their own policy, allowing employees to be in multiple unions. Chuck's people were taken care of, and as a bonus, he had stuck it to an outsider. People who weren't part of Chuck's team, but who seemed eager to interfere with it whenever possible, were a particular sticking point for him.

Spencer recalls, "He'd make awards for employees. He'd come in every week and give us trophies for 'the best crew of the week.' Every other week, he'd come in with jackets for all of us. Chuck commanded loyalty from his staff, but if you were loyal to him, he'd be so loyal to you. Best boss I've ever had.[17]

"One day Chuck was playing drums in his office, and I just walked in and listened to him. Suddenly Chuck just stops and looks up, and he says, 'What the fuck do you want?' There's a guy standing behind me. He's not part of our company, and that bothered Chuck. He loved his crew, but he really did not immediately trust anyone from outside."

Newspaper columnists who covered TV would occasionally print letters from readers, offering their column as a sounding board for television viewers. The letters about *The Gong Show* were rarely fan mail.

Someone ought to gong NBC's Gong Show. *It stinks!*[18]

I think The Gong Show *is the dumbest show ever on TV. I think it should be taken off the air.*[19]

I think the host, Chuck Barris, stinks. He smiles too much, he never knows where the cameras are, and his jokes are rotten. He always puts down the people trying to do their acts.[20]

I think Chuck Barris deserves to be gonged himself. He is such a jerk on The Gong Show. *Why doesn't the network get somebody else to do the show?*[21]

17. Personal interview. 2 Feb. 2019.
18. "Giving The Gong Show The Count of Ten." *The Philadelphia Inquirer.* 22 Aug. 1976.
19. Ibid.
20. Ibid.
21. Scheuer, Steven H. "They Can't Gong Chuck Barris, He's the Boss." *Miami News.* 1 Jun. 1977.

This Barris fellow makes me sick to my stomach, changing his silly hats and flopping all over the place.[22]

I'm a college student and I love TV. I really do. But I think that The Gong Show *is positively disgusting. How can human beings subject themselves to such humiliation? And why would any station carry such a horrible program? Am I wrong about this?*[23]

The average syndicated newspaper columnist in the 1970s, reacting to another viewing of The Gong Show. PHOTO BY AND COURTESY OF VINCE LONGO

Why doesn't Chuck Barris just crawl into a garbage disposal and disappear? Signed, F.U.[24]

There was also the endless stream of criticism about the way Chuck Barris humiliated the contestants on his shows. This was a knock he had been bearing all the way back to *The Dating Game*.

Syndicated columnist Gary Deeb wrote, "A typical Barris show…features a group of psychologically degenerate contestants who don't mind

22. "Shull's Mailbag." *The Indianapolis News.* 17 Nov. 1977.
23. "A Look at 'The Gong Show.'" *The Messenger.* Madisonville, KY. 28 Apr. 1978.
24. "Shull's Mailbag." *The Indianapolis News.* 21 Mar. 1978.

parading their deficiencies on coast-to-coast television...and so the contestants yell and jump up and down and acts boorish, and the audience laughs and laughs and laughs. An exercise in degradation."25

Gong writer Jaime Klein said in 2016, "Every show gets criticized. If you're going to work in television, somebody hates your show. It comes with the territory. But the criticism of *The Gong Show* just annoyed me.

The Vatican Four; the nuns did a choreographed routine while the priest lip-synced to Tom Lehrer's "The Vatican Rag." ROBERT BURROUGHS COLLECTION

They said we were cruel to the contestants. We didn't con these people to come to the show! It wasn't a ruse! They signed up for it, they were coming to us...These people signed up and auditioned knowing that they'd be on national TV, and that these judges were ready to bang a gong and tell them that they were no good. And they went right ahead and did it anyway."26

Larry Gotterer is quick to point out a logical gap in the criticism. If Chuck Barris' shows were mean to contestants, they wouldn't have had contestants. "We did things differently, and to a critic, 'differently' must

25. Deeb, Gary. "Gong Show Forum for Jackasses." *The Akron Beacon Journal*. 25 May 1976.
26. Personal interview. 8 Dec. 2016.

be bad. Contestants loved Chuck, and I mean all the contestants on all the shows. Everybody just liked him."[27]

Chuck defended his empire to Mike Wallace when *60 Minutes* profiled him for a story. "On game shows, at least we don't pistol whip, we don't rape, we don't murder, we don't punch ladies in the face or kick people like they do in beloved and prestigious prime time. The shows entertain

Lisa and the Insomniacs. BOB BODEN COLLECTION

and provide a certain amount of prizes and good things for these people."

Chuck didn't fully cut himself off from TV critics in search of a chat, but he could be less than cordial to them. Frank Swertlow of *Chicago Daily News* recapped his own experience of interviewing Chuck Barris at an upscale restaurant: Chuck showed up thirty minutes late, argued with the maître di because he refused to wear a tie, left unannounced, and Swertlow was forced to pay for Chuck's meal. Chuck responded to Swertlow's write-up by dedicating an episode of *The Gong Show* to him. The billboard on the stage read IT'S SOURPUSS SWERTLOW DAY.

Chuck articulated his increasingly hostile attitude toward the press in a memo to his staff, asking them not to give interviews.

27. Personal interview. 24 Apr. 2019.

> ...[O]ne of the things I asked everyone to adhere to was NOT TO TALK TO ANYONE FROM THE MEDIA UNLESS I HAVE GIVEN THAT INDIVIDUAL PERSON <u>MY</u> PERMISSION. IF YOU HAVEN'T RECEIVED <u>MY</u> PERMISSION, THEN THE ONLY THING YOU CAN SAY TO THE PRESS, THE RADIO, THE MAGAZINES, THE CABLE TELEVISION, THE NEWSPAPERS, THE LOCAL TV, THE NATIONAL TV, IS…"I HAVE NOTHING TO SAY."
>
> From now on, anyone who says anything will be fined $100 on the spot and then I will evaluate where he or she can stay with the company. And don't get tricked. If someone from the press tricks you, you will be fined just the same; for two reasons: (1) You ought to have known better in the first place, and (2) I can't very well fine the media person, can I?
>
> The reason for this blast is <u>not</u> that we have anything to hide. Obviously, we don't. And if you were to speak to anyone from the press, etc., and told that person anything [they] wanted to know, there is nothing you can say that would be wrong. But the media…would love to FIND something wrong, and they have a knack of taking YOUR nothing and turning it into something altogether different, out of context, detrimental. And since it is not your job to be a spokesperson for the company, don't make yourself vulnerable to lose your job over something that's not your job in the first place. When you're out there on your own, talk to the media all you want, but when you are with us, just keep your mouth shut. The press' bright lights and cameras are fun and exciting…until the next morning when you read or hear what you have said.

"To me, Chuck was like Mozart," muses Lynnette Karnes. "He was doing all these things that the public loved and appreciated. But anybody who had any sort of clout or voice in the business would complain about it because it confused them. They just saw him as a bad boy. And Chuck found that criticism very hurtful."[28]

To Chuck's mounting frustration, he found that the people who liked *The Gong Show* could irritate him just as much. It wasn't so much the loss of privacy and being recognized in public — that comes with the territory when you're a TV star — it was that people just seemed to presume that Chuck was always on the hunt for talent. People would do bird calls, or start doing terrible celebrity impressions, or warble a tune, or whip out

---

28. Personal interview. 3 Oct. 2019.

their harmonica, or tap dance, or ask him to pick a card. If they didn't perform, they sure were ready to describe their acts to Chuck in detail. He just wanted to eat lunch and read.

Chuck told Mike Douglas, "I was sitting on a plane, reading the newspaper. And a guy ran up the aisle and started to do a lizard. See, because the thing is, we don't do a normal audition. We get the lunatic fringe

Pro wrestler Rock Riddle, who sang while breaking boards. ROBERT BURROUGHS COLLECTION

dancing about my person. 'Hey! Watch this!' I guess that comes with the territory. That scares me…How would you like to have people jumping out and doing lizards in front of you every five minutes?

"I thought about this once. This is all relatively new. Fifty years ago, nobody knew anybody. Before films, there weren't any recognizable celebrities. I think they should make a study, because I don't think the human body or the human mind is capable of taking this kind of change in their life. It's a change! Boy, it's immense. I mean, I sit there in a car, and people stare at you at red lights…I like to go out to the movies, and I can't stand in line anymore. I have to wait until the last person's in, then run up, get a ticket, and dash into the movie."[29]

In the early days, maybe Chuck could have played off the way he felt by taking a page from Rodney Dangerfield's book and saying, "I don't get no respect," but after a year or so on the air, it wasn't funny to Chuck anymore. Respect was turning into a big deal for him. If the lack of respect was hurting, the staff felt his pain. They saw a side of this man that no one else seemed to see.

"Chuck was so enormously generous in so many ways," says Jefferson Beeker. "We were getting our NBC salary, and Chuck was using us regularly for the character bits on the air, so we were making a bunch of extra money for that. But then Chuck would give us bonuses for the smallest things that we just considered part of our job.[30]

"For example, they taped five episodes in a day. There was an episode where Chuck got hit in the face with a shaving cream pie toward the end. Then once the credits rolled, there would be a fifteen-minute stopdown while everyone changed clothes, got their make-up retouched, and got some water. Well, Chuck comes backstage covered with shaving cream, and the make-up and hair people got him all cleaned up, reapplied his make-up, and touched up his hair. I took care of his clothes, so that he was spotless and fresh-looking for the next episode. That was our job. We were there to do that. When we got our checks, we found that Chuck had kicked in some extra money for each of us, because he was so impressed with how well we had cleaned him up after that one episode.

"I was sitting at home one day and I got a call from a liquor store saying they had a delivery for me. I said I hadn't ordered anything, but they told me it was a gift. Chuck had a case of wine sent to me, just as a token of appreciation for the work I was doing on the show."

Chuck's loyalty to his staff, Beeker sensed, was a way of filling a void. "One thing I remember was it seemed like we always taped on holidays. We didn't tape on Christmas Day, but we taped close to it. We taped on Easter Sunday. We taped on other holidays — days that you would spend with your family. We knew Chuck did not have any family that he felt particularly close to. On holidays, that can be a lonely feeling. Chuck wanted us taping on holidays because that way he could be with the people he was close to. His staff was his family."

But...what about his actual family?

29. Mike Douglas. 1978.

30. Personal interview. 10 Apr. 2019.

Murray Langston says, "Della was such a sweetheart whenever I talked to her backstage. It's hard to think about what Chuck was going through with her. Thinking about it now, that may have been why Chuck didn't want to see anybody on the staff using while he was around. He saw what that kind of stuff was doing to her."

Beeker says, "Della was the sweetest girl. We loved her. But we knew

NBC page Shelley Herman with Della Barris. Employees loved her, but they saw how troubled the young girl was. PHOTO COURTESY OF SHELLEY HERMAN

there were problems. She was struggling in school. She was attending Westlake, which was an all-girls school, and she hated it there. Chuck, at one point, asked me if I could come to his house to give Della tap-dancing lessons, which was odd. She may have had a little crush on me, because after the first lesson, she asked me to stay and the maid cooked dinner for us. A little crush there, but also, she was very, very lonely. After a while, she lost interest in tap dancing and I stopped giving her lessons, which I was fine with, but I think she just really wanted somebody at the house to talk to."[31]

31. Ibid.

Della's troubles in school were rooted in two issues. When she lived in Europe, she did homework when it was cold and rainy outside. She didn't have trouble concentrating on it because, after all, what else did she have to do? Trying to study in California, where it was constantly sunny, was difficult. She felt like she was missing out on something. In her early teens, she was interested in boys, and being at an all-girls school frustrated her.

Chuck's way of dealing with her issues, he later conceded, was stupid. He asked Della where she'd rather go to high school. She answered Beverly Hills High School.

Chuck didn't want to leave Malibu. He rented Della her own apartment on Rodeo Drive, so she could live in Beverly Hills, on her own most of the time, and attend Beverly Hills High School. One week later, she was hospitalized. She was 14 years old, and she had overdosed on cocaine. Della had started using cocaine, pills, and alcohol to try to fit in at Beverly Hills High School. But the hospitalization had turned her into a laughingstock, and left her with a new nickname among her classmates: "Odie," a pun on O.D. Della's own search for respect had turned her into an outcast.

All Chuck did was go back to work and keep rolling out more television shows. For as many ideas and as many forms of media as Chuck had pursued in the past decade and a half, Chuck Barris Productions' fortunes were increasingly dependent on only three properties: *The Dating Game*, *The Newlywed Game*, and *The Gong Show*. Most producers who have an explosive hit like *Gong* would have producers and syndicates banging on their doors and taking whatever that producer had to offer. Not for Chuck. His ideas were still too far out.

In 1978, Chuck told Mike Douglas about some of his ideas that had been shot down recently. "They've rejected a bunch. I once had a show that I wanted to do where we'd have a manhunt. We'd do a half-hour and commit a crime. Have a robbery, something like that. And then [we'd] have the actor who portrayed the criminal go out somewhere in the country and we'd give you clues to where he was. And if you could find him…you'd win $100,000. The networks wouldn't do it because they were afraid somebody might shoot this guy."[32]

More perplexing to Chuck was that on the rare occasions that executives courted him, they didn't really want him or the kind of ideas that he had already succeeded with. They courted Chuck Barris hoping he would produce something more inside-the-box.

32. Mike Douglas. 1978.

Chuck told writer Peter H. Brown, "You know, one of the executive bigwigs came to me a while ago and asked me why I wasted my talent on the shows I produce. The guy said, 'You're so good; why don't you come over to the network and do something with substance to it?' Whaddaya want me to do, buddy — create something like *Charlie's Angels* or *Laverne & Shirley*?"[33]

Rhett and Scarlett on the stage of the Forum for The Chuck Barris Rah-Rah Show. PHOTO COURTESY OF JEFFERSON BEEKER

Chuck Barris' pursuit for respect was about to come to the forefront. The American public didn't quite realize what drove Chuck's next move, but his staff picked up on it as they came together to help the boss shape a new idea called *The Chuck Barris Rah-Rah Show*.

Chuck had parlayed his deal for three more prime-time specials on NBC into a pilot for the network for a splashy weekly variety show that would pick up where another show had left off.

Chuck touted, "I kind of always thought that [the networks] should do 'Ed Sullivan Revisited.' You have great acts, well-known acts, and unknown acts, and good talent. Giving all sorts of people a break. It's

33. Brown, Peter H. "Television's Thriving Theater of Humiliation.

not *The Gong Show* in that sense. It's just an hour of acts, one act after the other."[34]

Each week would have a dazzling array of guest stars; among them, many of *The Gong Show* judges, doing the type of performing that got them the notoriety that led to the judges' table to begin with. Jaye P. Morgan sang, Fred Travalena did impressions, Rip Taylor did some brutally punny stand-up comedy. Mixed in with the beautiful people were lesser-known performers with memorable acts, nearly all of them booked straight from the files of *The Gong Show*. Instead of the "professional nightclub engagement" touted at the dawn of the series, *Gong Show* contestants who turned out to have a modicum of talent would now be rewarded with prime-time network television exposure, and shared billing with some of the top names in show business.

Larry Spencer says, "I was involved in writing *The Rah-Rah Show*. Chuck obviously felt that some of these acts that had been on *The Gong Show* were serious and relevant."[35]

A pilot program was shot on October 19, 1977. To make it feel like a grand event, Chuck opted to go bigger than the confines of the NBC Studios in Burbank. *The Chuck Barris Rah-Rah Show* was taped on the stage of The Forum, a 17,000-seat venue in nearby Inglewood. The pilot included guests George Carlin, Dale Evans, the Bay City Rollers (Della's favorite band), and The Duke Ellington Orchestra. The pilot also included 2-4 The Show Trio (a three-man band playing Spike Jones-inspired tunes) and Rhett & Scarlett.

Larry Spencer says, "George Carlin was unforgettable. George Carlin walked onstage and just stared at the audience in silence for six minutes. He got huge laughs."[36]

Jefferson Beeker remembers, "Being on that show was terrifying. The Bay City Rollers were the white-hot group in music at that point, so Chuck booked them for the pilot to ensure a full audience. Seventeen-thousand seats, tickets were free because it was a TV taping, and we went out onstage in front of these 17,000 people who came to see The Bay City Rollers.

"Thankfully, right as we started talking, there was an audio problem and they had to stop tape. We just stayed there onstage while we waited for them to make the repair. That was the most wonderful thing that

---

34. Ibid.
35. Personal interview. 2 Feb. 2019.
36. Ibid.

could have happened. We stood onstage so long that we got acclimated to being in front of that massive audience and we weren't worrying about it anymore. They restarted tape and we went right into the routine, and it was perfect."

It looked like NBC was going to have an opening for the show quickly. *The Richard Pryor Show* premiered on NBC in the fall of 1977, boasting

Chuck meets Mr. Television. The legendary Milton Berle appears on The Chuck Barris Rah-Rah Show. ROBERT BURROUGHS COLLECTION

an astonishing cast including Robin Williams, Paul Mooney, Sandra Bernhard, Edie McClurg, Tim Reid, and Marsha Warfield. But Pryor's relationship with the network went sour; and his battles with censors were nearly constant.

Jefferson Beeker recalls, "I was hired as a day player for Richard Pryor's show. We had two back-to-back seventeen-hour days of taping, and out of two seventeen-hour taping days, NBC did not have twenty minutes of broadcast-suitable material for what was supposed to be an hour-long show."[37]

Pryor pulled the plug on the show after only four episodes, creating a gap on the show's schedule. The first week after *The Richard Pryor Show* ended, NBC filled the gap in the schedule by airing *The Chuck Barris Rah-Rah Show*. Other filler followed over the next several weeks while Chuck hammered out a deal with the network. Another *Rah-Rah Show* aired during Christmas week and bombed in the ratings. But when NBC's planned midseason series *The Hanna-Barbera Hour* (an hour of cartoons in prime time, which, in the late 1970s, was considered a sign that a network was desperate) fell through, the hour went to Chuck. On January 28, 1978, *The Chuck Barris Rah-Rah Show* had a permanent slot on the NBC schedule, Thursdays at 8… Well, maybe not that permanent.

Cab Calloway, the hidee-hidee-hidee-hi man, appears on Rah-Rah. ROBERT BURROUGHS COLLECTION

At first glance, it looked like another hit on Chuck's hands. Although the series didn't tape at the 17,000-seat Forum the way the pilot had, it might as well have. So many people showed up for the first taping at NBC Studios that the spillover was taken into an unoccupied adjacent studio to watch the taping on a closed-circuit monitor.

---

37. Personal interview. 10 Apr. 2019.

The problem with Chuck Barris was that he couldn't seem to decide what he wanted the show to be, in a sense torn between the show he wanted and the show he had. Look at the guest list. Redd Foxx, Michelle Phillips, Ray Charles, Phyllis Diller, The Oak Ridge Boys, Patti LaBelle, Victor Borge, Milton Berle, Henny Youngman, Chet Atkins, The

Jaye P. Morgan, in her element on The Chuck Barris Rah-Rah Show.
ROBERT BURROUGHS COLLECTION

Temptations, The Mills Brothers, Johnny Paycheck...and The Bandit Impressionist...and The Bait Brothers, two svelte men who squeezed into a large pair of pants and danced in unison...and Harry Kipper, the man who poured food all over himself...and a man who puts a stocking over his head and does an impression of a corkscrew....and Gene-Gene the Dancing Machine and The Unknown Comic...

Chuck Barris wanted to do a relevant, respectable, legitimate variety show, but he wanted to do it as *The Gong Show*. He wanted a crowd-pleasing show, with all the trappings of a show they hated. Whatever your own opinion of *The Gong Show*, columnist Lisa Tuttle's review of *The Chuck Barris Rah-Rah Show* was an apt one: "*The Gong Show* by any other name is still *The Gong Show*."[38]

Or was it? Since it wasn't a talent competition, there were no judges, which meant no wisecracks from Jamie or Jaye. Chuck did away with Larry Spencer's gag introductions, instead introducing each act with a fawning "I love this group" or "Here's a fave." At the end of each act, Chuck didn't interact with the performers at all. The show veered from act to act without taking a breath. Blink while former contestant Kevin Parker is playing "Johnny B. Goode" on an acoustic guitar, and you'd open your eyes to find comedian Gallagher smashing a watermelon. *The Chuck Barris Rah-Rah Show* was the worst of both worlds. For people who hated *The Gong Show*, it was too much like *The Gong Show*. For people who loved *The Gong Show*, it was too different from *The Gong Show*.

There was one oddly egotistical bend to the *Rah-Rah Show*. There was constantly a camera on Chuck. "Of course there was," you might say. "He was the host." The host introduces the acts, and then the host disappears until the end of the performance to introduce the next act. Chuck introduced the acts, and the director always kept a camera on him to get shots of Chuck somehow participating. When bands played, we got shots of Chuck clapping his hands. When dancers took the stage, we got shots of Chuck off to the side, getting down. Chuck seemed to be trying to share the spotlight instead of simply giving it.

Lynnette Karnes says, "My main memory from *Rah-Rah Show* was that I offended Milton Berle. I was sent down to call the next act to the stage for each performance. I went down one night and yelled, 'Milton Berle to the stage please! Has anyone seen Milton Berle?' He was standing right in front of me. He says, 'I'm the king of comedy! Don't you know

---

38. Tuttle, Lisa. "'Tell Me My Name' Weighs Adoptee's Rights." *Austin American-Statesman*. 20 Dec. 1977.

who I am?' And I looked right at him and said, 'Well, no, sir, I don't.' I was 23 and he was shocked that I didn't know who he was."

The Chuck Barris Rah-Rah Show ended after only six weeks. Its final episode was ranked 68th out of 69 prime-time programs in the Nielsen ratings for that week.

CHAPTER 12

Where Did They Come From?

Above: Chuck Barris moved on from the failure of The Chuck Barris Rah-Rah Show. *There were still plenty more acts to be gonged in his other work.* ROBERT BURROUGHS COLLECTION

Maureen Orth was a writer for *Newsweek*, and like a handful of reporters at the zenith of *The Gong Show*'s popularity, she thought that sitting with the staff while they held auditions might make for an interesting article. After sitting next to Chuck Barris for a few hours as he watched a teenage belching virtuoso, a singer too drunk to finish her song, and a tattooed guy who specialized in barnyard mimicry, Orth was stupefied when Chuck turned to her and asked, "What can you do, Maureen?"[1]

Orth wasn't expecting to become part of her own story and didn't know how to answer. "I can do my old high school pompom routine, I suppose."

Chuck answered, "When?"

Orth was as bewildered as anybody to find herself returning for the next round of auditions, wearing a sweater she hadn't put on in 17 years, and wielding a pair of towels — the closest thing she had to pompoms. She did a routine she had concocted specifically for the show and got herself booked. She listened to other acts brimming with confidence — one said, "I know I won't get gonged; I'm a music major" — but Orth was no performer by trade. She had been arguably roped into this. She was hardly over the hill, but she was just old enough that she knew she couldn't pull off looking like a college cheerleader. All of that did a strange thing to her morale, though, as she recounted in her *Newsweek* story — she went onstage so fully prepared to get gonged that she was looking forward to it.

Milton DeLugg and the Band with a Thugg blared "On Wisconsin!" for her as she did a minute's worth of high kicks, shook her towel-towels, and told the judges, "Gimme a G! Gimme an O! Gimme an N! Gimme a G! What's that spell?"

In her head, she had imagined a judge timing the moment perfectly and banging the gong in response…but that's not what happened. Arte Johnson, Jaye P. Morgan, and Steve Garvey were devouring the performance, so she simply did a few more kicks and took her bow. She got a respectable score of 26 but lost in a tiebreaker to a singer.

For her *Newsweek* story, Orth described the feeling of losing, but surviving, *The Gong Show*: "'I did it, I did it!' I said to myself as I joined the other contestants onstage for the frenzied awards ceremony…It was a feeling I hadn't had since the last winning play of that football season sixteen years ago."[2]

---

1. Orth, Maureen. "Gong Show Contestant." *Newsweek*. 1977. Retrieved from *https://maureenorth.com/1977/02/gong-show-contestant/*

2. Ibid.

So many who had turned up their noses at *The Gong Show* and tsk-tsked it for the way it embarrassed contestants couldn't fathom why anyone would appear on the show, knowing what they could be subjected to. But Orth had experienced the answer first-hand. Even in a losing effort, there was something to be said for the exhilaration of having 90 seconds of national television time all to yourself to show off. *The Gong Show* was the only outlet available to most people who had a secret desire to perform, and to be seen.

To read the press surrounding the show at the time, there wasn't much to be gained in the way of respect. These contestants put themselves out there to be heckled, jeered, judged, and yes, gonged, and for their bravery, syndicated columnists called them "psychological morons"; "psychologically degenerate contestants who don't mind parading their deficiencies on coast-to-coast television."[3]

Michael Sherman was already a seasoned performer by the time *The Gong Show* came along in 1976. "I started as a comic in the 1960s. I came awfully close to being on *Laugh-In* in the late 1960s. They called me back twice, and then I got a call saying they'd keep me in mind. Well, fifty years later, they haven't called me yet.[4]

"I had an act in nightclubs where I would play different records and lip-sync to them, and I would act out a little scene for all of them. I had a couple of songs I performed with. One was 'Speedy Gonzales' by Pat Boone. Another was 'John and Marsha' by Stan Freberg. When I learned about *The Gong Show*, I decided to audition with 'Mulambo No. 1' by Yma Sumac. I wore a Viking helmet, Groucho glasses, and a wig with braids, and I got frightened by a rubber snake. Part of the joke was that the song was played at the wrong speed. I had it on a record album, which meant it was supposed to be played at 33 1/3 RPM. I'd perform the act with the record set at 45 speed. That was perfect for *The Gong Show* because played at 45 RPM, that song is exactly 90 seconds.

"I was sure I'd be gonged. Not only did I survive, but I also got perfect tens from all the judges. I won $516.32. The first person I told was my best friend, Skip Stephenson, who went on to be one of the co-hosts on NBC's *Real People*. Well, my appearance was taped before the show had started airing on NBC. I went straight to Skip's place and told him 'I won *The Gong Show!* I can't believe it!' He said, 'What's *The Gong* Show?'

3. Deeb, Gary. "Gong Show Forum for Jackasses." *The Akron Beacon Journal*. 25 May 1976.
4. Personal interview. 1 May 2019.

"They brought me back a few weeks later for a special episode with acts that scored 30 points. I didn't win that time, but they brought me back again for a nighttime show with Gary Owens, and then another nighttime show. I was on four times. Then they brought me back for *The Chuck Barris Rah-Rah Show*.

"I did the same act for every appearance because that's what they wanted. I got kind of hot from that, if you can believe it. I got booked

Michael Sherman reminiscing in a Los Angeles diner in 2019. Still a Gong Show *contestant after all these years.* PHOTO BY THE AUTHOR

for a few TV shows to do that, including *Cos*, Bill Cosby's variety show, where I played a patient in a mental institution with Henny Youngman. It didn't really launch my career though. I never got a shot at a show like Johnny Carson's. But I never gave up performing. I'm 80 now and I still act. I'm still available to do impressions too. I did an hour and ten minutes at a senior center yesterday."

Chuck D'Imperio has enjoyed an extensive career as a disc jockey in upstate New York. But in 1976 he was an aspiring singer responding to a newspaper advertisement. "I had just moved to Los Angeles. I was working at the Biltmore Hotel and living with friends in Venice, doing whatever singing showcases I could. I was a classic struggling artist. I had no money, but I was having a wonderful time. [5]

"*The Gong Show* wasn't even on the air yet when I auditioned. I saw a notice in a show business trade newspaper for an open talent audition. The ad said they were looking for acts for 'a Ted Mack-like variety show on NBC.' I showed the ad to my friends, and they encouraged me to try out because I had nothing else to do.

"I went to Old World Restaurant, met with an assistant, and got in line. Once it was my turn, they brought me into the dining area. There was a section that had been walled off with black curtains, and when you stepped through the curtains, there was Chuck Barris sitting in a director's chair. He and I talked a little bit and ended up riffing on each other because we had the same first name. I'm 6'6" and Chuck Barris was kind of short, so he called me Big Chuck and I called him Little Chuck.

"Then it was time for me to audition and I really wasn't very prepared.
'Do you have a resume?'
'No.'
'Do you have a photo of yourself?'
'No.'
'Did you bring sheet music?'
'No.'
'Do you have a phone number?'

"I didn't even own a phone at that point. I gave them a phone number for the Biltmore Hotel and told them when I usually worked there. Then for my audition, I sang. Now since the show wasn't on the air yet, I didn't really know what it was all about, so singing was all I did.

"On a Sunday, I get a call at the Biltmore from Chuck Barris himself. I want to say Chuck was a regular there for the restaurant, so he felt comfortable just making the call himself. Chuck tells me, 'I like you. You have a great personality; I want you to be on the show. But do you have something funny you can do while you perform?'

"I told him, 'I really don't.'

"Chuck explained what the premise of the show had evolved into. He told me, 'It's fine if you just want to sing. But I'll be honest with you, we have a lot of singers at this point, and a lot of them are ahead of you. If you can come up with a gimmick for yourself, I can put you on the show for Friday's taping.'

---

5. Personal interview. 29 Apr. 2019.

"He said I could take the night to think about it and call him the next day. I talked to my friends and one of them made a good point. If they already have singers lined up and this show fails, you'll never get on, so I should do something funny.

"One of my roommates said, 'You always sing in the shower. For the show, what if you got into a shower on the stage and sang?'

Shower singer Chuck D'Imperio. PHOTO COURTESY OF CHUCK D'IMPERIO

"I called Chuck the next day and suggested that and he said, "I love it! You're on! Be here on Friday!"

While *Gong Show* contestants were usually on their own for props and costumes, Chuck D'Imperio had obviously auditioned without a shower, and since Chuck Barris had imposed the need for the gimmick upon him, the show accommodated the contestant for this unique situation.

D'Imperio continues, "*The Gong Show* had a full rehearsal with all the acts for five episodes. When it was my turn, Chuck Barris came backstage and led me by the hand to the stage."

As they walked, the self-proclaimed Little Chuck explained to Big Chuck, "We gotta make sure this works, but if it works, it will only work once. We're bringing up a shower stall from a men's room in another part of the complex. We'll cut a square in it. You'll be buck naked in the shower, and you'll sing like that."

An audition poster...who will be the next to answer Uncle Chuck's call?
ROBERT BURROUGHS COLLECTION

Some NBC crew members measured D'Imperio and cut a square into the shower curtain so that his face and chest would be visible. D'Imperio explains, "For the rehearsal, I got in fully dressed. Some NBC engineers brought in a garden hose and attached it to the shower to see if it would fit. I sang my song, but Chuck refused to run the water during the rehearsal because, as he said, 'If this works, it'll only work once.' I sang 'Bad, Bad Leroy Brown' and it went great.

"For the show, they gave me a pair of flip-flops and a bathrobe with *The Gong Show* across the back, like a boxer's robe. Now, I might be remembering this wrong, but I don't remember anybody else getting gonged for that episode, and I was the last act to go on, so I was thinking 'Uh-oh, the judges are saving it for me.' I got in the shower, took off the robe, and started trembling because I was freezing.

"Chuck announces, 'All the way from Rutland, Vermont...' I have no idea where that came from. I'm not from Rutland, Vermont. I've never been there. I never said it, but that's how Chuck Barris introduced me. I'm in that shower as the stage curtain pulls open, the band is cooking, and water started shooting out at me. Ice cold water. I had a moment of panic because I looked down and saw that the water was hitting my chest

Jamie Farr, striking a pose typical for a Gong Show *judge watching an Elvis impersonator. Raymond Michael was a fortunate exception.* ROBERT BURROUGHS COLLECTION

and going out the opening, so it was hitting the stage floor. I was worried they'd stop taping to fix that. I gently tapped the shower head to the left so it would hit the wall instead. That worked, except the water hitting the wall made such a loud rattling sound that I couldn't hear the band. So, I just belted out 'Bad, Bad Leroy Brown' as hard as I could.

"I was getting soaked. I looked over at the judges — Arte, Jamie, and Jaye P. that day — and I think that's it for me. But instead, they're walking toward the shower stall, and they start doing a dance around it. Arte, who was short, did a gag where he jumped up and down to try to face me. Jaye surprised me by sticking her head in the stall very briefly. I finish my song, the curtain closes, and Chuck Barris announces a commercial break while an assistant comes backstage and gives me the robe and flip-flops.

"Chuck pulls me through the curtain, and we wait. The judges haven't even announced their scores yet, that's for after the commercial break, but I look off-stage and I see the cue card person making a card that says, 'Today's winner is Chuck D'Imperio.' We came back from the commercial, and all the judges held up 10s for me. Jaye P. Morgan says, 'I didn't think much of his singing, but what I saw through the curtain was worth a ten.' I got $516.32, the trophy which I still have, two Mr. Coffee machines, Turtle Wax, and 100 one-pound boxes of elbow macaroni.

"Almost 30 years have passed and I'm in New York as a disc jockey. Chuck Barris has written a book and a publicist is calling radio stations looking for DJs who want to interview Chuck. This publicist doesn't know me or anything about me, she was only calling to ask if I wanted Chuck for a guest and I immediately said 'Yes' but I didn't tell her anything. I figured I'd save this for the show.

"Chuck is a guest on the show, I introduce him, and the first thing I say is 'Chuck, I want to tell you that in 1976, I was a winner on *The Gong Show*.' I didn't think he'd remember anything — he saw so many acts — but he asked me what my act was. As soon as I started describing it, he interrupts and says, 'And we had to drag that shower out of the men's room and haul it up to the studio!' He absolutely remembered my act!"

Raymond Michael was on the show in 1976, performing what was, in many ways, the quintessential *Gong Show* act. He was an Elvis impersonator. "I was an actor while I was a college student. I did plays, musicals, and operas. I was also on the college football team — we won a national championship.

"A hypnotist came to the school, and he wanted a football player to be hypnotized as part of the show. He had gone to the coach to ask that a player be part of the show, and the coach told me to do it since I had stage experience. The hypnotist asked me to be Elvis. My kind of music was opera. But I had a little sister who loved Elvis movies, and I had a roommate who listened to 'Blue Suede Shoes' all the time, so I was set.

"I did the impression, and after the show I was approached by a guy who worked in Vegas, and he wanted to sign me for a show he was developing. Hal Holbrook's one-man show about Mark Twain was quite popular at the time and he wanted to do a one-man show about Elvis.

"We thought that *The Gong Show* would be a good way to get me some national exposure. I got to skip the audition process. We mailed in a reel-to-reel film of me performing my act and that was enough to get me booked. I scored 29 points. Not enough to win. But it was good exposure, and I've been impersonating Elvis for longer than Elvis was alive. I'm still doing it."

Al Lampkin is an actor and retired magician who appeared on the show twice. "My agent booked a lot of stuff for that show. Very early on in the series, Chuck Barris' staff had reached out to talent agencies to recruit contestants. They wanted professional talent for the show because they were worried about how people would react to being gonged, and they felt that professionals had thicker skin. 'Professionals won't cry' was their thinking.[6]

Rip Taylor may have found the gong mallet more savory than some of the acts he had to endure. AUTHOR'S COLLECTION

"The first time I was on the show, I appeared with a friend of mine, Ken, who was tall and skinny. He was going to be Stan Laurel and I was going to be Oliver Hardy. Chuck Barris was at our audition. I remembered him being very friendly and very straightforward with us. We got booked for a Sunday taping, and that was a problem for me. I had just joined Church of Jesus Christ of Latter-Day Saints, and I told Ken, 'Right now, I'm trying really hard not to take jobs on Sunday.' Ken said, 'Well, tell them that.'

"I explained my problem and it didn't bother Chuck's staff at all. They said they'd get back to me. They called back that same day and said 'Okay, you're doing the Saturday taping now.' We did the show, and as we're

6. Personal interview. 11 Apr. 2019.

sitting backstage, we got to talking to the other contestants and we found the oddest thing. All of them had been booked for Sunday's taping, and all of them had been moved to the Saturday taping. I guess they had a very precise way that they wanted each show booked and that they didn't want to shake that up too much by switching one act. When they had one contestant who needed to be moved, they moved all the contestants to that same day, so they got exactly the episode they wanted.

"Aside from the fact that we played Laurel and Hardy, I don't even remember what the act was anymore. We got gonged, but I had fun. They brought me back on the show a few weeks later as a magician, which was my actual profession. I didn't even audition for that second appearance. I had fun the first time, I got along with the staff, they saw how well I took it when I got gonged. When my agent told them, 'By the way, he's also a magician,' I think they just said, 'Can he come back for another taping and do that?'

"I completely skipped the audition process and appeared on the show a second time, doing a clumsy magician routine. That was never really my act. It was a bit I had come up with for a magicians' convention, where I bungled all my tricks, and the big ending was that my table broke. It went well.

"Ultimately, it didn't really have any impact on my career. I was just thrilled to be working any show. The most lasting impact it's had: I'm in IBM — International Brotherhood of Magicians. And American Society of Professional Magicians, which is a group in Northern California. We did an annual Gong Show, where we would come together and do terrible acts. The other members would ask me about it because I had been on the real thing. As they were putting together the production, they'd say things like 'Al, you did the show, how should we set this up?'

"Years later, I was a guest on *The Tonight Show Starring Johnny Carson*, which taped in the same studio. It was such a drastic change. For *The Gong Show*, you're crammed into a large room with dozens of other contestants to wait all day for your turn, and when you want to go to the restroom, it's just this small, cramped room way down the hallway, and you have to make sure somebody knows you're going to the restroom. For Johnny Carson, same studio, but they put me in my own, plush, carpeted little dressing room with a bowl of fruit. It made me feel like I had really come up in the world."

Andy Swan is a clown whose brother steered him toward his chosen profession. "I was a freshman in high school. My brother had taught himself how to juggle. He grabbed three rocks when he was at the beach one day and just started playing with them until he figured it out. He showed me and I said 'You gotta teach me how to do that!' I have ADD but he showed it to me, and I just locked onto it and had it down in two hours. I began doing shows in high school. I got a standing ovation the first time I was onstage and that was it for me. I was going to do this for a living. I wasn't going to do anything else.[7]

"I watched *The Gong Show* for the first time and saw all these unusual

Milton DeLugg and the Band with a Thugg. With all the insanity erupting around them, it was easy to forget sometimes that the musicians showed remarkable versatility, adapting their style from contestant to contestant.
PHOTO COURTESY OF JEFFERSON BEEKER

acts, and the show was just so funny. They had that announcement. 'If you have a good or unusual act...' I didn't even wait for the end of the show, I called that number right away. I figured I needed something crazy and different to get on the show, so I told them I could juggle while lying on a bed of nails. I did that for my first audition. They called me back for my second audition, with Chuck present, and Chuck really surprised me. He told me, 'Your juggling looks great, you don't need to do anything special. Get rid of the bed of nails.'

---

7. Personal interview. 8 May 2019.

"I made it onto the show with a friend of mine playing my assistant, Muchero the Clown. During rehearsal, I was dropping stuff constantly. Chuck asked me, 'Are you okay?' I told him I was fine, but I really wasn't. I was so nervous, and the energy in that holding area where the contestants waited was amazing. I can still feel it when I think about it. Everyone was watching the taping on the monitors they had set up backstage, but I tried lying on my back and zenning out. I'd heard that Olympians try to picture what they're going to do before they go out and do it, so I tried the same thing, I pictured myself performing my juggling act on *The Gong Show*.

"I got called to go on and I found out before I went out there that we were taping in Johnny Carson's studio. Johnny was a big star, so I got overwhelmed thinking about that. I'm about to walk through a curtain just like Johnny and perform on Johnny's stage.

"I juggled a few different sets of things for the act. I started with clubs, and I was so nervous that twice, I caught the clubs on the wrong ends. But I got lucky because I managed to self-correct, and the audience applauded. It just washed over me and after that it was smooth sailing. The audience applause settled me down. I juggled plates, I added a chair, and then my big finish was flaming torches. At the end, as I got on my knees and started to collect them, I grabbed one of them the wrong way. The audience thought I was doing it that way on purpose. No way! That was a mistake.

"Louie Nye, Jaye P. Morgan, and Jamie Farr gave me perfect scores and I nearly jumped out of my shoes. Chuck announced me as the winner of the day. I got the money, which I reinvested into my act because I was starting to grow it and I had spent a thousand dollars in the past month for new stuff. And I won a pallet of chocolate mints. It was more than any one human being could eat, so I gave them away to all the kids in the neighborhood and I was the most popular guy on the block. I got some exposure and ended up getting booked for some college shows from it. And then years later the show got rerun on cable and people saw the rerun, so I got exposure and bookings out of it again!"

Sean Hannon was an aspiring actor who made two appearances on the show early in his professional career. "I always wanted to be an actor, from the time I was little. I did plays in the park when I was a kid. I was in *A Midsummer Night's Dream* when I was nine. When I was a teenager, I joined Theatricum Botanicum, Will Geer's outdoor theater group in Topanga, California.[8]

---

8. Personal interview. 6 May 2019.

"I hadn't seen *The Gong Show* but word of mouth about it started to spread around the other actors in the group. There was this talent show on NBC that allowed you to do pretty much anything, good or bad, as long as it was entertaining, and they were holding open auditions. We also found out it was guaranteed money if you were a member of AFTRA. I watched a few episodes to get a sense of what I was about to get myself into, and then started trying to come up with an act.

Even if it was just a lark, a victory on The Gong Show *really meant something to the people who accomplished it. Sean Hannon is seen here in 2019 with his Golden Gong trophy.* PHOTO COURTESY OF SEAN HANNON

"The first time I was on the show, I called myself Rhetch Butler. A girlfriend told me I looked like Clark Gable, so I dressed as Gable in *Gone with the Wind* and I sang 'I Can't Dance, Don't Ask Me.' I was so prepared to get gonged that I had a gag ready for it. I didn't tell anybody. I got gonged by Arte Johnson, and as Chuck came over and started to walk me offstage, I set off the cap gun in my holster, shot myself in the foot, and fell to the ground and crawled offstage.

"At the next commercial break, while I'm backstage, a production assistant comes to me and says, 'Chuck's looking for you.' I instantly began trembling. I prepare myself and figure I'm about to get yelled at. I go walking and looking for Chuck, and right as the show is about to start taping again, we find each other, he's on one side and I'm on the other, and he's about to walk back onstage, and when Chuck sees me, he just beams at me and gives me a big thumbs-up. And it told me that I understood exactly what the show was, and that Chuck appreciated that about me. Years later, I watched the episode and for the first time, I saw that Chuck did this double-take and giggled while he was getting ready to introduce the next act. He really got a kick out of what I did.

"I had enrolled in Los Angeles Community College and was taking theater classes. They had a great theater program there. I became really interested in a make-up course and all the things you could do with it. I came up with an idea where I would act out a scene from *The Waltons*, and I would play both Grandpa and John Boy. And because I spent so much time around Will Geer when I was at Theatricum Botanicum, I really got a chance to study his mannerisms and his way of speaking, so I had my Grandpa Walton impression. One half of my face would have old man make-up and hair, the other half would be done like a young man, and I'd wear half of two costumes put together. You could come back on the show if you did something different the next time, so I auditioned with this scene and got on a second time.

"I came to the studio, and they did something nice for me. I had told them in the audition that applying the make-up for this bit took about two and a half hours, so on the day of taping, instead of having me in the green room with all the other acts, they gave me a private dressing room so I could prepare and have all the space I needed for putting everything together.

"The act went great. The audience responded well to it and the judges liked it. My only regret is it didn't occur to me to tell the technical team the nature of the act, so they didn't shoot it properly. I should have explained that the gag works best if they're shooting me only in profile, so only one character or the other is visible at any time. They shot me in three-quarter profile, so there was always a little bit of the other character visible.

"But I won! I got $516.32. Also, for both of my appearances, I won all the small prizes that got announced during the show. I was surprised to learn how that worked. They don't just send you a box of stuff. Those prizes are shipped separately by the manufacturers, so for what felt like months, packages just kept showing up at my door. Come home one day and there's a box of La Choy Noodles. The next day there's a crockpot. The next day there's a vacuum. They just kept coming. Also, Will Geer loved the act. He showed it to Earl Hamner, the creator of *The Waltons*, and he loved it too.

"Being on the show didn't impact my career in the sense that it gave me new opportunities. Talent agents looked at *The Gong Show* as an outlier, so it wasn't like you'd put a clip of your *Gong Show* act on your demo reel. But doing that show was a great learning experience. I learned to go with my gut and trust myself, and it gave me confidence later. I auditioned for a movie called *Fire and Ice*, which was a rotoscoped movie. They cast actors and then animators traced over all the footage. My agent said they wanted people who moved well, so I wore dancewear underneath my flannel shirt and my jeans. I began to feel out of place in that outfit, so I stripped down to the dancewear and walked into the room, which made everyone do a double take because that's not what I was wearing when I had first shown up. But I nailed that audition and got the role. Everything in my audition reading just clicked because I had confidence. That willingness to trust myself came from being on *The Gong Show*."

Kurt Abell was a music student at Fresno State. Originally attending on a full scholarship to play the bassoon, he discovered a new passion when some friends took him to a club one night during his freshman year. "There were some guys playing banjos onstage, and I thought they looked like they were having a lot of fun, so I bought a banjo. I mastered it in about ten months. I even began giving lessons.[9]

"Some new friends who played the banjo went to *Gong Show* auditions and got booked on the show. My friend Dave Marty played the William Tell Overture blindfolded but didn't win; he lost the tiebreaker. Another friend played my own arrangement of 'Swanee,' and he didn't win.

"I watched the show, and the announcement came on saying 'If you have a good or unusual act…' so I called the show and said I play the banjo while hanging upside-down. I had never done that, but I thought it would get the show's attention. They had me come in for an audition.

"I went to a swap meet and found a tuxedo with tails. The label said it was made in 1926. I wore the tuxedo with tails to the audition because I thought it would look funny if I wore that while playing the banjo, but on my way there, I put two and two together and realized if I'm upside-down and wearing a tuxedo, then I'm a vampire. I came up with the name Count Banjola.

"Old World Restaurant was this dilapidated building…it may have been condemned. It wasn't a pleasant-looking space, and it was obvious

---

9. Personal interview. 7 May 2019.

there was no way for me to do this upside-down. At least not safely. I did my audition and right at the very end, I said, 'Please don't forget that I do this upside-down.'

"I got home and immediately got a phone call from Chuck Barris. He asked, 'Can you really do this upside-down?' I said 'Yes, I do it all the time.' Again, I had never done it in my life. I came in for a second audition,

Kurt Abell, a/k/a Count Banjola. AUTHOR'S COLLECTION

with Chuck Barris and Milton DeLugg both present. I played 'Alabamee Bound,' which sounds like a flashy tune, but it doesn't actually take much to play it. Chuck loved the act and told me to stick around. He picked up a guitar, and we just had a jam session; Chuck, Milton, and me. And then I got the nod to be on the show.

"I came in at 6:00 am on taping day for make-up, and I was in the chair for about three hours. They made me up so well that later, after my mom saw the show, she recognized my banjo before she recognized me.

"Suddenly it was time to rehearse, and I needed to be upside-down, and for the first time, somebody asked 'How do we do this?' I was familiar with how stages were constructed; good stages, at least. I told them to throw a rope around a curtain rod, loop it around my feet, and hoist me. They lifted me up and I began spinning in circles, which surprised me. And Chuck saw my reaction and he said, 'You've never done this before, have you?' I told him the truth. 'No, but if you split my legs and tie the rope around the other one, I should be fine.'

"It was such a complicated set-up that they made me the opening act of the episode, but I still had to hang upside-down for thirteen minutes; that's the set-up and the actual performance combined. It hurt and I was dizzy the entire time I was playing, but I won. It came down to a

Chuck Barris welcomes another newcomer to the Gong Show *spotlight.*
AUTHOR'S COLLECTION

tiebreaker, and I won over a female singer. They dumped confetti from the ceiling at the end of every show, and what I learned that day is that on TV, confetti dropped from the ceiling looks like lots of little pieces. It's just this solid block that pretty much breaks apart as it's falling, so the confetti really hit you when it comes down. That's probably why Chuck wore those hats on the show. He needed protection.

"I remember what Jaye P. Morgan said at the very end, as the credits were rolling, Jaye walked up to the singer who lost, and she says 'Go out in front and make sure that camera can see you. This is your moment.' She was a sweetheart.

"They brought me back for the nighttime show. They dropped me that time. The guy who did the rehearsal got sick. The guy who replaced him got instructions about lowering the rod, but I guess nobody made it clear to him that there was a person attached to the rod, so when the time came he just released the brake and I plummeted. And they kept bringing me back just as a favorite act. I was on five times. I also got booked on *The Chuck Barris Rah-Rah Show*. I was put in Johnny Carson's green room to wait to go on. I was back there with Cab Calloway, Earl Scruggs, and the Nitty Gritty Dirt Band. I wish we had cell phones back then; it would have been one hell of a photo.

"That 15 minutes of fame has followed me for forty years now. I still get advertised at gigs as 'Count Banjola from *The Gong Show*.' And personally, it gave me confidence. I used to be a shy person until I was on *The Gong Show*. I got married in 2008, and it turned out that the first time I was on the show, my wife was in the audience, and she remembered me. Her mom was a contestant that day."

Kurt's wife, Athens Abell, tells the story of joining her mother, LaVern LeVasseur, for her moment in the spotlight. "My mother and I loved *The Gong Show*. My mom always had a dream of being onstage, but never had a means of getting there. She missed out on Ted Mack. She got me on *The Hocus Pocus Show*, but I guess living vicariously through me wasn't enough. When *The Gong Show* made that announcement, 'If you have an unusual act…,' my mom thought it was her calling.[10]

"Mom sent her info to Chuck Barris Productions, and not long after that, they called us to come to Old World Restaurant, which was this ugly, condemned restaurant in West Hollywood. My mom and I were both raised in religious, protective environments, so West Hollywood was a shock to us. As we arrived, we saw a guy sitting on the curb with his feet in the gutter.

"The restaurant was seedy and smoky, and I loved it because it was all these sights I had never seen. It was real, and it was raw. It wasn't the glamorous version of Hollywood. Have you ever seen *The Godfather*? It looked like the restaurant where Michael had to get a gun from behind the toilet. You walk in and there's an old man sitting there greeting everybody, and you can tell from his voice that he's been smoking for longer than I've been alive. The restaurant was dingy, it smelled like smoke, and the plastic chairs were sticky. I saw the largest rat I've ever seen. You went into the bathroom, and it stunk in there. It wasn't even human stink. It was mildew and cigarettes.

"We waited out in the restaurant until we were called in to step through these velvet curtains, and when you stepped through, it was a ventilated,

---

10. Personal interview. 7 May 2019.

well-lit room where Chuck Barris was sitting. I was surprised at how small he was in person. I was already 5'6" by the time I turned 12. I was 15 when Mom auditioned, and I was looking down at Chuck. His personality on the show was so big that it made him seem taller.

"I remember expecting that I would get star-struck when I met Chuck, and then I didn't. It had a lot to do with the way Chuck conducted him-

Jaye P. Morgan wants to see more! AUTHOR'S COLLECTION

self. He was so down-to-earth, and he behaved like a guy who was just there to do a job.

"Mom wore a harem outfit and pantomimed to Ray Stevens' song 'Ahab the Arab.' I was mortified by the outfit because this was my mother. She was 5'7" and about 270 at the time, long before fat was accepted, and Chuck was completely impressed by her. She got on the show. What I loved about the experience was the way that Chuck Barris and his staff treated the contestants. They didn't treat the contestants like they were just there to serve their purpose. The contestants were all made to feel incredibly special and important.

"She got gonged. The judges, Jamie Farr, Phyllis Diller, and Rip Taylor, came to get her, brought her to the gong, handed her the mallet, and made her gong herself…it played so well that they actually called my mother and asked if she would be on the show as a recurring character, and she'd get gonged every time. And it would be a meta-joke where this same contestant was on the show over and over and over again, doing the same act and getting gonged every time. She considered it but because of her religious beliefs at the time, she couldn't. Her religion was very restrictive of what she could do on Saturdays and Sundays and that was when *The Gong Show* had most of the tapings."

Larry Keen, born and raised in Wood County, West Virginia, attended West Virginia University, got a masters' degree in biochemistry, and ran off to Los Angeles to become a singer. The journey took him and a friend to *The Gong Show*. "We both had bookings previously with a prestigious agency called the New York Coffeehouse Circuit. You toured mostly college towns. Jim Croce, Don McLean, and Billy Crystal all did tours. And I had just done a tour with Jay Leno. I had a partner in music named Richard Pollack. He was from Fairmont, West Virginia. We both moved to Los Angeles to start music careers, and both of us became union musicians. We had a record deal and it had just fallen through. And then Richard found out that if you were a member of a performers' union, *The Gong Show* would pay you whether you won or lost. [11]

"We went down to the restaurant on the day of auditions, and we were there all day. It was like auditioning for *American Idol*, you just had to wait and wait. We played a great song called 'No Better Feeling' by Ron Sowell, who folks from West Virginia would know from *Mountain Stage*. He was the bandleader. I played guitar and Richard played banjo. They told us that whatever your act was on *The Gong Show*, it had to be no more than 90 seconds, so we played the song at a really fast tempo.

"Chuck was at the audition, and he loved the guitar I was using. Guys who know guitars would recognize this; it was a '49 D28, and I had a leather strap that was made for me with fringe that hung down to the floor, and you could really make it swing. Chuck came over to me after our song was done and asked to play it.

"We got on the show. At rehearsal, Chuck explained how they formatted the show. They taped five episodes in a day, and Chuck said they tried to have 'two acts per episode that were actually good.' Chuck told us he was saving us for the last episode to be taped that day, but depending on how things went, something might come up and we might be called out for the fourth episode instead.

---

11. Personal interview. 12 Apr. 2019.

"While you're waiting, you're backstage with all of the other acts who were going to be onstage for the five episodes. There was a pair of boys, looked to be about 16 years old, redheaded, freckles, in kilts, who were going to play the bagpipes. Their mother was so intense and domineering. And she was convinced that these two boys were about to become big stars from playing the bagpipes on *The Gong Show*.

But these judges have seen enough. AUTHOR'S COLLECTION

"The fourth episode tapes and these two boys with the bagpipes score 29 points. A perfect score on *The Gong Show* was 30. Toward the end of that fourth episode, Chuck comes backstage and says, 'We have three extra minutes, can you guys go on now?' We went out there and did our song.

"The judges loved us. Jaye P. Morgan held up a sign that said SPANK ME. I didn't realize they showed that on camera. And then I did. My mother and her whole bridge club were watching when it aired. The judges give us 30 points. We won the trophy, and we got $516.32. The union guarantee was $250, so actually, winning was bonus money.

"After the show, the mother of those bagpipe kids gets right up in Chuck's face and tells him, 'I'm lodging a formal complaint!' And she goes into this whole tirade about why it was unfair that we were on the show and that we shouldn't have been competing against her boys.

"I will never forget this. Chuck Barris stood there as quietly and politely as he could, and just nodded his head. 'Mm-hmm...yes... uh-huh...' And he listened to her whole complaint. And when she finally finished, all he said was, 'Madame, get the fuck out before I throw you out.' And he turns around to us and says, 'Now, where were we?'

"He invited us backstage to his dressing room and we had a jam session. It was really a lot of fun. Chuck really loved playing music, although honestly, as far as technique went, he was marginal. There's a tell that musicians have when they aren't very good. They speed up their tempo for no reason, as if they're trying to keep up with the people they're playing with, and Chuck did that a lot when he played, he'd speed up out of nowhere. But for a guy who wasn't very good at playing the guitar, he really loved it. That was such a wonderful day. Like I said, the record deal had just fallen through, so to go on TV and play well enough that we got a trophy and a check for it really meant a lot for us."

Paul Zeglar began pursuing acting in the 1960s when he attended NYU. His career took him first to the Second City improvisational troupe, where he performed with Bill Murray and Betty Thomas, and then to Ace Trucking Company with Fred Willard. His appearance on *The Gong Show* happened practically by accident.

"I got a call from my agent. *Sanford and Son* was casting a small role for an episode. The episode was about Fred and Bubba going on *The Gong Show* and I was auditioning for the role of another *Gong Show* contestant. I got the role. For the *Sanford and Son* episode, I wore a Boy Scout uniform and did a dance while holding a tea kettle that played 'Yankee Doodle.' This was completely the writers' idea. It was the character I was playing.[12]

"But Chuck Barris guest-starred as himself for that episode, and when he saw my performance, he thought it was so funny that he came to me afterward and said, 'Could you come on our show and do that for real?' So, I did. I was on the show twice, once in the daytime and once on nighttime.

"The daytime show was fantastic. The judges were Paul Williams, Jaye P. Morgan, and Jamie Farr. They marched in time with the music coming from the tea kettle, and then they did this great bit where they marched from their seats over to the stage, took me by the arm, gave me their mallets, and made me gong myself. That's hilarious!

---

12. Personal interview. 12 Apr. 2019.

"The nighttime show wasn't as fun. I survived on the nighttime show, and I scored 13 points. Well, what's the fun in that? When you were a contestant on *The Gong* Show, you hoped for two things. Either win or get gonged. Who cares about the people who don't get gonged but then don't win? A few months later, I got a call from *TV Guide*. They were doing a group photo on the set of *The Gong Show* for a feature called 'The Worst

Paul Zeglar, dubbed "the worst of the worst" by TV Guide. ROBERT BURROUGHS COLLECTION

of the Worst' with the most memorable *Gong Show* acts. And I was part of that group photo. They noted in the caption that the judges made me gong myself, so that's my claim to fame. It really had no impact on my career at all, but it's been a fun thing in my past. And just for showing up, I got a very nice Polaroid camera."

Jim Richardson had been a musician since signing up for the elementary school orchestra. He started on the cello, then switched to clarinet before the high school bandleader switched him to saxophone. His prowess on the saxophone would lead Jim to a career as a professional musician…and for two shining minutes, an appearance on *The Gong Show*.

Richardson says, "There was a jazz musician I really liked named Rahsaan Roland Kirk who would play two and sometimes three saxophones at the same time. I listened to all his records. He was a magnificent musician."[13]

"In the 1970s, I was in a Vegas show group. The bandleader critiqued me one night. He said, 'Jim, do something different.' Do something different? I reached over and picked up a second saxophone, and I played two saxophones at the same time. I did it badly, but it got such a great reaction from the people sitting in front of me, and the bandleader loved it. He said to work on it.

"The secret to playing two saxophones at once is that it's really more of a coordination exercise. You really don't have to blow very hard to get a sound out of a saxophone, so the same breath will pretty much produce a sound from two at once. From there, you just figure out where your fingers need to be on each one to create the harmonies and you're set. And luckily, I had just joined a rock band; rock music isn't very complex, so I figured out how to play a lot of pieces with two saxophones at once because there weren't many chord changes. And I'm somewhat handy so I added two extra holes to the alto sax so I could get two more notes out of it and that allowed me to do a little more."

"I wasn't a big TV watcher. A few of my friends told me I should try out for *The Gong Show*. I watched a few episodes and thought, 'Oh, this is a piece of cake, I'll win that $500.'

"Chuck Barris was there when I auditioned. It was strange. He had a golf club and a ball, and he was just putting the golf ball around the room while the acts were performing, and he'd say 'Oh, excuse me' and go around them. We didn't know how seriously we should take him or if he was testing us or what, but he kept hitting that ball everywhere while we were performing. As silly as it was, I do remember him just being very straightforward and honest with the acts when it was time to give his opinion.

"I made it on the show, but I made a mistake. I played an original piece, and it was too complex and too sophisticated for the show. It drew more attention to the music itself, and the fact that I was playing two saxophones took a backseat. Looking back, I should have played a simpler tune because then everyone would have focused on the novelty of playing two saxophones at once. So, I didn't get gonged, I got my score from the judges, and I didn't win. Well, the problem with that is it doesn't give

---

13. Personal interview. 16 Apr. 2019.

you anything to talk about. 'I won on *The Gong Show*' is something to tell people about. 'I was on *The Gong Show*, and they gonged me so hard and the audience booed me offstage.' That's something to talk about. 'I was on *The Gong Show*, and I didn't win, but they didn't gong me.' Well, come on, how much fun is that?"

Jim Tobin is a drummer and a California native who appeared on the show in 1977 as part of the unforgettably-named band Pickens & Reid and The Boys with the Noise. "I was jamming with friends when I met up with Rick Pickens and Jimmy Reid. They were a duet in Orange County. And then they added the Boys with the Noise, and I became part of the group. Some talent scout came to see us one night and he was looking for bands to play Whiskey Creek in Mammoth Lakes, which is where the skiing is in California. We had that gig for two years; they kept us on and off-skiing season.[14]

"Unbeknownst to any of us, Rick called *The Gong Show* office and asked if we could come in and audition. We had to drive all the way from Orange County to Los Angeles. Chuck Barris wasn't there. They asked us if we could come back the next week and audition for Chuck. And I thought, 'Well, that's why we're here now.'

"We came back for the second audition, which meant driving all the way from Orange County to Los Angeles again. Chuck liked us and put us on the show. The only catch was he didn't want me to play the drums. Chuck didn't like to stop tape for any reason, and it takes a long time to set up a drum kit. He asked if I could play something else. I played the washboard on the show. Backstage at *The Gong Show* is the craziest sight I've ever seen. They taped five episodes in a day, so there were 30 acts back there, all practicing their acts and performing at the same time, wearing wild make-up, wearing costumes. It looked like an acid trip in *The Twilight Zone*.

"It began really hitting me that we were about to be on national TV, and I started getting worked up and nervous. Two of the other band members were nervous too. One of them finally just said, 'Let's go outside for a few minutes.' We went out there and we smoked half a joint, and it worked. I felt focused and ready after I smoked that, and I think it helped the performance. If you watch the tape, I'm a little glassy-eyed, but I put on a good show.

"They had told us at the audition that we had to keep the act down to 90 seconds. We had a big introduction that we had prepared. When we went

---

14. Personal interview. 17 Apr. 2019.

on the show, we did the introduction, which was we all ran onstage with brooms and we announced ourselves. 'And now the band that's sweeping the nation…' When the show aired, they cut out the introduction.

We got 30 points. Eva Gabor loved us. She said she wanted to take us home with her. She gives us ten. Peter Lawford said he wanted to take us home with him. He gave us ten. Arte Johnson loved us, he gave us ten. We were a lock to win the $516.32. Well, then they brought out a woman who sang 'I Got Rhythm' and they loved her and gave her 30. And then a tap dancer came out. To be honest, I didn't think the tap dancer was all that great, but they gave her 30. And when it came time to break the tie, the tap dancer won. We weren't winners that day, but we did get a Hoover vacuum and a ton of Turtle Wax. For the next year, I had the cleanest truck in California.

"A few months later, some tourists from Florida came to Mammoth Lakes on their vacation and watched us play. They recognized us from *The Gong Show* and told us they thought we were robbed. So that made us feel good. But ultimately the show didn't affect our careers. I went on to write two songs for Jimmy Reed, though."

Arte Tedesco was a journeyman guitarist from Pennsylvania who was discovered in Ruidoso, New Mexico, when a film crew shooting on location for a Walter Matthau film hired him to provide the entertainment during breaks in shooting.

"I never set out to audition for *The Gong Show*. They asked me. Somebody in Pennsylvania called the show and gave them my contact info and said I should be on. The producer asked me if I wanted to come in for an audition.[15]

"Chuck Barris was there, sitting in a tall director's chair. I knew we had a 90-second time limit, but I didn't realize they'd enforce that for the audition. I had a version of 'Rocky Raccoon' that I liked to perform. In my version, I speed up the song as it goes along, until finally it has a machine gun beat, and I do some scatting along with it. I get 90 seconds in and I'm only just starting the really fast part. Chuck cuts me off and says 'Next!' I said, 'I didn't get to the good part yet!'

"Chuck was a little surprised that I talked back like that. He gets out of his chair, takes a few steps forward, and draws a line in the floor with his foot, and he says, 'Don't cross that line.' And he sits down, and he says, 'If you only have 90 seconds and you haven't reached the good part

---

15. Personal interview. 30 Apr. 2019.

yet, then start it in the middle of the song. Try again.' And he let me start over again. I did exactly what he told me, I started from the middle. And this time he was happy with it, and I got booked on the show!

"I still remember what it looked like backstage. They had all the acts for five episodes in one giant room. You see people juggling, and next to them are two women painting each other, and next to them are a couple of people writhing around with live snakes, and next to them, there's a baroque quartet. It's a human menagerie back there.

"I got a great reaction, but I only got 28 points. Two of the judges gave me tens. Juicy Jaye only gave me an eight, which she spelled ATE on the card and made a prurient remark with, so basically she gave me that score so she could do a joke with it. But that was fine because I lost to a soft-shoe dancer and honestly, that guy was really good. It never really did anything for my career, although I hit it off well with one of the other contestants at the taping session that day, so I ended up with a girlfriend for a little while."

John Schneiderman had been playing "anything with strings" since his grandmother handed him a ukulele. He was a child prodigy who performed on the radio when he was five. "I hit my growth spurt really late, and I discovered people weren't as interested in a full-grown person who played the banjo."

"When *The Gong Show* came along, I had just started college. I was 18 years old. I had seen the show and $516.32 was good money for a college student. I went there to win. I played all kinds of stringed instruments, but I decided a banjo was the best fit for what *The Gong Show* was. I did two auditions for the show. Chuck was there both times. And he loved me. Both times, he grabbed his guitar and played along. I knew I was a lock to get on.[16]

"Backstage at *The Gong Show* on taping day was not the happiest place in the world. I was a serious musician, but I understood what the show was, I knew it was a total joke. But I was shocked by the number of people backstage who really believed in what they were doing, believed that they were great at it, and didn't know how ridiculous it looked. There was a woman dressed as Dorothy from *The Wizard of* Oz, and she had a full-size poodle with her. And she sang 'Somewhere Over the Rainbow.' You could tell before she went out there that she honestly thought she was a great singer and that today was the day she was going to become

---

16. Personal interview. 29 Apr. 2019.

a star. And she went onstage, she was completely off-key, the audience roared, and she got gonged. She was in tears backstage when it was over.

"There was another guy with a guitar who acted backstage like he was the new Johnny Cash, and nobody knew it yet. He went out there and got gonged, and I remember it was a struggle for Chuck to get him to leave the stage. He started complaining about how Milton DeLugg and the band were playing the song wrong and that messed him up. He was so angry.

"I performed well, the judges gave me a nice score. Charlie Brill, I found out later, was learning to play the banjo as a hobby, so he had taken a special interest in me. I tied with another act, called Rinder Cella. He recited the story of Cinderella, but the joke was he switched the consonants around when he talked so it sounded funny. 'Rinder Cella wore geautiful bown and went to a bancy fall.' Here's what did me in. I was a college kid away from home, and they taped that show during the holiday break. All my friends were gone. Rinder Cella happened to have a bunch of his friends in the audience. To break the tie, they used the applause meter, and his friends made a lot of noise. The judges apologized to me when it was all over. Maybe I'm reading too much into this, but I still watched the show regularly after I lost, and I noticed they stopped using the applause meter very soon after that. I think the show decided they wanted to control who won in a tie after that happened.[17]

"They invited me back for the nighttime show, but it was taping during finals week, so the timing was all wrong. It was still an enjoyable experience overall, though. I won a set of towels and toilet bowl cleaner. I also won a crockpot, which my sister ended up with; and after more than 40 years it still works."

California Zephyr is a band based in Napa, California, but they've been on the road since 1975. Alan Arnopole is a founding member. "We played what would be called Americana music now. Back then we called it 'Good time country.' We were traveling the US and Canada in a tour bus, and we took every gig we could. We played in funky honkytonks, grand ball rooms, the Lone Star Café in New York, and the Calgary Stampede. We had a song called 'I Ain't Really a Cowboy, I Just Found the Hat,'

---

17. He might be right about this. In the July 1977 issue of *Broadcasting Production & Programming*'s cover story about *The Gong Show*, producer Gene Banks explains that the show recently jettisoned the applause meter because audience members sitting close enough to the microphones could throw off the reading.

and it became a regional hit. A few radio stations picked up on it and we became popular in a few parts of the country.[18]

"We were based in Northern California, and *The Gong Show* had an open call one week in San Francisco, so our manager called us and suggested that we go for an audition. We did 'I Ain't Really a Cowboy, I Just Found the Hat' on camera for Chuck and his staff to review. They

Who's winning the Golden Gong today? BOB BODEN COLLECTION

weren't actually at the open call. We got a call back a week later to come to Hollywood to audition for Chuck in person. We had a gig the night before. We drove the bus overnight from northern California to Los Angeles to make the audition on time. Chuck had a guitar next to his chair and he pulled it out after our song and asked us to stay for a while for a jam session. We weren't expecting that, but we stuck around and futzed around on our instruments for a while as Chuck played with us. I remember we all played 'Johnny B. Goode' with him. Chuck really liked us. And finally, he put the guitar down and thanked us for coming and sent us on our way.

"We got the call a month later to come back down to Los Angeles to be on the show. We took the tour bus to NBC Burbank. I remember

18. Personal interview. 3 May 2019.

stopping on the way in to look at Johnny Carson's parking space because it was marked with a sign in the lot. We waited in the green room with all the other acts, which I remember being a very friendly, positive atmosphere. Everybody came to have fun and liked to talk about their acts. Nobody was nervous. The mood in the room was more like, 'Well… here we are.'

"They taped five episodes that day. I can't remember exactly when we went on, but it must have been late in the day because I remember a group of people showing up with these 20-foot-long hoagies to feed all of us who were still waiting backstage. We did get to watch the show as it was being taped on these large screens in the green room. I remember a pair of singers named Major and Minor. To this day, I don't know if this was a put-on or what, because part of the gag on *The Gong Show* was that you couldn't be sure about any of it. Major and Minor were a man and a woman who sang, and their song was absolutely fingernails on chalkboards. It was awful. And when they got gonged, the man…who, I'm guessing, was Major, stood up and said very dramatically, 'I know what you're all about, Chuck Barris, and I'm going to have you canceled!' And he storms off stage. And in the green room, everybody who hadn't gone onstage yet was just cracking up. Nobody could believe he was taking the show that seriously.

"We did our song. The judges were Pat Paulsen, June Allyson, and Dick Shawn. June Allyson gave us 10. Pat Paulsen gave us 10 and said, 'This is the kind of band you'd like to go down to the river and stomp frogs with.' Dick Shawn gave us 9. But one of the other contestants was a woman who was very well-proportioned in the chest area and Dick gave her 10 so we lost.

"We got five cases of sparkling grape juice, though, and when the show went into reruns, we got some residuals, which was nice. And we loved Pat Paulsen's line so much that we used it in our publicity for years afterward. For a few years, we used the appearance for notoriety because *The Gong Show* was so white hot at the time. We advertised ourselves 'as seen on *The Gong Show*.' Ultimately, the show didn't really help or hurt our careers. It just was."

CHAPTER 13

Hey...
Aren't You...

Above: Chuck introduces another act...and possibly creates another career.
ROBERT BURROUGHS COLLECTION

For Larry Spencer, two *Gong Show* contestants stand out in his memory, for reasons having nothing to do with their performances.

"We had a contestant on the show who — I don't even remember what his act was, but we found out after the show aired that the FBI had been looking for him, and they caught him because an FBI agent saw his appearance on *The Gong Show*.[1]

"On another day, a guy came up to our offices on Cahuenga Boulevard, and he got around the security guard and goes up to the receptionist and says, 'I want to talk to Chuck right now!' He had already taped his appearance on the show, but the episode hadn't aired yet. And he said 'I want to talk to Chuck, and I want my episode aired right now! You're holding up my career!'

"Chuck wasn't even in the building. He stormed past the guards, goes into my office as I'm walking out of my office, so our paths crossed, but as soon as I'm out of my office, he slams the door, locks himself in my office, pushes my desk against the door to keep anyone from breaking the door down, and he lights everything on fire. All the scripts, everything I had written for the next taping, all of it went up in flames. We called the police and called the fire department and got him out of there, but he burned so much stuff."

It takes a truly special show to entice people to risk significant prison time to get seen on television. Remember, YouTube and the dawn of social media were still decades away. in a universe where "the entertainment industry" amounted to film, commercial radio, and four channels on your television, opportunities to showcase a unique or silly talent were very few and very far between. To abuse another cliché, an appearance on *The Gong Show* genuinely was a once-in-a-lifetime opportunity.

As much as Chuck insisted that *The Gong Show* was nothing more than "a chance to be seen coast-to-coast on tee-wee" (his peculiar affectation for the word "television"), history would prove that Chuck had created something with the potential to turn people into stars.

Vince Longo remembers, "We were doing auditions at the restaurant, and it was very early in the series. And we were told that a large band was coming in. We said we were ready for them, and the first member of the band to walk through the curtain had a rocket ship strapped around his torso. It was Oingo Boingo."

A quirky new wave band, The Mystic Knights of the Oingo Boingo, appeared in only the third taped week of the series, performing arguably the Gongshowiest *Gong Show* act that the show had seen to that point.

---

1. Personal interview. 2 Feb. 2019.

A man in tux and tails with a heavy German accent, along with another tuxedoed man and a woman so scantily clad she appeared to be wearing only an accordion, announced that they'd be performing "Hayden's Trio for Accordion, Piano and Triangle." Before they even played one note, a man with a smoke-spewing rocket strapped around his waist charged onstage, followed by a dragon, and a brass section with parachute pants

Larry Spencer in character as "The Villain" in one of Chucky's Fables. He must have made a convincing villain if an aspiring contestant tried to set his office on fire. PHOTO BY VINCE LONGO, COURTESY OF LARRY SPENCER

and painted faces. They collected $516.32 that day.

In a matter of years, the group would streamline their name to Oingo Boingo. Their music would become a staple of '80s film soundtracks, like *Fast Times at Ridgemont High* ("Goodbye, Goodbye"), *Back to School* ("Dead Man's Party"), and *Weird Science* (the title song). The trombonist in the *Gong Show* performance was Danny Elfman, the prolific film and television composer best known for scoring much of Tim Burton's body of work, including *Pee-Wee's Big Adventure*. Speaking of which…

Betty and Eddie's Sensational Sound Effects strolled onto the stage, approached a radio microphone and acted out three brief scenes, an alien invasion, a family picnic, and a dog trying to do a trick. They earned a standing ovation from Jaye P. Morgan, a perfect score from all the judges and $516.32. Betty and Eddie even earned a return invitation for the nighttime show and won an additional $716.32. A few weeks later, Les Chats showed up. They were a pair of extremely literal cat burglars in black outfits and masks, plus pointed ears and tails. Together tiptoed around the stage, scatting a version of "Alley Cats." Then there was Jay Longtoe, decked out in full Native American regalia, complete with headdress. He

Native American lounge singer Jay Longtoe, one of the many Gong Show *alter egos of Paul Reubens.* PHOTO BY AND COURTESY OF VINCE LONGO

did a rain dance very much inspired by the low-rent lounge singers populating nightclubs in that era. He schmoozed with the audience and sang "Soon It's Gonna Rain" from *The Fantasticks* before letting out an abrupt war whoop and dancing straight up on the tips of his toes. Suave and Debonair was a quartet of men in white and gold with top hats, singing a tune boasting of their good manners. And then there was Dancin' Feet, a troupe whose moves weren't so far removed from the fancy footwork of Jay Longtoe.

All those acts involved one Paul Reubens. Reubens was an aspiring theater actor who had made his way into The Groundlings, an improvisational troupe based on Melrose Avenue in Hollywood. Word had trickled out that Chuck Barris paid guaranteed money to unionized performers, and many members of The Groundlings were using performance workshops to fine-tune ideas they had for *Gong Show* acts.

After "Betty and Eddie" made their first appearance on *The Gong Show*, Reubens and his performing partner, Charlotte McGinnis, took out a full-page ad in *Variety*. Surprisingly, this isn't the part of the story where Reubens was launched to stardom as a result of the appearance and the ad. They got one phone call, met with a manager and that was it. Being on *The Gong Show* ultimately didn't make much of an impact on Reubens' career. But he kept going back for more because the money was good.

Chuck Barris was willing to bend the rules a little bit, just as he had for *Dating Game* contestants. Game shows were strictly regulated by the FCC and by the major networks because of fallout from the 1950s quiz show scandals. The networks all imposed strict limits on how many times a person could be a TV game show contestant, and how long a former contestant had to wait before auditioning to be a contestant on another show (generally the rule was that you had to wait a minimum of one year between appearances, and that you certainly couldn't be on the same game show multiple times unless you were a "returning champion").

Reubens didn't know first-hand whatever Chuck Barris did to prevent those rules from applying to *The Gong Show*. But no NBC representative at the studio seemed to bat an eye when Reubens showed up repeatedly to be a contestant. Reubens, by his own count, would appear as a contestant on the *The Gong Show* 14 times.

Reubens said in 2017, "I've told people for years that Chuck Barris supported a lot of struggling artists."

The Groundlings Theater on Melrose Avenue still stands and still holds regular performances. The green room backstage, where performers relax before going on, was painted with the free paint that all contestants received as a parting gift at one of those 14 tapings.

A few other members of The Groundlings showed up under the names Pepita and Grandpa. "Grandpa," wearing a heavy rubber mask to make him look appropriately old, made a stoop-shouldered stroll onto the stage and talked about his infatuation with Pepita, a prostitute on Sunset Boulevard. As Pepita swigged tequila and smirked at the audience, Grandpa recited a poem about getting ditched by Pepita, who realized he was flat-broke and went back home to Chihuahua to find something else to do with her life. Pepita was Teresa Burton. Grandpa, utterly impossible to recognize in his *Gong Show* performance, was Phil Hartman, just under a decade from his career-making break on *Saturday Night Live*.

Robert Schimmel was one of the all-time great stand-up comics — #76 according to Comedy Central's ranking, a frequent guest of Howard Stern who had, as his brother Jeff succinctly puts it, "A dirty, dirty act." And as Jeff tells it, *The Gong Show* paved Robert's path to stardom.

Jeff Schimmel says, "My brother had come to LA in 1978 just to visit our sister, who lived on Fairfax Avenue. At the time, he was living

Robert Schimmel's rise to stand-up fame included a quick stop to play the piano on The Gong Show. PHOTO COURTESY OF JEFF SCHIMMEL

in Scottsdale, Arizona, and selling stereos. He had always been the class clown in school, but he had never really thought about being a comic. While he was in LA, he and my sister went to the Improv, and it was open mic night. You could put your name in a hat, Budd Friedman would draw the names at random, and if your name was pulled, you could come onstage and do two minutes. Unbeknownst to Robert, my sister had slipped his name in there.[2]

"He went up there and did two minutes. Budd Friedman told him 'Come back any time!' Now, what Budd probably meant when he said that was 'Come back to another open mic night.' Robert took it to mean he should quit his job in Arizona and move to LA, which is what he did,

---

2. Personal interview. 17 Apr. 2019.

and he brought his wife and his baby daughter with him. The day they arrived in the city, Robert said, 'Let me show you the club where I'm going to start my career.' And he drives his wife to the Improv. The Improv had burned down the night before.

"Robert gets a job selling and installing stereo equipment to support himself. At the time, *The Gong Show* was huge. Robert auditioned for it. He played the theme from *Love Story* on the piano with his nose. It was something he did first when he took a girl somewhere and wanted to impress her. He was proud of it. He did it in my dorm building when I was in college because he spotted some girl, and he wanted her to notice him.

"He got on the show. He told this story later. Now my brother could be prone to exaggerating, but here is the story as he told it to me. A woman dropped dead while he was there. One of the other contestants. [This was indeed the same show on which Esther Wolf was supposed to perform.] She was backstage near the curtain. And there's this panic and everyone is surrounding her and tending to her. But the call comes out. 'ROBERT SCHIMMEL TO THE STAGE PLEASE... ROBERT SCHIMMEL TO STAGE!' And my brother just had to step around her body and go out to do his act."

"Being on *The Gong Show* launched his career. You need to understand why. At comedy clubs, the emcees like to introduce the comics by saying what they've done recently. And if you introduce a comic by naming a TV show they've been on, it gives them a little allure and the audience is interested. Well, all they could ever say about my brother was 'He's done open mic nights at other clubs.' *The Gong Show* was a feather in his cap. 'You've seen him on *The Gong Show*!' And again, that show was huge at the time, so it got the audience's attention when they heard that. So that opened a lot of doors because now he had a hit show that he could attach his name to, and that got him other gigs.

"This is an aspect that *The Gong Show* doesn't get nearly enough credit for. *The Tonight Show Starring Johnny Carson* was never going to book a newcomer. *The Gong Show* provided this forum for a bunch of new talent who were never going to be given another opportunity like that.

"Being on that show really meant something to Robert. The next real TV exposure he got was a show called *So You Think You Got Troubles* hosted by Jay Johnson, the ventriloquist. And that's good TV exposure, but he totally treated it as just a gig. He was there to pick up a $500 check. Two years later, he was on *Star Search*. Now *Star Search* was a popular show in 1984. But he treated it as a total goof. He did not give a shit that he was on *Star Search*, however popular it was. But *The Gong Show* truly mattered to him. He cared about being on that show. He was proud of it.

And when he really hit his peak as a comic, it wasn't something he tried to hide. It wasn't something from early in his career that embarrassed him. He was proud of the fact that he had been on that show. It was a fond memory for him.

"His wife was really embarrassed by it, though. Robert's wife was always kind of embarrassed by everything he did, because his act was really, really

After watching so many acts, maybe Jamie Farr just figured he could do better. ROBERT BURROUGHS COLLECTION

dirty. He'd be outside the club after a show, and she'd just want to hide. *The Gong Show* was the same thing — he viewed it as a triumph and his wife was so embarrassed by it. She just looked at him and thought, 'God, why can't you just be a dentist?'"

Joey D'Auria might not get a second look if you saw him walking along the sidewalk, but for two decades, he was one of the most beloved figures on children's TV. He was Bozo the Clown. And his journey to the legendary role started with his appearance as a contestant on *The Gong Show*.

D'Auria got his career off to a good start as a teenage actor in summer stock performances in Maine and Vermont. After attending the American Academy of Dramatic Arts in New York City, he took a rocky road west; first, a dinner theater in Ohio that went out of business; he got hired for another dinner theater in Denver, but as he pulled into the parking lot for the first time, he saw the sheriff putting a padlock on the door. Finally, Beverly Hills, where, like Chuck's first production office, he settled into an address that sounded nicer than it was.

D'Auria says, "I got lucky. I found a good paying job that allowed me to maintain my apartment and take classes with an improv group called Off

A publicity still snapped in a calmer moment at the studio. PHOTO BY AND COURTESY OF VINCE LONGO

the Wall. I got to do scenes with Robin Williams before anyone knew him. We were told to do a scene where he was angry with me, and he starts the scene by yelling, 'You ate my bicycle!' Where do you go with that line?[3]

"Word got around the class that Chuck Barris wanted *Gong Show* acts so badly that he was willing to pay the AFTRA minimum for anyone willing to do a stupid act and possibly get gonged and booed offstage. AFTRA minimum at that time was the same as my rent so I figured if I came up with one stupid act a month, I won't have to worry about my apartment.

"I started watching *The Gong Show* to get a sense of what I was getting myself into. One of the things I noticed was that your act had to

---

3. Personal interview. 10 May 2019.

be 90 seconds, and a lot of the acts that got gonged were funny ideas for a few seconds, but they became boring after a while. There was one act who came out with glasses filled with water, and you immediately think he's going to rub his fingers around the rims to make music. Instead, he grabs them and shakes them like handbells. Now that's funny, but after ten seconds, he's still grabbing them and shaking them.

"I had one idea. I bought a large matchbox and a Mormon Tabernacle Choir album. It was 33 1/3 RPM, but I had the audio man play it at 78 RPM to make it fast and high pitched. I called my act a flea choir. I tapped my baton, opened my match box, and then the audio man played the record so it sounded like fleas were singing.

"I was on another show as Professor Wolfgang Von Bimbo. I used an ax and destroyed a rocking chair to the beat of the William Tell Overture.

"Then I came up with Dr. Flame-O. I had a bunch of candles around the apartment, because I came of age in the 1960s and all of us have a lot of candles in our homes. Some were used more than others, so all the candles were different heights. And it occurred to me that if I put the candles side-by-side, they looked like a pipe organ. I thought, 'I'm going to burn my hands to music.'

"Backstage, I was sitting next to a homely girl. Very pleasant but very homely. She turns to me and says 'I'm going to be a star. I know I'm not attractive, but Barbra Streisand isn't either, and she's a great singer.'

"She went onstage. Now, the audience at *The Gong Show* was encouraged to scream and boo. They didn't want polite audiences. Because she was plain-looking, the audience was already kind of on her when she walked onstage. She sang the big hit song of the day, which was 'You Light Up My Life.'

"And she sang it badly. Oh my god. She was tone deaf. Benefit of the doubt, maybe the audience unnerved her. But the audience just booed and shouted. I remember watching the episode when it aired, and honestly, television didn't do justice to that sound. In person, the booing was overwhelming. That audience made Simon Cowell look like Rebecca of Sunnybrook Farm. She got gonged, and once she was backstage, she ran off in tears.

"I said to myself, 'Thank goodness I already know I'm going to get booed.'

"To open the act, I push my candles onstage, and some of the audience is already hollering as I walk out there. I say, 'Ladies and gentlemen, give me just a moment to tune up.' I held one hand over one of the candles and went 'Ahhhhhhh…'

"One audience member yells, 'He's hurting himself!' The audience goes 'YAAAAYYYY!' And then the act is me, moving my hands back and forth over different candles, and yelling in pain, but changing the key of the yell for each candle, and I yelled the melody of 'Smoke Gets in Your Eyes.'

"Jaye P. Morgan, Fred Travalena, and Pat McCormick all gave me tens. Jaye said, 'That was the best hand job I've ever seen on TV,' which got edited out. I walked out there expecting to get gonged, and I blurted out, 'You liked that?!' Chuck elbows me in the ribs and says, 'Be quiet! They liked you!' Chuck liked me so much that I got booked for *The Chuck Barris Rah-Rah Show*. I went on before George Carlin.

"Then I got a day job at a restaurant called the Variety Arts Club, it was a vaudeville-themed restaurant and private club owned by Milt Larsen, who had been a writer for *Truth or Consequences* and at that point, he was writing for Jim Nabors' variety show. Milt had a private table where he'd bring Jim and their business associates for lunch all the time. I'm pouring everybody's water and I hear Jim ask Milt about the funny act that he wanted to book for the variety show. Milt says, 'I saw it on *The Gong Show*. El Flame-o. I need to talk to Chuck Barris and get the guy's real name.'

"I say, 'Are you talking about the man who held his hands over candles and yelled in pain to 'Smoke Gets in Your Eyes'?

"Milt says, 'You know him?'

"I say, 'Well, first, it's Dr. Flame-O. And second, sir, I am Dr. Flame-o.'

"That table just broke up laughing. Milt said, 'Only in Hollywood can the actor you're looking for turn out to be your waiter.' I did the Dr. Flame-o bit on Jim Nabors' show.

"George Carlin came to the restaurant one night. As I served him, I said, 'We've worked together before.' He gave me a look and I said, '*The Chuck Barris Rah-Rah Show*.' George says, 'You were the guy with the candles! That was one of the funniest things I ever saw!' He was there with a group of friends, and I gave them a private tour of the club when dinner was over. George left me a $100 tip. Later, I got to open for George at a comedy festival in San Diego. My dressing room was this little hole in the wall, and George says, 'Get out of there, you're with me.' He had me moved into the gigantic star dressing room with him.

"In 1982, I was working at Milt Larsen's club and Milt explains that Johnny Carson was getting ready for his New Year's Eve show. Johnny always liked to book a magician for New Year's Eve and Milt had lined up three magicians for Jim McCawley, Johnny's talent booker, to watch. One of them made a bit of a mess as part of his act, so Milt asked me to do Dr. Flame-o to kill some time while they cleaned the stage for the next magician. I went out there and did Dr. Flame-o. Jim McCawley was notorious among nightclub performers because he did not react to anything at all. It's true. He didn't come anywhere near a smile that entire night. But he came to the club with Tim Conway, and Tim Conway doubled over watching me. Afterward, a cocktail waitress said Milt wanted to see

George Carlin on The Chuck Barris Rah-Rah Show. *Joey D'Auria would make a lasting impression on George that night, as he discovered some time later.* ROBERT BURROUGHS COLLECTION

me, and Milt said Jim McCawley wanted me on *The Tonight Show* for New Year's Eve.

"The next day, I got a call from a talent manager who wanted to represent me, and she poisoned my career. She wouldn't accept any acting roles for me that were less than five lines of dialogue, which meant I couldn't get hired for anything. I don't know how my life would have turned out if my wife didn't see an article saying Bob Bell was retiring and they needed someone to replace him as Bozo the Clown. I mailed the producers a tape of the Dr. Flame-o act, and for some reason, they saw that and agreed this man should be in charge of entertaining children, so we moved to Chicago, and I was Bozo the Clown for the next 17 years. I also played Max Prince in Neil Simon's *Laughter on the 23rd Floor*, which is the work I'm the proudest of."

Mare Winningham is a prolific actress, familiar to film and television viewers for her roles in *St. Elmo's Fire, Turner & Hooch, Grey's Anatomy, American Horror Story*, and *Hatfields & McCoys*. And before all that, she slung a guitar around her neck and sang The Beatles' "Here, There, and Everywhere" on *The Gong Show*, going by the alias Sharon Shamus.

She told the story when she was interviewed by Johnny Carson. "I was sixteen at the time…My sister dared me, and a couple of classmates. I dressed up as this very awkward, backward…someone to feel sorry for. And I had this green shirt on, and these black cat eyeglasses. And if I don't wash my hair every day it's a disaster. And I didn't wash it for two days, and it was really oily…And hopefully if I could get past all the teeters and the whispers, I sing. And I was going to sing as heartfelt and as believable and exciting as possible.

"The way it worked out was just horrific. I went out there. My mom went out there with me because I was a minor at the time. I had a different name. I was Sharon Shandler. I wouldn't dare go out there using my real name, looking like that. And I went backstage, where everyone takes themselves real seriously…You know, they kept coming up to my mom and saying 'Geez, does she have to wear that? She could be an okay-looking kid, I mean, come on.' And everyone was trying to make me over while getting in the spirit of the thing.

"And she says 'No, you know, she can't see without those. Literally, I could not see *with* these glasses. I borrowed them from a friend down the street. I couldn't see anything. I walked out with my little guitar. There were Girl Scouts in the audience. And I guess they figured that since I was their peer, that I was about their age, that they could do what they would with me.

"And they just started hooting and laughing and making a spectacle. I could barely get out the first few notes of the song. You couldn't hear anything....And I started to sing and I was real nervous anyway. But I just started to move with the song. And Paul Williams started to listen a little bit. And he kind of got into it and got the feeling for it. And he stood up and told the Girl Scouts to be quiet. They have a shot of him doing that. It was wonderful. And pretty soon, you could hear a pin drop. And I finished up the song...And I won five hundred bucks, which is like a million dollars when you're sixteen years old. And afterwards, Paul Williams came up to me, and he put his arms on my shoulders and he said, 'Sharon, no one's ever going to laugh at you again.'"

A 19-year-old stepped onto the *Gong Show* stage in 1978 and did a routine about the different shows you might see when you switch channels. First, he acted out a brief scene in which Benji the hero dog mauled a small boy for touching his nose; a quirky premise that got some laughs, and he did a rather credible-sounding angry dog. And then he changed the channel to an episode of *Star Trek* and, using only his mouth, did a dazzling barrage of sound effects — the phasers, warp speed, and the beams. And then a Disney cartoon, for which he performed a chainsaw-wielding Donald Duck attacking Mickey Mouse. For his big finish, he put on an afro wig and performed "Purple Haze" as Jimi Hendrix. No guitar skills needed, his mouth providing the instrumentation.

The whole act triggered the longest, loudest reaction any act ever got; the audience stamped their feet and cheered so hard that they drowned out Pat McCormick at the judge's table. McCormick gave a ten; the audience roared. Gary Mule Deer gave ten more; the audience roared. Michele Lee, feeling playful, teased that she hadn't given a ten, and the audience booed her. And then she held up her ten and the audience roared again. It was a star-making segment.

That was Michael Winslow. And his odd talent for creating his own sound effects led to roles in *Spaceballs* and, most prominently, the *Police Academy* films.

The before-they-were-stars stories don't stop at the stage of *The Gong Show* either. Even the acts that got rejected went on to fame. Weird Al Yankovic revealed to *Goldmine* writer Chuck Miller that he once auditioned for the show.

"I was in college," Yankovic told Miller. "And a friend and I drove down to LA for the day and auditioned for *The Gong Show*. And we did a song called 'Mr. Frump in the Iron Lung.' And the audience seemed to enjoy it, but we never got called back. So, we didn't make the cut for *The Gong Show*.

The judges' panel helped move a few careers forward. Allen Ludden, the former host of *Password* who had a few turns as a judge, had, a few years earlier, discovered a quirky talk radio host in Indiana who told him privately that he was considering moving to Los Angeles to start a career in stand-up. Once he made the move and established himself, Ludden took a special interest in his career and recommended him for bookings on game show panels.

Allen Ludden, who performed a few tours of duty as a judge on The Gong Show, *helped launch David Letterman's career through his connections in the game show world. Up-and-coming comic Letterman spent a week as a judge on* The Gong Show *himself.* FRED WOSTBROCK COLLECTION

Jefferson Beeker says, "I got called one day to go to a stand-up comic's house and measure him. He got booked for the show and we needed to make some tuxedos for him, but he had never been measured for a suit before, so he didn't know his sizes. It turned out to be David Letterman."

Even the members of the show's family saw their stock starting to rise. Rhett and Scarlett looked for a moment like they might be on their way to big things. Beeker says, "We were booked in a comedy club. Ruth Goldberg, one of Chuck's producers, thought we might make a good opening act for comics, and she booked us for a show at The Comedy Store, the famous comedy club in Hollywood, to see how we worked as a stage act. We

BOMBED. I can tell you what it feels like to bomb on the stage of a comedy club now. Just the wrong fit for that kind of gag. Here was the problem with doing it as a nightclub act. The reason Rhett and Scarlett were funny was because the most offensive words in the routine were bleeped. When you could hear what we were saying, the gags fell completely flat.

Murray Langston, as the Unknown Comic, fared much better. The character had become popular, and in an odd way, he had triggered the public's curiosity. The fact that his face was covered had spawned a reaction that Langston didn't anticipate. Fans had taken to speculating about the identity of the Unknown Comic, suspecting that maybe this was an elaborate long-term set-up by a superstar stand-up like Steve Martin or Andy Kaufman.

Rhett Butler and Scarlett O'Hara. A little of the act went a long way, as they discovered when they attempted to take the act to nightclubs. PHOTO COURTESY OF JEFFERSON BEEKER

The Unknown Comic's popularity surged, in part because of that curiosity, but largely because the act was just plain entertaining. The whole premise was that he was supposed to be a bad comic, but Langston's jokes were clever, spanning from actually funny to so bad that you admired his courage for telling it. The Sahara Hotel in Las Vegas called Langston and offered him $10,000 for two weeks.

Langston says, "I had been an actor before *The Gong Show*. I really didn't have a background in stand-up before I became the Unknown Comic. The gig went great, and I kept getting bookings. I really lucked out with the Unknown Comic. I'm a go-getter and I was determined to keep working in show business. When I got that first booking for *The Gong Show* it was just for the money, but it worked out better than I anticipated, and I just went with it. But if it hadn't been the Unknown Comic, it would have been something else."

The Unknown Comic transcended *The Gong Show* on television. He began popping up all over the place. "I was on *The Midnight Special*,

Mike Douglas, *Rock Concert, Make Me Laugh*...Paul Block from Johnny Carson's staff liked my stuff, so I got booked on *The Tonight Show*, which ended up being a strange experience. I got eight rounds of applause during my act, but Johnny himself didn't like me. In general, Johnny didn't like prop comedy and he didn't like comedians who did gimmicks. I only did

The Unknown Comic got some unexpected mileage out of an act he had only whipped up for a quick $250. ROBERT BURROUGHS COLLECTION

The Tonight Show twice, and the second time, David Letterman was guest-hosting, and we knew each other from comedy clubs where we crossed paths. But years and years have passed and I'm still putting that bag on my head and doing the act."

CHAPTER 14

NBC Bangs The Gong

Above: Chuck prepares to bring on the next offender.
ROBERT BURROUGHS COLLECTION

September 20, 1977: a date that will live in *Gong* infamy.

That day, a pair of young ladies — Chuck remembered them being 17 or so — appeared on the show, calling themselves Have You Got a Nickel.

Before explaining what they did in their act, perhaps it's necessary to get Chuck's own explanation of why he even booked them for the show. It was a cunning strategy he had devised for dealing with NBC censors, and on this day, it backfired in an odd way.

Chuck told the Archive of American Television, "We had a man and a woman from Standards & Practices who would come down to see all of our acts. Invariably, they would cancel one act. I never understood why. But they would cancel <u>one</u>. And I couldn't see anything wrong with airing it. So, I started to bring acts that they would cancel, that were totally abominable. And these two would say, 'You can't have that act on television.' I would say 'Okay' and get rid of it. I brought [Have You Got a Nickel] down…and I don't know where the censors were. They must have went out and had a cigarette."

Chuck, in the hopes of getting a few acts on the show that he wasn't quite sure would make it past the censors, had booked Have You Got a Nickel to provide the censors with the target. They were supposed to reject the two women, and the rest of the performers would be in the clear to appear on that day's taping. But when the censors didn't say a word, Chuck decided there was no harm in letting the young ladies do their thing on the show.

The two brunettes skipped out on stage in t-shirts and short shorts, both wielding popsicles. And then they licked the popsicles. Slowly licked the popsicles. Then licked the sides of the popsicles. Then sucked on just the tips of the popsicles. Then twisted the popsicles. Then inserted the popsicles in their mouths as far as they could go. It was the most unsubtle 90 seconds the show had presented in the past 14 months.

Chuck smiled at the memory. "The stagehands that were sweeping up stopped sweeping and just looked at them! They couldn't believe their eyes."

The show aired in the eastern time zone and within seconds, WKYC, the NBC affiliate in Cleveland, was swamped with angry phone calls. A WKYC employee called WMAQ, the Chicago NBC affiliate, which regularly aired the show three hours later, to give them a heads-up about the offensive segment. But the staffer who took the call didn't relay the warning to station general manager Lee Hanna, who was blindsided when he saw the act as it was airing, braced himself, and fielded all the angry phone calls coming into his station.

An exasperated Hanna told *The Chicago Sun-Times*, "I don't understand how it ever got past Standards and Practices in New York."[1]

The words of warning quickly made their way to NBC's affiliates in the Pacific time zone. KNBC faded to black just a bit early and aired public service announcements in place of the segment. A number of other affiliates on the west coast opted for reruns that day.

Acts like this began getting the attention of NBC station managers and the censors. PHOTO BY AND COURTESY OF VINCE LONGO

For the record, the young ladies finished with a score of 12 — a zero from Phylis Diller (who complained that she didn't understand the act), a two from Jamie Farr, and a 10 from Jaye P. Morgan, who said she got her start in show business the same way. One of the women was so appreciative that she gave her popsicle to Morgan, who did her own thing with the popsicle as Chuck wrapped up the segment.

Larry Spencer remembers, "After the taping ended, I asked one of them for a date. She said no."

The next day, Chuck was summoned to the office of NBC Entertainment president Herb Schlosser. Sensing the reason for the meeting, Chuck walked into Schlosser's office smiling and sucking on a lollipop.

1   Jenkins, Alan. "Gong Show Routine Prompts Complaints." *The Palm Beach Post*. 22 Sep. 1977.

Schlosser didn't mince words. "I want ratings, not cocksuckers!"

Michael Brockman was still an executive at ABC, but word reached him about what had happened over on the other network that day. Brockman, who had passed on *The Gong Show* pilot two years earlier because it "didn't feel like a daytime show," thought the incident was emblematic of the problem he saw with it.

Gypsy Rose Widoff, who "stripped" down to a flesh-colored body stocking.
BOB BODEN COLLECTION

Brockman says, "Put aside the taste factor. It was obviously in poor taste to put that on television. But even if you're not talking about taste, it's bad business to show something like that on daytime television. Who's the target audience for daytime television in the 1970s? Adult women. That's who you gear the shows to. Advertisers buy time on daytime TV because they want to reach that audience. Do adult women really want to watch that?"

The Popsicle Twins, as they came to be known, weren't even the only source of agita for Lee Hanna of WMAQ in that month. During September 1977, the station began airing the nighttime *Gong Show*. Because syndicated television was conducted through mail in those days — copies of the master tapes were shipped to the station — Hanna was able to screen those episodes in advance and put his foot down twice.

For Episode N201, he refused to air a performance by Miss Dolly, an overweight woman who gyrated in a bikini. He called the segment "physically revolting." (Though some could argue that instituting "fat shaming" as an official station policy was equally revolting.) For Episode N208, an act called Ada and Alice, in which a "blind" farmgirl sang to her animals, was deleted from the broadcast. There was nothing offensive about the song itself, but as it happened, the camera got a close-up of a chicken right as it defecated on the stage, and Chuck Barris' staff didn't bother editing the moment. Hanna called it "degrading and tasteless."

Lee Hanna at WMAQ wasn't just being a fuddy-duddy; in the late 1970s, he had legitimate cause for concern about the content of the nighttime *Gong Show*. In 1975, the FCC instituted a "Family Viewing Hour" policy, stating that broadcast television between 8:00 pm and 9:00 pm Eastern time had to be suitable viewing for entire families. In 1976, a federal court ruled that the FCC's policy was overstepping its boundaries and canceled the policy, but as a show of good faith, for years afterwards, the major networks generally attempted to keep that hour of television family friendly. Local TV stations that aired syndicated programming during the hour before the prime-time line-up generally also wanted to keep that hour family-friendly, and the nighttime *Gong Show* was airing right in that slot across the country.

The Gong Show did make some minimal effort to make the nighttime show more appropriate sometimes. The average viewer didn't spot it, but the nighttime show's contestants, all of whom had previously appeared on the daytime show, would occasionally have to perform modified versions of their acts. A conspicuous example was an escape artist who appeared on the NBC daytime *Gong Show* singing the song "Please Release Me" while hanging from a cross. When he appeared on the nighttime version, he was tied to a small post instead.

Chuck always seemed to enjoy having a little fun with the censors. He kept NBC's video editors on edge for months with what he called his 'wee-wee doll,' a stuffed character in a trench coat that could be opened to reveal its penis. He would occasionally flash it at the audience or a nearby stagehand for a quick laugh, being mindful of keeping it out of view of the camera, but then he would carelessly let his arm drop while hanging onto the doll and the coat flaps would come apart.

Dog acts delighted Chuck because it gave him a chance to engage in a sneaky trick. He would slip backstage and rub Alpo on his crotch just before the performance. At the end of the act, when Chuck joined the contestant to hear what the judges had to say, invariably, the dog, sniffing something familiar and wonderful, would bury its snout deep into Chuck's pants while Chuck feigned shock and tried to get away from the dog, usually with a struggle as the dog just followed him wherever he went. Chuck acted helpless when it was really what he wanted the whole time. And what were the censors going to say? Every dog owner knows it's what dogs do. How can *The Gong Show* control an animal's instincts?

Adult star Carol Connors became a semi-regular on the show after her breathtaking performance of the song "Something in the Way I Move." She later starred in a Gong Show *porn parody, the title of which could be easily guessed.* BOB BODEN COLLECTION

Yvonne Longo says, "The censors had to be aware of what Chuck was doing because he did it every time we had a dog on the show."

Chuck himself acknowledged that he was in danger of pushing this only so far. He told writer Frank Swertlow (yes, the same "Sourpuss" mentioned earlier), "You can really put yourself out of commission if you cross a certain line. You can be so distasteful that people will not watch you...I just don't know what my boundaries are."

The problem was Chuck himself didn't seem to have a discernible line that he stayed away from, and *The Gong Show* sometimes came across as a show blissfully unaware of what it should and shouldn't be doing.

Granted, some of the battles with censors seem charmingly out of date now. The billboard onstage was adorned with the message "WHAT THE HELL?" one day and at the network's insistence, "Hell" was blurred out. Chuck and a male staffer acted out a bit leading to commercial once where they spoofed the spaghetti scene from Disney's *Lady and the Tramp*. Chuck munched on one end of a licorice rope, the staffer munched on the other, and just as their faces came thiiiiiis close…they stopped.

One of the most vitriolic complaints about *The Gong Show* was one of the most endearing qualities of it, looking back. Viewers and critics griped, "They'll let anybody on this show." In hindsight…yes, they let anybody on the show. In what other television show during the 1970s could you find drag queens? And more remarkably, in what other television show of that era could drag queens blend in, without any semblance of disgust? Granted, even then, there was a censor fight…while NBC almost always allowed *Gong Show* contestants to use whatever stage name they wanted, drag acts had to tack a distracting "Mister" onto their names, with Chuck introducing them that way at the start of the act.

While *The Gong Show* conceded that fight, Chuck was still willing to put himself out there as an open ally to the homosexual community, by introducing one episode with a joyful middle finger to the most visible homophobe of the decade. Anita Bryant, a popular singer and orange juice spokeswoman, had gained notoriety early in 1977 by referring to homosexuals as "human garbage" and leading a coalition called "Save Our Children," dedicated to protesting and repealing ordinances that prohibited discrimination based on sexual orientation.

The billboard on the *Gong Show* stage read "IT'S NOT ANITA BRYANT NIGHT!" Chuck opened the show by emphatically announcing that tonight's program was not dedicated to Ms. Bryant. And then Chuck took a big bite out of an orange and introduced the first contestant…Mr. Tootie Finell, a drag queen who quite fittingly belted out "Respect."

The daytime show also had a pseudo-tribute to Bryant. For "IT'S NOT ANITA BRYANT DAY!" on NBC, Chuck announced that he was dedicating the next act to the singer, in case she happened to be watching. And then he welcomed a gender non-conforming stripper.

Chuck was accepting of the transgender community, although the way he expressed this came out sounding very much like a sentence from the mouth of Chuck Barris. Here was his introduction of a transgender contestant on episode #N208:

> CHUCK: This is amazing. This next act was actually a man not too long ago. I can't get over those things. I mean…heh…I mean, I'm from Philadelphia, and we don't understand that stuff…but he's here now…as good old Brandy Lee.

Brandy Lee scored 29 points, with Jaye P. Morgan expressing approval in her own unique way too. "I hate a guy with bigger tits than mine." The joke hasn't aged gracefully, but Jaye P. Morgan needled everybody who walked on that stage. Brandy Lee got treated like anybody else in that moment.

Larry Spencer says, "We never got, to my knowledge, any kind of backlash for having gay or transgender contestants. Honestly, I think it's

"Mister" Tootie Finell, who helped The Gong Show *send a rare but earnest message.* BOB BODEN COLLECTION

because we were *The Gong Show*. If it was on some other show, it might have caused a problem."

But Chuck kept hunting for new buttons to push. He booked a folk duo named The Bearded Lady, one of whom was an obvious man in drag… and if it wasn't obvious enough, he performed with his genitals hanging out of his hiked skirt. NBC censors slapped the word "OOPS" over the offending region for broadcast. A stand-up comic performed with a bike horn in his pants and squeezed his crotch after every punch line. A stripper freed herself from a straitjacket. A man calling himself "Shartie" did a silent sketch with an inflatable doll.

Jefferson Beeker, a/k/a Miss Scarlett, noticed the show was getting edgier too. "In the beginning, the words that got bleeped in our sketches were just nonsense words, since we knew the audience at home wasn't going to hear them anyway. It started getting more risqué, because Chuck realized that nobody was going to hear it except the studio audience.

"I remember looking at the cue cards for our bit one day before a taping, and I said, 'This is getting awfully blue.' Peter reasoned, 'Yeah, but it's just the studio audience.' Well, yeah, but we would rehearse with the cue cards backstage, and Della Barris, who was 14 at that point, would do the cue

Peter Mins and Jefferson Beeker put away their Civil War garb for this segment. Here they play Dubert and Pucky, a ventriloquist and his dummy.
PHOTO COURTESY OF JEFFERSON BEEKER

cards for us. She's 14 and we're saying these words to her. She may not have even gotten the jokes yet, she may have just known that they were supposed to be funny."[2]

"So, the Rhett and Scarlett sketches keep getting bluer and bluer until a day when I just looked at that script and thought 'Wow.' But we did the bit."

The next day, Beeker, who, after all, was still hired from day to day to work various NBC shows, returned to the studio complex to work on whatever other program needed him that day. He was told to go upstairs for a meeting with NBC's head of production services.

2   Personal interview. 10 Apr. 2019.

Beeker faced the executive, "a very corporate type" as he recalled, in the standard-issue suit and tie. The executive greeted him. "Jefferson, I want to talk to you about your participation on *The Gong Show*."

Beeker tentatively replied, "Okay."

"Did it not bother you that you were saying these particular words on the show?"

Monsieur Le Poof, who farted hard enough to extinguish a candle from across the stage. ROBERT BURROUGHS COLLECTION

Beeker made his defense. "Well, apart from whether it bothered me or not, I knew it wouldn't go out on the air."

The executive continued his cross-examination. "Do you speak like that in your everyday language?"

Beeker responded, "That's not the issue. It all gets edited."

The executive asked, "Why did you say these things?"

Beeker told him, "The material was written by the executive producer. He's the boss of the show. I'm an actor on this, performing material that is given to me."

The executive took that point and made another. "Suppose someone in Switching Central, as you tape the show, accidentally puts you out on the air live."

Beeker answered, "If you hired an idiot in Switching Central, I have no control over that."

The executive changed tactics. "There were minors in the audience."

Beeker had an answer for that too. "It says very clearly on the ticket that you must be a certain age to attend the taping. I don't have control over who you let in."

The executive went to the only approach he had left, a threat. "We have to think about this and see if you'll be allowed back on the lot."

Chuck and the Unknown Comic. Murray Langston wasn't shy about getting the censors' attention with his routines. BOB BODEN COLLECTION

Chuck Barris found out about the threat. Chuck, who adored his staff like no other tycoon in television, boarded a plane and went straight to New York to see Madeline David, the NBC daytime boss who had greenlit *The Gong Show*, to complain about the way Beeker had been treated.

To Chuck's delight, the fuse was extinguished before he even had a chance to light it. David greeted him by saying, "I love those Rhett and Scarlett bits! Keep doing them!"

Chuck returned to Los Angeles, and Beeker's job was secure. That would normally be the end of it, and NBC probably would have been content to let all of this be swept under the rug and forgotten. Not Chuck. For a few episodes after the confrontation, Chuck would introduce Rhett and Scarlett by telling the audience, "Ladies and gentlemen, these two have caused some trouble. I can't tell you why, but they're in big trouble. Here's Rhett and Scarlett!"

For one episode, Chuck announced that the show was instituting a Penalty Box for acts that had caused problems for the show. Sitting in the penalty box were Rhett and Scarlett, both with tape across their mouths.

The next day, NBC's head of production services saw Jefferson Beeker in the hallway and said nothing more than "Good morning, Mister Beeker."

Beeker, as wardrobe coordinator, found himself dealing with censors for other reasons. Despite NBC's own edict that wardrobe couldn't "help" the contestants in anyway, periodically, a woman would show up for rehearsal wearing an outfit that gave the network some concerns, and they would break their own rule by asking wardrobe to provide a sweater or heavy scarf before letting her go on the show.

UNKNOWN COMIC: Hey, Chucky Baby! You know, a lot of people are wondering who I am. Well, my name is Joe! I don't have a last name, though. My name used to be Joe Dingle-Dangle. Yeah, that's right, my name used to be Joe Dingle-Dangle.

CHUCK: Wait a minute! Just a minute. Everybody has a last name.

UNKNOWN COMIC: I know, it's a weird last name, isn't it? I'll tell you what happened. I went to Yale and I got a BA degree, so I became known as Joe Dingle-Dangle, BA. Then I went to Harvard and got a Ph. D., so I became Joe Dingle-Dangle, BA, Ph.D. Then I was a hero! I was drafted into the service, and I was awarded the DSC. So, I became known as Joe Dingle-Dangle, BA, Ph.D., DSC. Well, then I got VD. Well, when Yale heard about the VD, they took away my BA, so I was just known as Joe Dingle-Dangle, Ph.D., DSC, VD. Then Harvard found out about the VD, so they took away my Ph.D., so I was just known as Joe Dingle-Dangle, DSC, VD. Then the Army found out about the VD, so they took away the DSC, so everyone just called me Joe Dingle-Dangle, VD.

CHUCK: Well, then what happened?

UNKNOWN COMIC: Well, the VD took away my Dingle-Dangle, so everyone just called me Joe!

CHUCK: Get out! Shut this curtain!

Danny Lies says, "I don't think there was a conspicuous effort to make the show edgier, naughtier, more offensive. I think it really was just a natural evolution. Chuck didn't want the audience to get used to the show, so he prided himself on trying to do something new with every show and looking for something viewers hadn't seen before. And looking for taboos to break was just a way of finding something new to do."

Larry Spencer says, "Chuck really wanted to make his shows off-the-wall. I mean, more so than usual. He began pushing hard. At one point he came to me for help developing an idea he had for a talk show. He'd be the host, but instead sitting in a chair, he'd be lying in bed for the entire show."[3]

May 30, 1978: Another date in *Gong Show* infamy. Gene-Gene the Dancing Machine came out to boogie. Nothing unusual about that.

Chuck Barris threw himself into a full-body convulsion at the side of the stage, spinning, shaking his feet, and throwing his arms out in something resembling the rhythm of "Jumpin' at the Woodside" by Milton DeLugg and the Band with a Thugg. Nothing unusual about that, either.

And then Jaye P. Morgan stood up. During the run of the show, Jaye P. Morgan, apparently fancying the movie *Annie Hall*, switched her wardrobe from evening gowns to suits & fedoras. As the music blared and the audience focused their attention on Gene, director John Dorsey, sensing that something was about to happen, kept one camera fixed on Morgan. She removed her hat...then her necktie...then the jacket...and then the shirt. No bra underneath. Jaye P. Morgan had just flashed the viewers of *The Gong Show*.

At least, that's how NBC treated the incident. Jefferson Beeker's argument from his own confrontation with the network brass absolutely applied — barring an extremely incompetent technician manning the console at that exact moment, NBC viewers were never going to see what Morgan had done. And indeed, when the show aired, the word "OOPS" covered the screen. Morgan wasn't even visible; in editing they cut away from her to the "OOPS" graphic.

Vince Longo remembers, "I was onstage taking photos. One of the cameramen was a friend of mine, Les. And the audience is getting into Gene-Gene, and I notice Jaye P. standing up and starting to take stuff off, and I start snapping photos right away. I kneel to get a better angle because I can see what she's about to do. And then right as that blouse comes open, Les picks that moment to dolly back his camera. Completely

---

3   Personal interview. 2 Feb. 2019.

ruined the shot. All the photos I took on that stage, and I don't have a photo of that moment because Les' ass got in the way."

It wasn't an isolated incident. Morgan had disrobed onstage once before.

Michael Brockman had just jumped from ABC to NBC, replacing Madeline David as vice president of NBC Daytime and Children's

Noted troublemaker Jaye P. Morgan. AUTHOR'S COLLECTION

Programming, when Morgan's first incident happened. Brockman recalls, "An older NBC employee pulled me aside one day and begins making a case to me because he says something is happening at *The Gong Show* and it concerns him. And he makes this speech to me about the prestige of the network, and its lengthy history, and the reputation of the network, and the quality of our program. And he finally gets to the point, which is that during commercial breaks at *The Gong Show*, Jaye P. Morgan is stripping. I was not aware that this was happening. I thanked the employee for telling me, and I went to Chuck."

Although Brockman didn't really know Chuck Barris all that well, he felt comfortable dealing with Barris directly. They had crossed paths at ABC when Chuck was still an executive and Brockman was an up-and-coming administrative clerk. As Brockman climbed the corporate ladder and Chuck built his empire, they crossed paths increasingly, and Brockman remembered finding him charming, even though they never got a chance to know each other very well. Although Chuck was fiercely proud and protective of his creation, Brockman found him easy to deal with when the network had to confront him about issues with content.

"It's all in the tone," Brockman says. "Chuck did not create the problem, but he was the executive producer. The right way to approach him is to let him know that you are not blaming him, but that the issue needs to be dealt with. I told Chuck that this wasn't appropriate because you can't just think of the studio audience as your fans who all love the show, you have to treat them as the general public."

While *The Gong Show* had a rabid fanbase that did indeed turn out in droves for tapings, it's also true that the audience members at TV show tapings aren't always fans of the show. Often, they're tourists, enticed by a studio tour or a brochure at the hotel to come see a taping of a real live TV show while they're in town. Blindsiding them with a striptease during the commercial break could put a bad face on the entire network.

Chuck promised Michael Brockman that it wouldn't happen again. Jaye P. Morgan promised Chuck that it wouldn't happen again.

But Morgan, with a somewhat questionable explanation of what went wrong during that May taping, explained, "I forgot that I had promised that I wouldn't do it."

Danny Lies says, "That was Jaye's nature. She loved pushing people's buttons. That's why Chuck adored her so much."

That episode, numbered #D462, concludes with a telling camera shot panning the entire set. From day one, *The Gong Show* had always concluded with wide, full shots of the stage, with all of the contestants assembled, along with the host, the scorekeeper, confetti thrower Jerry Marin, and any of the "non-contestant talent" featured that day, chatting it up, or mugging for the camera, and often dancing to the theme music. During the close of this episode, the party was going on without Chuck or Jaye P. Morgan. As everyone else danced and enjoyed the ninety-second party happening center stage, the camera swept over and saw Chuck and

Chuck Barris looked around and suddenly realized that maybe it was all just too much. ROBERT BURROUGHS COLLECTION

Jaye P. Morgan, both seated on the floor and slouched back against a wall of the set, talking quietly to each other about who-knows-what, and both looking visibly tired. With no credible aspersions to cast against either one of them, mind you, the only way to describe the scene is to borrow some drug slang. Both of them look like they're coming down.

In his memoir *The Game Show King*, Chuck Barris describes his state of mind during this taping. Chuck remembered the exact moment he entered his mid-life crisis because it happened as tape was rolling.

In 1993, Chuck wrote, "It was during that show's final commercial break, while the makeup lady patted my perspiring face with handfuls of Kleenex, that I began to wonder why I was hosting *The Gong Show* and acting the way I did. Today when I think back, I'm more confused than ever, frustrated and sad. I still don't know why, back then, I insisted on being such a profound ham so that now, years later, the mere thought of those antics of mine can make me moan aloud with embarrassment."

What vexed Chuck the most in that moment was how he started to realize how thoroughly his own performance as host contradicted every edict he ever handed to an emcee. When he oversaw *The Dating Game* and *The Newlywed Game*, he had advised hosts Jim Lange and Bob Eubanks to be okay with being bland. Viewers liked the sameness of the shows. There was no reason to try to make every episode the best one ever, or to push themselves to try something different as host. Leaning back was just fine.

What did Chuck Barris do when he became a host? He became obsessed with making every *Gong Show* something different. More shocking acts, more bawdy gags, more noise, wardrobe changes at every commercial break, more, more, more. And Chuck, with a need for control, had run himself ragged in the office, insisting on writing the scripts for the comedy sketches himself, even as he still had a business to run. *The Newlywed Game* was still going strong, and he had just sold a revival of *The Dating Game* for the fall of 1978, as well as a Gong-ized pageant called *The $1.98 Beauty Show*. With all that going on, Chuck had still chosen to drown himself and his show in excess. He had worn himself out.

On July 21, 1978, *The Gong Show* aired its 500th and final episode on the NBC Network. Locking down a reason that the show was canceled proved surprisingly hard. Many have, in the past, attributed it to The Popsicle Twins. Even Larry Spencer, when asked, said that The Popsicle Twins were "the reason they gave us" when the bad news reached Chuck Barris Productions.

In one way, that doesn't quite hold up to scrutiny. The Popsicle Twins performed their act in an episode taped in August 1977, eleven months before the final NBC broadcast. After it aired, Chuck Barris still managed to secure a deal for an hour of prime-time TV every week with *The Chuck Barris Rah-Rah Show*. It seems unlikely that he could have pulled that off if NBC was that angry.

In another way, the blame might be warranted. Vince Longo says, "The Popsicle Twins generated a lot of negative publicity towards the show. We got a lot of ill will in the press, and it snowballed after they were on. They weren't the thing that got the show canceled, but they got that ball rolling."

Even Susan Simons, NBC's Compliances representative at *The Gong Show*, says, "I never heard a reason myself. Nobody ever told me why that show got canceled."

Jaye P. Morgan's flashing has also been attributed as a reason, but that doesn't quite work either because the incident came far too late. Budd Granoff, executive vice president of Chuck Barris Productions, announced to the press as early as April that the network had canceled the show. The only true consequence the show endured from that was that NBC prohibited Jaye P. Morgan from appearing on any of the remaining episodes of the daytime show.

"Hollywood Cowboy" Chuck Barris, who appeared as a contestant on his own show, and fell victim to the gong, on the final NBC broadcast. ROBERT BURROUGHS COLLECTION

Another excuse bandied about was a change in management at NBC. Madeline David, the show's biggest advocate was still in charge, but in 1978 Fred Silverman was appointed President and CEO of NBC. He outranked Madeline David, and he hated *The Gong Show*. That's all true, but again, the timing doesn't line up with that explanation. Fred Silverman joined the network in June, two months after Budd Granoff announced the cancellation.

The call to cancel *The Gong Show* was made by Michael Brockman. And Brockman says that the reason he ended the show was a fairly universal one: "Ratings were down."

He elaborates, "Again, this goes back to the problem that I saw with that show when I saw the pilot. You have to think 'adult women' when you're picking shows for daytime television, and this didn't feel like a daytime show. Now that's not to say that no women watched it, but that wasn't its strongest audience. Meanwhile, the ABC O&Os had picked up the nighttime version when it first went on the air. And if you looked at the nighttime show, it had a huge audience. The nighttime show got great ratings, which made sense because it had more viewers to grab from. More men were watching. Teenagers were watching.[4]

"I was looking at the ratings books and I was looking at the daytime *Gong Show*'s ratings, and you could see it was trending downward in daytime. As an executive, I always tried to stay ahead of things when I saw a show trending downward. I began looking at shows to replace it right away, and I would even look at shows to replace the replacement in case the replacement failed. In 1978, you could see that the daytime *Gong Show* was starting to slide. I canceled it."

Larry Gotterer says, "When NBC canceled the show, we knew it was going to keep going in syndication, but we were going to have a few weeks off until the new season started. I had not been home to see my family in such a long time, and the flight I booked was for Saturday, June 24, which ended up being the date that Chuck scheduled for taping the final NBC daytime show."

Larry Gotterer didn't understand why Chuck Barris approached him on the preceding Monday and told him, "Cancel your flight."

Gotterer, believing he understood Chuck's reasoning, told him, "Listen, I know you don't want me to miss the final show, but it was the only flight I could get, and it's just been so long since I've seen my family."

On Tuesday, Chuck greeted Gotterer at the office by asking, "Did you cancel your flight?"

On Wednesday, "You've canceled your flight, right?"

Thursday came around. "Did you cancel the flight yet?"

On Friday, Larry Gotterer arrived and found his office too full to walk through. Chuck had moved all of his own belongings into Gotterer's office — his costumes, his hats, his knick-knacks, everything.

Gotterer finally asked something he had never got around to asking in the preceding week. "Why do you need me to cancel my flight?"

Chuck told him, "Because you're hosting the final episode."

Gotterer said, "Are you joking?"

---

4   Ibid.

Chuck told him, "No, you're the host."

Gotterer, trying to make sense of his boss' order, said, "I don't believe you. Show me the script."

Chuck confidently answered, "No script, I just need you to go out there and suck."

The Gong Show would go on. Enough stations had signed on for another season of the nighttime show. But the final NBC episode was a farewell to the show as viewers knew it; one last wave of glut and goofiness from Chuck Barris. The entire episode was framed as a "Chucky's Fable" segment. Chuck sat in a rocking chair, reading *The Land of Ferb and Fenwick Gotterer*, a tale with more symbolism and truth to it than any of the other ridiculous fables on the series. Larry Gotterer played Fenwick, a man who approached the effeminate king of Ferb and described an idea for a talent show with one great act after another. After early auditions failed to turn up any worthy entertainers, the king threw Fenwick in prison, only to pardon him when Fenwick suggests a talent show featuring lousy acts. The rest of the show was presented as an episode of *The Gong Show*, "from the land of Ferb, almost live!" Larry Gotterer, as Fenwick, hosted the entire show.

Chuck Barris' employees appeared on camera with one small role or another throughout the half-hour. And Chuck himself appeared as a contestant, the lead singer of a band called The Hollywood Cowboys. Chuck, leaving subtlety at the door, sang "Take This Job and Shove It," and flashed his middle finger at the camera during the chorus. Jamie Farr gonged him.

Larry Gotterer says, "I have no formal training for acting or any other type of performing. Chuck told me he needed me to go out there and suck, and that was absolutely what I did. I threw it to commercial at the wrong time. I introduced an act that wasn't ready yet. I started to announce the winner at the wrong time. And at one point after I made a mistake, I looked behind me, and Chuck was on the floor laughing at it.[5]

"What I'll never forget was that I had prepared myself for the way the audience would react to me. The studio audiences always loved Chuck. They got excited to see him. I reasoned that when I walked onstage, the audience was going to boo because they'd realize that they weren't really going to get to see the show that they had come to see. But Chuck had built up the story so well in the opening segment that the audience got

---

5   Personal interview. 24 Apr. 2019.

really into it and accepted it. When I walked out as the host of the show, they gave me a big round of applause."

At the end of the half-hour, the king suddenly announces that "he's tired of laughing," and Fenwick Gotterer's show is canceled. End of fable. End of series. Chuck concluded by introducing Gene-Gene the Dancing Machine. In one last act of defiance, "Gene" was actually Jaye P. Morgan in Gene's sizeable clothes. As the credits rolled, Chuck took a pie to the face, and Jaye P. Morgan unflinchingly licked it off him.

CHAPTER 15

Gong To The Movies

Above: No rest for the canceled...NBC may have booted the show, but The Gong Show *marched on in syndication.* AUTHOR'S COLLECTION

Chuck Barris Productions sprang into action quickly. They packaged the 495 aired episodes of the NBC *Gong Show* — only John Barbour's week was omitted — and sold the reruns for local stations to air any time during the day, while continuing to offer the nighttime *Gong Show*, which had ranked number-one with adults 18-49 according to Arbitron (the firm which gathered data for syndicated television).

Vince Longo says, "I expected the rerun package to become the next *You Bet Your Life*. Groucho Marx had put *You Bet Your Life* reruns into syndication in the early '60s and they aired late at night on stations for years and years and years. And *The Gong Show* was such a different show. It was unique. I thought our reruns would go on forever."

The 1978-79 season of *The Gong Show* was, in so many ways, going back to the basics. Chuck Barris emerged from the curtain in his tuxedo and stayed in that tuxedo for almost the whole show; maybe he'd just take off the jacket toward the end. And maybe he'd put on a wacky hat once in a while, but no dressing down and no costume changes. The graceless grin and the stiff hand-clapping mannerisms were all still in place, but he had roped himself in a little bit, allowing himself the same freedom that he had allowed his other hosts. He wasn't trying to stand out or top himself anymore. He wasn't trying to force each episode to be the best one ever. *The Gong Show* was still as *Gong Show*-y as ever — Chuck even agreed to an idea that the staff had pitched to him after an exhaustively repetitive few weeks of auditions and presented "Elvis Impersonator Night" for a nighttime show — but the process that got each episode on the air was now much less draining than it had been for the man in charge.

Gone were most of the recurring acts. The Whispers, Rhett and Scarlett, Father Ed, and Fillipe De Fox all disappeared, though they retained their actual jobs backstage. Larry didn't have any more instruments to break, and Chucky had no more fables to read. Gene-Gene the Dancing Machine and The Unknown Comic remained, possibly because they were so identified with the show at this point that Chuck viewed them as indispensable. But there was another probable reason they remained; neither of them needed any prepared material. Gene-Gene simply boogied into the commercial break without saying a word, and Murray Langston always wrote his own jokes for the Unknown Comic segments. Chuck's self-imposed obligation to pound out extra scripts for all those other sketches had gone away.

That desire to do something a little more respectable came to the forefront with a few episodes of the 1978-79 season, where Chuck attempts to modify the show's format a bit. In addition to the zany acts competing for the grand prize — which was now $716.32 — a few episodes featured guest stars performing their acts. No zany payoff, no twist, just the guest stars doing what they did. Willie Bobo and his orchestra played some tunes and stand-up comic Gary Mule Deer did his routine. But the guest stars fell by the wayside quickly and the show just stuck with funny acts,

Roping it in. Chuck still donned the hats and got rid of his jacket occasionally, but during the 1978-79 season, he was noticeably trying to recalibrate his hosting performance into something resembling normal. AUTHOR'S COLLECTION

an occasional dance, and an occasional guy in a paper bag mask telling bad jokes.

While Jefferson Beeker would never be seen on a first-run episode of *The Gong Show* again, the syndicated rerun package proved to do wonders for him. "I used to have the contracts, because I had to fill out a paper every time Chuck had me appear on camera, but I know I was on more than 100 episodes of the NBC *Gong Show*. And I got paid for each of those shows. When Chuck sold the show into reruns, I got residuals. Residuals diminish over the years with each rerun, but the way it works is, for the first few times the show is rerun, your residual is 100% of what you were originally paid. For the first few years of those reruns, I was getting a bunch of money from them, on top of the money I was still getting from NBC."

The unionized contestants that Chuck fervently pursued were entitled to residuals for the reruns too. Paul Reubens later told *Variety* that the windfall of residuals from his 14 episodes came at an unsteady time in his life. Being on *The Gong Show* so many times provided such a nice financial

The L.A. Knockers, a dance troupe. BOB BODEN COLLECTION

cushion that Reubens stopped his search for a second job and lived off his residuals while he developed material for his act at The Groundlings.

In the fall of 1978, Chuck Barris introduced his new concoction, *The $1.98 Beauty Show*, a weekly prime access time offering. Rip Taylor, the flamboyant, confetti-throwing Las Vegas comic who frequently turned up as a *Gong Show* judge, was the master of ceremonies for a weekly spectacle. (Chuck had originally offered the role of host to another *Gong* judge, Jamie Farr, who declined because he was worried it would kill his acting career.) Women of all shapes and sizes could be contestants.

Getting the show made proved to be deceptively difficult. While the phones rang non-stop from people who wanted to be on *The Gong Show*, *The Dating Game*, and *The Newlywed Game*, rounding up women who wanted to be a part of the new show was such a daunting task that, to Chuck's frustration, two days' worth of run-throughs and rehearsals had to be called off. He sent out a scathing memo to the staff, a firm reminder that yes, fun-loving Chucky Baby was the boss.

> Today, a run-thru for "$1.98 BEAUTY" was canceled because "we didn't have enough people." I guess that means that through the regular channels, not enough people came into the halls. Apparently not a lot of thought was given to irregular channels; nobody put their mind to work trying to figure out how to fill this day. Shows are too tough to sell and too tough to mold into a hit to just kiss off an audition day with the simple "we just didn't have enough people" line.
>
> Next Tuesday and Wednesday we will hold "$1.98 BEAUTY" auditions. We tape October 5 & 6 and desperately need the girls. I WANT ONE HUNDRED AND TWENTY GIRLS DURING THOSE TWO DAYS OR THE FOLLOWING PEOPLE WILL BE DOCKED TWENTY PERCENT OF THEIR SALARY:
>
> (Here, Chuck lists 10 employees whose paychecks are now on the line for this show.)
>
> All the above are responsible in one way or another for the contestants on "$1.98." Their responsibility to the show goes beyond just the one job they are responsible for. They all have heads and can put them together and find solutions.
>
> In a way, the company is responsible to each other, so if other people might have an idea that would help bring $1.98 girls in and save the above from a twenty percent cut, suggest it.

The threat worked and the staff managed to pull together an eccentric weekly beauty pageant. During the swimsuit competition, announcer Johnny Jacobs read lengthy jokes from the typewriter of Larry Spencer to introduce each of the women. They performed bizarre acts for the talent portion, with Milton DeLugg and the Band with a Thugg providing the music, and three celebrity guests serving as judges. At the end of the night, Larry Gotterer, decked out in a medieval messenger costume, complete with pink and purple tights, received the judges' final scores on a silk pillow and trotted them over to Rip Taylor.

Gotterer remembers, "When we shot the pilot, Chuck told me to do a silly, high-stepping walk. And he warned me to keep a straight face. He said if I did so much as crack a smile, he'd replace me. But I had to take the scores from the judges, put them on a silk pillow, go down three steps, and to a high-stepping walk across the stage to deliver them to Rip. I got as far as about three steps, and I tripped and fell flat on my face. But I made sure I didn't break. I stayed completely in character and just reached up and handed the envelope to Rip from the floor. Chuck found that so funny he made it a running gag on the show. I'd bungle it slightly every week."

At the end of the night, one of the lucky women was crowned The $1.98 Beauty, receiving a bouquet of carrots, $1.98 (from a change dis-

Larry Gotterer escorts a contestant onstage during the pilot of The $1.98 Beauty Show. ROBERT BURROUGHS COLLECTION

penser attached to Taylor's waist) and a tiara, as Rip Taylor gushed out a parody of Bert Parks' legendary "Miss America" theme. "You win the prize! You take the cake! You get the crown and a dollar ninety-eight!"

Hold on…joke introductions…silly acts…Milton DeLugg…three celebrity judges…a ridiculous-sounding cash prize…this show seems awfully familiar, wouldn't you say?

Gong Show writer Jaime Klein said in 2017, "I think what happened with *$1.98* was that the audience actually saw through it. It was striving to be *The Gong Show*, and even fans of *The Gong Show* looked at it and figured out that we were just trying to deliver more of the same, but in a different package. *$1.98* had this 'It's been done' aura to it through the whole thing."[1]

1. Personal interview. 8 Dec. 2016.

Above: The Clark Twins, a pair of $1.98 Beauties...although technically, that would make each of them a 99-cent beauty. Below: Christmas comes early on The $1.98 Beauty Show. ROBERT BURROUGHS COLLECTION

As far as the press was concerned, it was just Chuck handing them more ammunition. It was bad enough that *The Gong Show* existed, but now Chuck was subjecting America to two of these shows?

> *From a strictly feminist perspective, this program makes the Atlantic City spectacle seem like a National Organization for Women consciousness-raiser. Bodies of virtually every age, contour, and girth are stuffed into bikinis and trotted about like exhibits at a cattle auction. Performing talents are stretched to the most grotesque lengths; an over-ripe baton twirler named Trixie scored exactly three catches in twelve attempts. All the while, emcee Rip Taylor leeringly twirls his handlebar mustache and an off-camera announcer machine-guns sexist jokes. Introducing one buxom lass, he quips: "Maxine's wildest dream is to tie her shoes without falling over."*
>
> Newsweek, December 4, 1978

In 1979, Chuck Barris struck a deal to switch his syndicated programming from ABC-owned and operated stations to CBS owned-and-operated stations. As part of the deal, the nighttime *Gong Show* would expand to twice a week, *The $1.98 Beauty Show* would get picked up for another season, and the CBS stations agreed to air a new series (but an old idea) from Chuck Barris called *3's a Crowd*.

A full-page advertisement in *Broadcasting* Magazine's March 5, 1979 issue touted the thriving and busy schedule that Chuck Barris' company would have for the 1979-80 TV season: two new episodes of *The Gong Show* each week, *The $1.98 Beauty Show* once a week, *The Dating Game* once a week, *The Newlywed Game* five days a week, *3's a Crowd* five days a week, plus a slate of new shows in development: a revival of *How's Your Mother-in-Law?* to be hosted by Pat McCormick, a writer for Johnny Carson who frequently sat on the *Gong* panel; something called *The Divorce Game*; and a project with the working title *Chuck Barris Hour Talk Show*.

Chuck, still hearing network and syndication executives asking him for something "more traditional," the same request that had led to *The New Treasure Hunt*, obtained the rights to a '50s game show called *Dollar a Second*, in which contestants earned one dollar for every second they remained onstage, answering trivia questions and trying to complete zany physical stunts before an "outside event," a random occurrence beyond the contestant's control, stopped the game. Chuck also bought the rights to, of all shows, *Camouflage*, the game that he dubbed "the worst ever" when he had seen it as an ABC network executive, and prepared an updated version for syndication.

Chuck Barris Productions was cranking out so much content that the company switched to "four-walled production," which Danny Lies helpfully explains. "A lot of television production involves rentals. You rent the equipment, you rent the studio space. In 1979, the company was

Rip Taylor crowns this week's $1.98 Beauty. AUTHOR'S COLLECTION

doing so many things that Chuck leased a studio from Television Center Studios on Prospect Avenue. They renamed that studio 'The Chuck Barris Stage.' And it was just our studio for our shows. We bought equipment. We bought stage lights, for example, which were incredibly expensive, but since we were just doing so much work and we were doing it out of a single studio, Chuck decided it would save everyone a lot of work if he just bought equipment outright. We owned everything in there."

All the deal-making and shows in production got Wall Street's attention. The stock for Chuck Barris Productions — the one that had seemed oddly undervalued at less than $4 a share a year and a half earlier — had shot up to $19. Chuck's cut of all that money came to over $32 million.

And at the bottom of the trade magazine ad, seemingly blending in as if it's just one more project on the slate: *The Gong Show Movie*.

What?

In an unusual turn for a game show producer, Chuck Barris managed to secure a three-picture deal with Universal Studios. He already knew exactly what film he wanted to make; he wanted to adapt his novel *You and Me Babe*. He was overruled by Universal Studios and told that he had to make *The Gong Show Movie*. But even the movie executives who handed down the order didn't seem to know what that should be, and

"I oughta be in pictures." Chuck Barris assumed a total takeover of production on The Gong Show Movie. ROBERT BURROUGHS COLLECTION

neither did Chuck. He was the self-proclaimed Duke of Daytime. What did he know about making a movie? Chuck hired a more experienced hand, writer/director Robert Downey to put it together.

Danny Lies remembers, "Chuck abruptly left the offices one day and said he was going to go 'look at locations,' which I didn't understand. That was the first time I heard about the movie. Chuck had a wonderful thing he did for all his employees who had moved to California from other parts of the country — since we were so far away from our families, he would let us come to his house on Thanksgiving and we'd have dinner with him. Robert Downey was at dinner and Chuck introduced him to everybody, and that's how we figured out what was going on."

Larry Spencer says, "Linda Howard was the first to know there was going to be a movie, and then the rest of us found out. It was very strange.

It wasn't a big announcement. We found out, really, through word of mouth. The news just spread through the office that there was going to be a movie. Honestly, I remember being disappointed that Chuck didn't tell me and ask me to help write it."

Jefferson Beeker remembers, "In the earliest stages, it was going to be a documentary. There was a day when we were told to expect a film crew

The Kanakke Kuties, an angel and a stripper who performed "Delta Dawn." Would they be one of the too-hot-for-TV acts featured in The Gong Show Movie? BOB BODEN COLLECTION

backstage doing some shooting. By the time the movie was finished, it had completely changed."

The film crew, including Robert Downey, followed Chuck through a day of *Gong Show* auditions. Vince Longo, at his usual post as a Shock Troop, sat near Chuck and carried out his usual duties of watching the acts and waiting for his boss to make his decisions.

One of the auditions that day was an insult comic with a single target: Chuck. He laid into the boss as the documentary cameras rolled. It was totally off-putting. Yes, The Unknown Comic regularly hurled insults at Chuck, but it's different when the victim is in on it. And there was just a purposefully nasty vibe to everything this comic was saying. At least the Unknown Comic prioritized laughs from the audience. This comic just tore Chuck apart without a punch line in sight. Chuck had finally had enough. He got up and left the room.

Downey gleefully told his film crew, "Follow him out! Follow him out!"

The film crew followed Chuck outside...and so did the comic, who continued his assault to the dismay of Chuck, who was unable to escape the onslaught. By the end of the whole incident, the truth about the act

An absolutely terrifying balancing act, Christina & Friend. BOB BODEN COLLECTION

became known. The comic was a plant, hired by Downey to come to the audition and ambush Chuck to get an honest reaction out of him.

Vince Longo says, "The next thing you know, Robert Downey isn't directing the film anymore. Chuck is. That was the biggest mistake Chuck made. Before that, Downey had been going around the studio for the taping, watching the crew doing all their jobs, and filming the staff dealing with the contestants. I said to Yvonne, 'This might be a really good movie.' We came to work one day, and Downey was out there with a camera shooting the acts in their costumes waiting in line to audition. That was probably a great shot he got, too. I was so excited. If anything, a documentary about the show would have enhanced our popularity."

Nearly all of that went into the trash after the incident with Downey's planted audition. But even after commandeering the project, Chuck still hadn't figured out what *The Gong Show Movie* needed to be. In a 1979 interview, Chuck seems to indicate that the focus will be on the acts deemed "too bizarre for television." There was probably a sensational idea buried in there that Chuck never pursued. In the nascent stages of the home video rental market, Alan Funt produced a series of direct-to-video episodes of *Candid Camera* featuring pranks not suitable for broadcast

Although it was no longer a documentary, The Gong Show Movie *would have some embedded touches of realism; Chuck's girlfriend was played by his actual girlfriend, Robin "Red" Altman.* ROBERT BURROUGHS COLLECTION

television, mostly involving nude women. Direct-to-video episodes of *The Gong Show* featuring acts that NBC — or now, the syndication firm — said no to probably would have drawn a bit of attention.

Armed with a $3.3 million budget from Universal Pictures, Chuck moved forward. While Downey remained credited, his own account was that Chuck completely overtook the writing stages. The movie turned into an odd blend of fact and fiction, documentary and drama. Some of the footage shot at the auditions was included in the film for a scene in which Chuck Barris (the character) had to go to work for *Gong Show* auditions — though Downey's ringer wound up on the cutting room floor. Actual segments from *The Gong Show* were incorporated too.

Jefferson Beeker says, "Once it became apparent that the footage that the film crew shot of us wasn't going to be used, I had a talk with Chuck. I told him, 'You know, Chuck, if you included Scarlett and Rhett in the film, you wouldn't have to edit it, you could just leave all the dialogue intact.' And I could see from the look on his face that I got his wheels turning. Chuck had unedited video of one of our segments from the NBC show,

Chuck, Mr. Didlo, and Red in a scene from The Gong Show Movie.
ROBERT BURROUGHS COLLECTION

and he just put the unedited video into the movie. And the best part of that was, again, we were in the union. We got money for being in that movie, and we didn't do one extra day of work to get it."

Other uncensored bits made it into the film, including cursing from Father Ed, some risqué jokes from the Unknown Comic, and Jaye P. Morgan's bare breasts in the unedited footage of the day that she flashed the camera and got herself booted from NBC.

Kurt Abell, a/k/a Count Banjola, was surprised by a phone call during a vacation in the Sierra Mountains. "I was on *The Gong Show* five times and did the act exactly the same every time; hung upside-down and played the banjo in my vampire costume. When I was there for my last appearance, I talked to Chuck and said, 'It would probably be funny if I just fell at the end of the act.' And Chuck kind of laughed at that and I went out and did my act.²

"I was hunting in the Sierra Mountains, and I got a call. 'You need to come home, Chuck Barris wants you to be in a movie.' I came home and called Chuck. He says to me, 'Remember that idea you had to fall at the

"You might remember me..." That's a then-unknown Phil Hartman talking to Chuck in a scene from The Gong Show Movie. ROBERT BURROUGHS COLLECTION

end of the act? We're shooting a movie and we're going to do that.'

"I came in for a full day of shooting. Movies can be kind of a boring process, it turns out. I sat in my dressing room for six hours just waiting and waiting around. I was across the hall from Kitten Natividad, the porn star, and I was still in my early 20s, so being near her was pretty nice. She was cracking jokes non-stop and wearing this outfit that showed everything. I said, 'Don't you get tired of people staring at them?' She said, 'I paid $8,000 apiece, people had better fucking stare at them!'"

The Gong Show Movie was now a full-blown movie, with actors, and sets, and scenery, and location shooting. The works. Like Chuck's novel

2. Personal interview. 7 May 2019.

You and Me Babe, the film would arguably turn out to be more fiction than fact. He was drawing from his own sources of stress and frustration for inspiration. Chuck is bearing his soul in the film. Yeah, it's an exaggeration, but Chuck laid out his frustrations for the world to see. Sometimes, a psychotherapist recommends putting your feelings in a journal. Chuck Barris made it a screenplay.

Rip Taylor, violinist Jack Bernardi, and the Bait Brothers, in the climactic scene of The Gong Show Movie. ROBERT BURROUGHS COLLECTION

The film opens with Chuck lamenting that he must "go make a goddamn fool of himself." A beggar bothers him, not for change but for an audition. He can't make it through a parking lot without being hassled by an aspiring songwriter. The waiters at the restaurant insist on singing for him.

A television executive, the rather-blatantly named Mr. Didlo, hassles Chuck about ratings…which are good, he admits, but they'll probably be bad soon. While visiting a hospital, a nurse goes out of her way to hold Chuck up just to let him know how much she hates his stupid show, although she never misses an episode.

There's a scene in the film where two men hold Chuck at knifepoint and force him to put them on the show as contestants. A movie viewer might see that and say "Oh, come on!" But how different is that from a man barricading himself in Larry Spencer's office and starting a fire to try to get himself on the show?

And if Chuck's mindset wasn't clear enough, the soundtrack even includes two original songs written and sung by Chuck Barris: "Why Me Oh Lord?" and "Sometimes It Just Don't Pay to Get Up."

Danny Lies says, "We didn't see the forest for the trees. Early in the process, I got to see the original script that Robert Downey had written, and the original script would have worked. Chuck began to see himself as an auteur and envisioned something loftier than what something called *The Gong Show Movie* should have been. He tried too hard to make it art, he didn't enough with the storyline, and he dove way too far into woe-is-me celebrity problems, and that third thing was the biggest mistake of all. Nobody gives a shit about a millionaire's problems."

Larry Spencer says, "I was in the movie. I play the Unknown Comic! Murray Langston had a booking for a stand-up show so he couldn't film a scene, so he sent me one of his suits, and he even went to the trouble of making a bag with holes for me, and I played him in one scene."

The film's spectacular ending sees Chuck going into hiding in Morocco after booking a flight out of Los Angeles (with former *Gong Show* contestant Phil Hartman playing an aspiring hijacker at the airport). To coax him out of hiding, Mr. Didlo comes to the Sahara, along with Milton DeLugg and the Band with a Thugg, Jaye P. Morgan, Gene-Gene the Dancing Machine, The Unknown Comic, The Bait Brothers, Chuck's real-life girlfriend Robin (he called her "Red"), the UCLA marching band, Dr. Jerry the Singing Chef, The Bait Brothers, Rip Taylor, Mabel King, and some of the characters who popped up throughout the film. Chuck's daughter Della was there too.

Danny Lies says, "Chuck hired me for the movie. I was his stand-in. We filmed the desert scene in Pismo Beach and Chuck said early into shooting that day that the actors didn't seem to get what we were doing, so he sent me around to relay instructions to all of them, with a production assistant following me as if I was the director. I was really taken aback that Chuck trusted me to carry out a duty like that, and I was surprised by how professional the actors were. They took everything I was saying to heart and delivered what Chuck wanted."

Together they sang "Don't Get Up," an ironic showtune in which they encouraged Chuck not to come back, while mentioning all the ways their lives would be ruined if Chuck stayed where he was. The film ends with Chuck Barris walking onto the stage of *The Gong Show* to a standing ovation, and introducing another parade of human oddities, like conjoined twins singing "Love Will Keep Us Together," and Count Banjola. The message is clear: *The Gong Show* will go on forever.

Except that's not what happened. By the time the movie had ended production, the Chuck Barris Productions staff knew that the lights were being turned out on *The Gong Show*...and *The Dating Game*, *The*

Della Barris and a cast of thousands serenade Chuck with "Don't Get Up," the peppy showtune that ends The Gong Show Movie. *The song proved an unexpectedly poignant coda for the series.* ROBERT BURROUGHS COLLECTION

Newlywed Game, The $1.98 Beauty Show, and *3's a Crowd.* One year after the full-page touting the lengthy slate of new shows coming out of the company, Chuck Barris was shutting everything down. The shows would still be sold into reruns, so on paper the company would still exist, but 15 years after the launch of *The Dating Game*, Barris' loyal staff found themselves looking for new jobs. Reality directly contradicted the ending of the movie...It really was too much for Chuck Barris to bear, and he really did need to get away.

The show that did him in, more than anything else, was *3's a Crowd*. The show was an idea that he had pitched to ABC in 1967 under the title *Three of a Kind*. ABC wanted no part of the idea, but Chuck wasn't willing to abandon it. The premise, as it was when Chuck had pitched it to ABC, was that a man sat onstage with his wife and his secretary. All three of them were asked personal questions, and the object of the game was to determine who knew the husband better, the wife or the secretary. ABC told him that the show went too far. Normally that would mean going to one of the other networks, but an ABC executive went further than just saying no. This was such a bad idea, he advised, that Chuck shouldn't attempt it, period.

Chuck forgot about the idea. Years later, he brought aboard a new business partner, Budd Granoff, officially titled the Executive Vice President of Chuck Barris Productions. (Per Granoff's *New York Times* obituary, his key contribution was that he was the first person to clue Chuck in that he should sell the reruns of his shows once they were canceled.)

Chuck described his rejected show, and Granoff apparently saw dollar signs. He insisted to Chuck that he could sell that show. Buoyed by Granoff's confidence, Chuck shot several new pilot episodes, under the new title *3's a Crowd*.

Jim Peck, the host hired for the endeavor, called it "*The Newlywed Game* with fangs."

Among the questions played on the show:

"Name your boss' (or husband's) favorite motel or hotel."

"How many times have you had your secretary buy your wife's anniversary present?"

"What is the closest you and your secretary have ever slept?"

"How many inches of your secretary's leg have you not seen?"

Although it was still Chuck Barris' company, *The Gong Show* and now *The Gong Show Movie* still took up all of his time. He put Mike Metzger in charge of *3's a Crowd*.

Metzger remembers, "That show was a mother. Chuck never should have done it. He put me in charge of producing and writing it. I tried to get out of it, but Chuck really persuaded me.

"The pilot episode was gangbusters. The husband owned a restaurant. His wife was pretty, but she was bitchy and honestly kind of a scary woman. His secretary was a gorgeous girl. The pilot was going okay, but then we ask a question to the husband — 'What's the most unusual thing your wife ever did at home that became the talk of your office?' It's the secretary's turn to guess how the husband answered that and she says, 'The <u>one</u> time that she made edible spaghetti.' The wife reached over and started to choke her! It was a very real moment."

"The husband in that trio was the owner of a restaurant in Hollywood that the staff loved going to," explains Ellen Metzger. "After that pilot taped, we all looked at each other and said, 'We can't ever eat there again, can we?'"

Granoff sent that pilot to independent stations across the country and immediately got commitments from 90 of them, plus the CBS owned-

Jim Peck, host of the infamous 3's a Crowd. AUTHOR'S COLLECTION

and-operated stations. Could it be that ABC was wrong? Did Chuck Barris have another hit show from the unlikeliest of premises?

The series began taping in the summer. Amazingly, they had a full supply of groups of three who showed up for auditions and eagerly showed up on taping days. Mike Metzger remembers, "We cast the show very strategically from the people who auditioned. We leaned very strongly toward the most stereotypical pairing, which was a plain, dumpy wife and a gorgeous secretary."

The New Yorker, of all publications, printed a comprehensive review of *Three's A Crowd* in one issue. Writer Michael J. Arlen admitted to becoming somewhat hooked on the show and watching it every morning while he exercised on a rowing machine. But even while acknowledging that he had turned into a regular viewer of what he dubbed "Jim Peck's Cabaret," it was clear from his essay that he was viewing it the same way that a scientist in a lab coat would be viewing rats reacting to stimuli. And he astutely noticed in his review that the contestants were "definitely not thin."

As Arlen recapped, Jim Peck asked a husband about the state of his wife's sex drive. He bluntly answered, "Terrible."

When the secretary was asked about the wife's sex drive, she answered, "I can't believe it's very high."

When the wife was brought out and asked about the state of her sex drive, she answered, "I think it's been pretty good…I mean, for us." She hit her husband in the ribs when she found that he had answered "Terrible."

Another wife answered the same question by telling Jim Peck, "Frankly, we've been having a problem about that, but I don't think it has much to do with my sex drive. It's more that he couldn't — you know — carry it out."

One wife, asked to name the droopiest part of her body, said, "My face. I drink too many milkshakes."

On the other hand, the typical *Three's a Crowd* secretary had no such hang-ups about her body. Asked what fruit or vegetable her body most resembled, a secretary answered, "I'd have to say a mango…because I've got a good figure. Also, I peel easily."

Her boss didn't match the answers. Asked what fruit or vegetable his secretary's body most closely resembled, he answered, "Two grapefruits."

One husband admitted that the secretary had invited him over to her apartment to try out her new jacuzzi. Another secretary timidly described "a pretty unusual kind of club" that her boss and his wife had invited her to, but that she didn't really want to describe it.

Jim Peck, speaking to a group of game show fans in 1996, recalled that, at his request, at the end of each taping, the contestants were not permitted to leave the stage until Peck was in his dressing room with the door locked. He didn't want to deal with what he had just been a part of. Ex-contestants called the Barris staff to vent their frustrations about the fall-out from their appearances. According to Peck, *3's a Crowd* was responsible for at least 12 divorces that the staff knew of, and at least one secretary was fired.

Feminists lashed out. So many strides had been made in the previous two decades to make women accepted members of the workforce, to give them the same opportunities that men were getting. And here now was a game show that perpetuated the stereotype that the women were only there so the boss had someone to diddle. Women picketed stations that aired *3's a Crowd*, which stunned even Chuck Barris, a man who presumably should have been stun-proof at this point. People hated his other shows, but they had never picketed his other shows. He was even getting death threats. Mike Metzger says Chuck even started keeping a gun in his desk.

In 1980, The National Organization for Women gave Chuck their Grand Gobbler "award" for his work in TV. NOW said that Chuck Barris Productions "consistently demeaned women and showed overall lack of good taste."

The show that brought down Chuck Barris Productions: 3's a Crowd, dubbed "The Newlywed Game *with fangs*" by host Jim Peck. ROBERT BURROUGHS COLLECTION

Shelley Herman, the NBC page who had worked tapings of *The Gong Show*, said in 2017, "Chuck did not deserve the reputation he wound up with, especially when you saw how he ran his company behind the scenes. I was a teenager when I first appeared on *The Dating Game* and started getting to know his crew. And what I always noticed was how valued the women were in that company. The women who worked for Chuck Barris rose in the ranks, they were given important duties, and Chuck trusted them to do it. He never looked over their shoulders."

"Chuck really loved the women who worked for him," remembers Ellen Metzger, who had climbed the ladder from bandit to associate producer during her time at the company. "It's true that the producers in charge of the shows were all men, but the associate directors, script people, and the people in charge of the money were all women."

That attitude was shared by the other men at Chuck Barris Productions. Director John Dorsey maintained a list of NBC technical crew members that he preferred to work with and crew members that he particularly did not want to work with. He passed that list along to the network

Chuck admittedly made himself an easy target for anyone who wanted to accuse him of sexism, but the people who knew him and worked with him saw something much different in the way he ran his company. ROBERT BURROUGHS COLLECTION

scheduling office, and technicians were accordingly scheduled whenever *The Gong Show* had taped in the Burbank complex. Dorsey was particularly proud of a taping in 1977 where all four cameras were operated by women; he maintained that it was a first for network television production.

In the past, Chuck could easily deflect bad publicity with the rationalization that people are watching. Whatever he did in the past, it was appealing. But *3's a Crowd* didn't even have that going for it. As Mike Metzger put it, "Episodes aired and day by day, viewers fell off like dead bees. It was the worst of both worlds. People were offended and they weren't watching."

Even Chuck himself concluded later that the problem with *3's a Crowd* was that the experience of watching it lacked joy. For a viewer, there was no vicarious good feeling. The show was such that even a "win" came with bad feelings. Chuck himself noticed the way that the men conspicuously cringed when their secretaries gave correct answers and their wives didn't. When the secretaries won, there was visible anger from the wives. Occasionally fights

Chuck Barris Productions was a lot more than Chuck Barris, who's not even present for the staff photo. As the boss concentrated on The Gong Show *and* The Gong Show Movie, *the staff brought his ideas to life at every taping of every show.* ROBERT BURROUGHS COLLECTION

broke out; the women clawed at each other. Game shows are supposed to be fun. *3's a Crowd* just depressed everyone, Chuck deduced.

Vince Longo says, "We taped the show without a studio audience, and they would add laughter and applause in editing. It was so quiet in that studio. The audio man said he could hear the shutter on my camera clicking. It was strange doing a show like that with no reactions. There was no excitement."

Larry Gotterer, a question writer for *3's a Crowd*, saw the show in a very different light. "It was an interesting premise to use for a game show because the whole basic idea of the show was that you knew the wives onstage were being cheated on. But when people criticized *3's a Crowd*, they spoke of the contestants as victims, as people that we set up to be humiliated and ambushed. That criticism loses sight of the way game shows are put together. The groups of three — the husband, wife, and secretary — had to call the production office and schedule an audition, like you would to be contestants on any other show. We interviewed them. They volunteered whatever info they felt like revealing about themselves. And then we had them play a sample game. And the material we used for the sample games was similar to the material used on the show — the questions in the sample game were built around the idea that the husband was cheating on the wife. After they had been through that, they went home and waited for us to call them. They came on the show having already put themselves out there to the staff, already knowing what to anticipate from the game, and they participated. They were willing participants.[3]

"Chuck loved that about the contestants on his shows. The perception that Chuck was this sociopath who hated his contestants was absolutely the opposite of reality — Chuck admired his contestants. Chuck loved people who were so comfortable with themselves and so confident that they were willing to go on TV and put their honest selves out there."

The damage done by *3's a Crowd* was visible and swift. In Baltimore, most of the Chuck Barris shows aired in the prime access time slots, either 7:00 pm or 7:30 pm. By December, nearly all of them were yanked from those slots. Only *Newlywed* was hanging on, and even that show was clawing for survival in Baltimore. In that same month, the station in Detroit stopped airing *3's a Crowd* altogether. The story was the same all over. In his memoirs, Chuck Barris remembered *3's a Crowd* as the show that "brought down" his entire company.

Vince Longo says, "We looked at the ratings data, and it was funny. We were a hit show in New York City and almost nowhere else. And we all said 'Well, doesn't that figure?'"

Mike Metzger adds, "After 13 weeks, we were ready to cut our losses. We had commitments to every station, but they weren't happy with their ratings, obviously. Budd Granoff was offering money to every station to buy out the commitments. And the stations agreed to take the money and we wouldn't have to finish out the season. Except for one station in a major market — as I recall, it was Dallas. The station manager in Dallas liked our show and would not budge. He insisted that he was going to hold us to our contract, and he was demanding 39 weeks of *3's a Crowd* like he was contracted for. Chuck Barris and Budd Granoff announced at

---

3. Personal interview. 24 Apr. 2019.

one point — and they were completely serious — that we were going to produce 26 more weeks of *3's a Crowd* to be broadcast on only one station in Dallas. I said, 'No, please, Chuck, just let it go. I want out.'"

A few staffers recalled that the show ceased production after only 65 episodes were taped. The show may have taken an extended break while the production company tried to resolve deals with the stations, but a studio master tape exists of the last episode taped — the slate at the beginning of the episode is marked as show #160, taped on March 6, 1980. That final episode ends with two Barris staffers, faces covered, dancing across the stage with the EXIT sign from the studio. The bicycling method for syndication was still in practice, which meant the show would be slowly mailed across the country to whatever stations still wanted them. A check of TV listings across the country shows that by December 1980, only two diehards — channel 7 in Wausau, Wisconsin and channel 19 in Victoria, Texas — were still airing *3's a Crowd*.

Chuck Barris reflected on the disaster during a 1986 interview on National Public Radio. "It was the very obvious triangle. Who knows the husband better, the wife or the secretary? Again, I was looking for humor. I was looking for spontaneity, saying lines that, you know, you could never write yourself. The preparation [for] the shows [was] fine. We went through the questions. Everything seemed to work well. But something happened between the rehearsal…and the air. It became serious. It wasn't funny.[4]

"I always prided myself in the fact that anybody that I ever did my show had fun doing them. These people were not having fun. They were uneasy, ill at ease, things were emerging from the show which were very unfunny and very embarrassing. And it came across through the screen like a rainstorm. I had that uneasy feeling, and I knew I was in deep trouble that I had created something that went against all those rules."

In March 1980, Chuck Barris Productions executive vice president Budd Granoff officially announced that Chuck Barris was shutting down production on everything. *The Gong Show*, *The Dating Game*, *The Newlywed Game*, *3's a Crowd*, *The $1.98 Beauty Show*, and even *Camouflage*, which had just premiered. Publicly, Budd Granoff blamed it on an oncoming bloat in the syndication marketplace.

"Everybody wants a strip!" Granoff lamented.

---

4. Chuck Barris interview. *Fresh Air*. National Public Radio. Aired 1986. Transcript accessed 14 May 2019 at *https://www.npr.org/2017/03/23/521229061/remembering-chuck-barris-self-proclaimed-king-of-daytime-television*

"Strip shows," despite the dicey name, has a completely different meaning in syndicated television. It simply means a show that airs five times a week, Monday through Friday (so, on a programming schedule, the show's title would appear in a single strip across all five nights). In 1980, Mark Goodson-Bill Todman Productions, the big bosses of television game shows, announced that their most popular prime access time show,

Was The Gong Show *approaching its expiration date anyway?* ROBERT BURROUGHS COLLECTION

Family Feud, would expand to a strip. The dynamics of prime access time changed almost overnight. Whereas most stations had programmed "checkerboard schedules" for prime access time, meaning strictly once-a-week or twice-a-week shows, they followed suit by offering *Family Feud* or by counterprogramming it with other strips, like *PM Magazine* or *The Joker's Wild*.

If a station manager suddenly only needed one show for a time slot instead of the five previously needed, it was easy to anticipate what was about to happen. Many syndicated shows were about to drop dead. Chuck Barris Productions maintained that they were simply going to beat the rush. Granoff stated, for the record, that the company was only going to take one year off. Once all the damage was assessed by mid-season 1981, the company would regroup and start plotting its next moves.

John Hill says, "When Chuck shut down the company, it was awful. From the day I started right up to that day, we had all been having the best time of their lives. And it was the only job I ever had up to that point. I didn't know anything else."

Even if *3's a Crowd* brought down Barris' company, it's possible that *The Gong Show* was headed towards its expiration date anyway. One critic referred to *Gong* and its ilk on television as "gimmick shows" with no substance beyond whatever idea the show used to attract viewers. And once the novelty of the idea wore off, audiences would get tired of the show and drift away.

For Jaime Klein, the big problem with *The Gong Show* was that it had been on for four years. "Where do these people come from?" wasn't a question that viewers asked anymore, because it was now obvious where they came from.

Klein said in 2016, "*The Gong Show* was losing its luster anyway. In the beginning, the fun of the show was that all these bizarre acts emerged out of nowhere, and you'd ask yourself where these people crawled out from. But more people began developing acts specifically for the purpose of appearing on *The Gong Show*, and I always felt that took some of the magic out of it."

Even though *The Gong Show* was shutting down, there was still a major motion picture to think about. The opening of *The Gong Show Movie* at Grauman's Chinese Theater on Hollywood Boulevard was equal parts movie premiere, class reunion, and goodbye party. The staff of Chuck Barris Productions was there, as well as the cast of the movie, as well as the best of the worst and the worst of the best from the past four years of *Gong Show* acts. Many of Chuck's favorite contestants, particularly the ones featured in the clip montages scattered throughout the movie, were invited.

Kurt Abell says, "I was invited to attend. All the contestants were asked to show up dressed for their acts, so I came fully in character as Count Banjola. The whole experience was how I learned how carefully orchestrated movie premieres are. On television, it looks like they're waiting for the limos to arrive, and they're surprised when the stars arrive. It turns out the whole thing is orchestrated; all the limousines are piled up on one corner of the street a few blocks away, and everyone's arrival is timed to the minute.[5]

"The limousines were arranged in perfect alternation, it would be a *Gong Show* act, then a star's limo, then an act, then a star, and so on. I

---

5. Personal interview. 7 May 2019.

was the last *Gong Show* act to arrive at the premiere. They rented a hearse for me to ride instead of a limo, and then once I arrived, Chuck was the last one.

"As I walked the red carpet, Army Archerd, who was the master of ceremonies for the premiere, approached me and asked me a question.

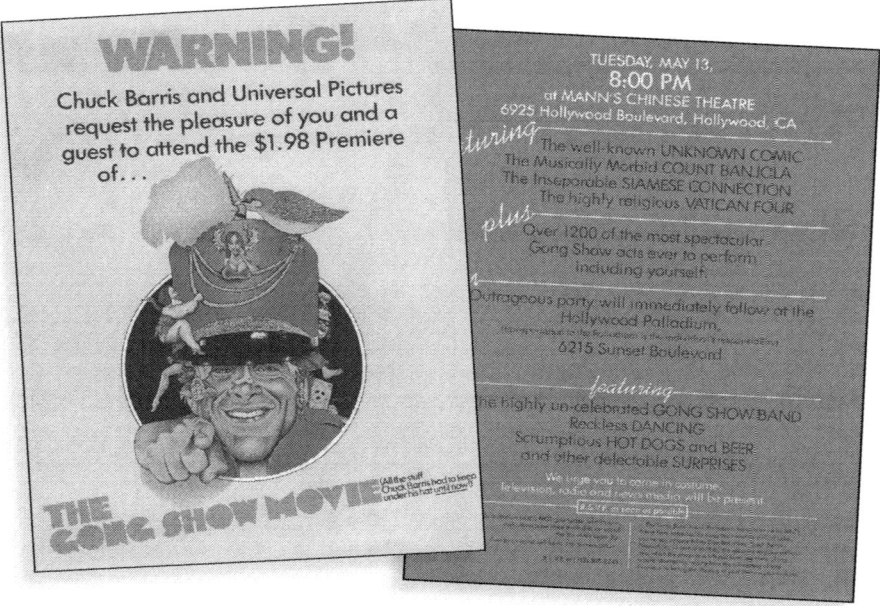

ROBERT BURROUGHS COLLECTION

And as he's asking me, I realize, I'm in character, and I've never given this character a voice. I have no idea what Count Banjola should say or sound like. If I say anything, it's not going to go well. Army finishes his question and holds the microphone toward me, and I just stare at him. He repeats the question, and I did the only thing I could do; I opened my mouth to reveal my plastic fangs, and I bit his microphone. That went over well.

"Once that part of the movie premiere is done, everyone goes inside and there's a lot of waiting around in the lobby before the movie starts. I felt an arm reach out and grab me. It's Chuck. He is hiding behind a potted plant in the lobby. I'm serious, Chuck was shy. And he pulls out some tobacco and says, 'Let's have a chew.' And I just chewed with him and talked for a while; we spat in the soil of the plant. And then once he relaxed a little bit, he emerged from behind the plant.

"At the end of the night, he gave me a gift. It was a picture taken during a *Gong Show* taping of me hanging upside-down right after finishing my act, and Chuck standing next to me, and he's smiling. There was a handwritten note on it. *This has sat on my desk for the past two years, and I'd like you to have it now. You were my favorite act.*"

The Gong Show Movie opened Memorial Day weekend in 1980 and was out of theaters entirely by June. For what few moviegoers saw it, it unintentionally served as a bookend to four years, nearly to the day, of

Chuck meets the press at the premiere of The Gong Show Movie. ROBERT BURROUGHS COLLECTION

zaniness from Chuck Barris and his gang. Chuck attended a midnight screening at a local theater after seeing a movie critic's review on a local station. The critic simply held up a garbage can lid and banged it with a hammer.

Chuck arrived at the theater. The ticket taker, who didn't seem to recognize him, tore Chuck's stub and told him pointedly, "You're not gonna like this one."

The gang's all here for the premiere of The Gong Show Movie. ROBERT BURROUGHS COLLECTION

Chuck found himself agreeing. For what was supposed to be a comedic take on his own personal issues with the source of his success, Chuck found the film coming off too seriously, and at times too angry. In his final analysis, about half the movie was fairly good. The other half, he could never fix.

"It was such a tired story," Jaye P. Morgan said in 2002. "…It was crap. It wasn't good at all."

In an odd way, the film had nothing new to say. People feel put upon by the stress of their jobs and sometimes feel they're committing too much time to their work. And the idea of a man bottoming out under stress and pressure until his friends come together at the end to show him that he was loved had been executed just slightly better by a little movie called *It's a Wonderful Life*.

To his dismay, the movie had only served to open a wound that Chuck could not close no matter what he tried. The past few years with Della had been a catastrophe. By age 16 she had already been in and out of rehab. She ran with the wrong crowd at school, and, from what Chuck could see, she may have been slowly turning into their leader. Midnight phone calls became common, and Chuck would drive in the middle of

Della and Bill Bridges in a scene from The Gong Show Movie. *Chuck would come to regret having his daughter appear in the film.* ROBERT BURROUGHS COLLECTION

the night to pick up Della from wherever she had passed out. The task usually came with forking over money for whatever had been damaged or stolen.

Early in 1980, he made what he later declared the biggest mistake he ever made as a father. Della showed up one day, shortly after Chuck started showing up for work again, and told her dad that she wanted to drop out of high school and leave Los Angeles.

Chuck, later in his life, replayed the memory over and over, realizing that Della wasn't 100% committed to what she was saying. In his book *Della*, Chuck suspected that Della was hoping for him to step up and tell her no. That he was going to force her to stay in school, and that he'd support her while she tried to kick her drug habit.

Instead, Chuck offered to set up a trust fund for her to support herself. He bought back $1.5 million worth of Chuck Barris Productions common stock and prepared to send Della on her way to wherever she was planning on going.

Despite all that strife, when Chuck wrote *The Gong Show Movie*, he wrote a part for Della, and she shot it. Chuck held an advance screening of the film in an auditorium on the campus of the University of Southern California. He and Della went together to watch the movie with 1500 other viewers, mostly students. For reasons that he could never make sense of, the moment Della appeared on the screen, the audience booed. Della ran out of the theater. Chuck followed her out and finally found her sitting next to a statue, sobbing.

Eventually, Chuck and Della went to therapy together. In his book *Della*, Chuck remembered the conversation they had as they walked toward the psychiatrist's office. At one point, Della asked him, "Am I really a walking nightmare?"

During the session, the psychiatrist asked Chuck to step in the hallway so he could talk to Della alone. She pulled out a baby bottle and sucked on it the entire time they talked. Once it was over, the psychiatrist talked to Chuck and gave his report: "You have a bipolar, drug-addicted tiger by the tail."

A brief time later, Della arrived at Chuck's house to get some things out of her bedroom. She didn't realize that after Chuck had allowed her to move into her own apartment, he put her belongings into storage. Della's bedroom was now a guest room, without any sign that she had ever occupied it. She was so upset, she never set foot in the house again.

Chuck, needing to decompress, went home to Philadelphia and treated himself to a hockey game. "…I went down to Philadelphia to see the

Rangers play the Flyers. I was sitting with [Flyers owner] Ed Snider, hoping this game would get my mind off things. In the middle of the game, Ed puts up on the scoreboard 'GIVE A BIG SPECTRUM WELCOME TO THE HOST OF THE GONG SHOW, CHUCK BARRIS.' And 16,000 people start booing. I couldn't believe it. I was shattered."

At the end of 1980, Chuck Barris' foray into film had bombed, his television company had shut down, and his daughter had disappeared. Taking stock of his life, it's hard not to think about a line that Chuck utters in *The Gong Show Movie* about the public's perception of him.

"They think I'm a clown."

CHAPTER 16

Respect

Above: Chuck in his office in the early 1980s. AUTHOR'S COLLECTION

Life after *Gong* wasn't so different for Jefferson Beeker. He had been a day player in wardrobe before and during *The Gong Show*. And one day in the early 1980s, he was hired to do some work for *The Tonight Show Starring Johnny Carson*.

As he adjusted Carson's outfit, he got the sense that the host was watching him. Not necessarily examining his fingers and watching the work he was doing. Carson was studying his face.

Carson finally asked him, "Were you Scarlett O'Hara?"

Carson also took a strong liking to Gene Patton. Patton had a natural charisma that appealed to Carson as much as it appealed to Chuck Barris, and he popped up in skits on Carson's show as Papa Doc and Idi Amin. He was no actor, which, of course, was part of his charm. He portrayed the ruthless dictators with a big grin and seemed to be perpetually suppressing a laugh. On April Fool's Day 1986, Johnny even sent him onstage after Ed McMahon's traditional "Heeeeeere's Johnny!"

Though Chuck Barris Productions had shut down, the company still had money flowing. Part of this was because of the low-tech operation that syndicated TV still was in 1980. While modern syndicated TV is done via satellite, with the shows being beamed for stations to receive and record them, and then air them whenever they wanted, syndicated TV back then was done through a process called bicycling; a package containing a tape of an episode and a list of TV stations went in the mail. Once a station aired the episode, they checked themselves off the list and sent it to the next station on the list. This was an incredibly slow process, obviously. *The Newlywed Game*, which had started producing five episodes per week for syndication in 1977, had, by the fall of 1980, produced so many episodes that there was a massive backlog. Even though the company was taking the year off, many cities were still going to be seeing new episodes of that show, and the revenue would still be coming into the production company.

And independent stations across the country, who didn't have Johnny Carson or *Nightline* or *The CBS Late Movie* anchoring their programming after 11:00 pm, quickly discovered how perfectly suited reruns of *The Gong Show* were for a late-night slot.

Lynnette Karnes says, "When Chuck did the Curtain Closer gags and filler skits using his staff, he did an amazing thing. He registered all of us with AFTRA, and he made our membership fees. So, when Chuck sold *The Gong Show* reruns, all of us got these checks in the mail. It's really nice at first. The first time an episode is rerun, your royalty is 100%. But the next time that episode is rerun, it's 75%, then 50%, and it keeps diminishing.

So initially I was getting checks in the mail for $250 or so apiece, and by the end of the 1980s, my mail always had a thick pile of paychecks, but they added up to five bucks."

Chuck also diversified his income quite a bit, though he rarely ever mentioned his other business interests. Few people realized, for example, that for a time, Chuck Barris Productions owned 27% of Ply Gem, a

Acts like The Buffalo Chips could live forever through reruns. BOB BODEN COLLECTION

manufacturer of exterior building materials. Baseball fans were surprised when Chuck's name popped up in the sports page in 1981; he was negotiating to buy the Philadelphia Phillies.

Chuck Barris Productions also benefited from some enterprising work by Danny Lies and Jimmy Commore. Lies says, "Chuck got a long-term lease on a studio, and bought all this equipment in 1979 for use on all his shows, and then in 1980 he totally shuts down production on everything, so the studio's not being used, and the equipment isn't being used. Jimmy and I began renting out everything. *That's Incredible!* used our studio and paid rent for it. We rented out the lights we had in there for different shows. We made so much money that we became a subsidiary of Chuck Barris Productions. We were listed as an asset."

As promised, in 1981, Chuck Barris Productions regrouped, with two shows ready to go that fall. One was a revival of their 1970s hit

Treasure Hunt. The other was a wildly different offering, a talk show called *Leave It to the Women*.

Leave It to the Women was an updated version of an old radio show, *Leave It to the Girls*, that Chuck had purchased the rights to. Host Stephanie Edwards and a panel of four women would welcome noteworthy and occasionally notorious guests to discuss women's issues. Critics seemingly

In television, there's life after death. The Gong Show *reruns kept the show in the public consciousness into the 1980s.* AUTHOR'S COLLECTION

missed Chuck while he was gone because they gleefully trashed *Leave It to the Women*, even while writing reviews that clearly exposed that they hadn't bothered paying full attention to it. Critic Howard Rosenberg explicitly referred to it as a game show in his scorching assessment, in which he said the show set women's equality back so far that the panelists should lose their rights to vote.

It would be curious to know what Rosenburg's tune would have been if he had known how little Chuck had to do with the show. The credited executive producer for *Leave It to the Women* was Linda Howard, Chuck's "general" that he had depended on whenever he found his own opinion wavering about potential acts on *The Gong Show*. Rosenburg stamped his feet and bellyached about how harmful the show was to the women's movement, unaware that Chuck had turned over the keys to a woman and let her run a show aimed at other women.

Chuck's willful absence was a sign of change for himself and the company. After an ugly falling-out with Barris that led to *The New Treasure Hunt* ending production in 1977 despite strong ratings, host Geoff Edwards returned to the company to host a reincarnation of *Treasure Hunt* for the 1981-82 season. He returned entirely because he was told Chuck wasn't going to be involved with the show. Mike Metzger was promoted to executive producer. Chuck was so uninvolved that it wasn't even his signature on the giant prop check awarded to big winners on *Treasure Hunt*, it was Metzger's.

The company was very publicly trying to reinvent itself into something a little more crowd-pleasing. *Treasure Hunt* and *Dollar a Second* (which Barris was still trying to sell in syndication, with Arte Johnson hosting) were closer to typical, traditional fare, even if they had a Barris bend to them — *Treasure Hunt* still wove sketch comedy into the show, and an adult male contestant in the *Dollar a Second* pilot wore a Buster Brown suit, complete with a curly blonde wig.

The project that Chuck was most excited about was one that he announced in September 1980: *The Million-Dollar Talent Search*. It would be *The Gong Show* again, except devoid of almost everything that made it *The Gong Show*.

In a way, it was going to revert the show back to the basic premise Chuck Barris started with before he ever went to that hockey game with Chris Bearde. *The Million-Dollar Talent Search* was going to be a genuine talent show. No off-key singers welcome. No goofy novelty acts or censor-testing gags. Just an array of genuinely gifted performers, amateurs and professionals alike. The judges would give them a score based on their ability and not necessarily based on a joke they wanted to make about the performance. No gong. There would be 26 programs in a season. Each of the winners of the first 25 programs would receive $10,000 in cash. For week 26, a massive season-ending event, all of the winners would be brought back, with the judges selecting an overall winner to receive a guaranteed $1 million worth of professional bookings at nightclubs and other venues.

Budd Granoff explained the need for the show to the Associated Press. "We saw so much exceptional talent during our auditions for *The Gong Show* that we couldn't put on."

This seemed like an odd explanation. *The Gong Show* never outright rejected talent for being "too good." A number of gifted performers popped up over the past four years, they were just in the minority overall.

More likely, the true need for the show seeped up when Chuck Barris told AP about his own role as host on the new show. "I'll have a tuxedo, combed hair, and black tie — and a warm, friendly, and ingratiating manner...I feel if we do this in the old style of Ed Sullivan, let them perform without a lot of hullaballoo or window dressing, we will succeed. There's also the competition aspect. People will be rooting for a particular act."

The crew of Chuck Barris Productions on the set of the 1981 reboot of Treasure Hunt. *Conspicuous by his absence: Chuck Barris.* PHOTO BY VINCE LONGO, COURTESY OF MIKE METZGER

It was antithetical to everything Chuck Barris had done before. The man who once told *TV Guide* that he refused to offer large prizes on *The Newlywed Game* because he didn't want contestants trying to kill each other was now touting a massive cash prize plus a life-changing business opportunity and emphasizing the sense of competition between the contestants. All while promising that he'd wear his tuxedo through the whole show, with nary a cowboy hat or pair of blue jeans in sight. A pilot was shot on November 19, 1980, at Caesar's Palace. A trade magazine ad enticing local stations to buy the show included a photo of Chuck in a perfectly-fit satin tuxedo, with his thick curly hair as neatly combed as it was capable of being. But not enough stations signed on, and *The Million-Dollar Talent Search* never happened.

Chuck then set his sights higher than syndicated television. With syndication proving more volatile to him than it used to be (he couldn't get the new *Dollar a Second* on the air, and the rebooted *Treasure Hunt* flopped so fast that production shut down after only 17 weeks were produced), he applied for a low-power broadcasting license from the FCC and started putting in bids to buy 28 stations across the country to launch a mini-network of sorts, called Channel America. The goal, one writer suspected, was to sidestep the hassle of selling shows altogether. Channel America would simply be a platform to air whatever Chuck Barris Productions were to come next. The project would never get off the ground.

It seemed that Chuck was trying to position himself as a new Dick Clark. He was trying to present himself as a neutral but crowd-pleasing master of ceremonies on the unsuccessful *Talent Search* project while trying to launch, or relaunch, a business empire. Station managers just weren't interested in doing business with him.

A trade ad for Million Dollar Talent Show, *Chuck Barris' attempt to "go legitimate."* AUTHOR'S COLLECTION

In the fall of 1983, producer Al Masini introduced a new weekly syndicated series titled *Star Search*, hosted by Ed McMahon. Each week, performers would compete against each other in several categories, with judges scoring their acts. Champions were crowned at the end of the show and awarded $10,000 apiece. At the end of the season, a championship show would crown grand champions in each category, who would receive $100,000 plus contracts for professional work. The idea was similar in many ways to Chuck Barris' *Million Dollar Talent Search*. To be clear, this isn't a statement of accusation or indictment toward Masini. The point to be made here is about perception. In the early 1980s, two TV producers reached out to local stations about syndicating a weekly talent show that would award big money and create new stars. Which one will get his idea on the air?

The one who broke out in the early 1980s with attractive and respected programs like *Solid Gold* and *Entertainment Tonight?*

The one dubbed "king of schlock" who was in the entertainment section of the paper once a week because one critic or another needed to get on a soapbox about cruelty on television?

Success begets respect, and with respect comes further success. Chuck

Rip Taylor, host of the never-aired Original Vaudeville Show *pilot, one of Chuck's attempts to revive* The Gong Show *without making it* The Gong Show. BOB BODEN COLLECTION

had success, but when he didn't get the respect along with it, he would only get a finite amount of that success. Taking time off from his company and relieving himself of the most stressful duties hadn't been completely helpful to Chuck's mood. If anything, he had started taking critics' barbs to heart. He admitted to one writer that he was still haunted by one biting review of *The Gong Show Movie*. "Life is cruel enough without Chuck Barris constantly around."

Chuck and his crew took another crack at reinventing the gong, mounting another pilot titled *The Original Vaudeville Show*. Chuck recused himself from the role of host, deferring to Rip Taylor. The set was designed to resemble an old theater, very much like the ones run by Roxy and Major Bowes. The acts were hula hoop virtuosos, ventriloquists, musicians; everything befitting a modernized take on an early 20th century entertainment form. The audience applause meter determined the winner. The winner had the option of accepting $1,000 or a mystery prize.

It was as if Chuck Barris was daring his potential critics to find fault. They loved to hate his performance as host, so he stayed away this time. It was a legitimate talent show, just like *Star Search*. The audience voted on the winner, just like they did for Ted Mack and Major Bowes. All for naught; *The Original Vaudeville Show* didn't drum up enough interest to make it on the air anywhere.

Chuck, who at one point lamented that the only way he was going to earn respect was to "take a bullet for the President," harnessed that frustration and turned it into yet another book. He retreated to the Wyndham Hotel in Manhattan for an extended stay. Every few days, he would call his secretary in Los Angeles and rattle off a list of things he wanted mailed to the hotel from his home. Ultimately, he moved cross-country via Federal Express. He expected to spend a month drafting the book, but instead, it took the better part of two years. Like Chuck's earlier effort at the typewriter, *You and Me Babe*, it was rooted in reality. But that reality would be woven into a new story that amused, bemused, and bewildered readers who couldn't be completely certain what Chuck was expecting them to believe.

The book was titled *Confessions of a Dangerous Mind*. (One critic zeroed in on the likely source of inspiration for the title, a documentary titled *Frank Terpil: Confessions of a Dangerous Man*, about an ex-CIA agent who had been indicted for selling arms to Colonel Khadafy and eventually secured a job as an advisor to Idi Amin.) Subtitled *An Unauthorized Autobiography*, the book was Chuck's stunning account of his own life: During a spell of unemployment (Chuck seemed to pinpoint it to the period after he had quit ABC and was trying to get his own production company off the ground), he answered a Help Wanted ad that turned out to come from the Central Intelligence Agency.

Chuck allegedly divided his time between his CIA duties and his television company until his direct supervisor, a man named Jim Byrd, suggested that there was a way to combine the two. Rather than send the matched-up couples from *The Dating Game* to upscale restaurants and nightclubs around Los Angeles, Byrd told Chuck to send the couples to exotic locations in Europe and Asia…and in case anyone objects to the notion of sending two complete strangers off to a romantic vacation in a foreign country, emphasize on the show that the vacations would be chaperoned. Chuck's staffers could chaperone them. And if he ever came up short-handed, Chuck himself could chaperone them.

The Dating Game, as Chuck described it, was the perfect cover for his assignments. When he chaperoned a couple, it was because they had won a trip to wherever he needed to carry out his next hit. His CIA work continued all the way through the rest of his years as a television kingpin until he finally had a nervous breakdown during a *Gong Show* taping. Shortly after, he killed Jim Byrd and another operative that he suspected of being a mole, and got out of the CIA.

Autobiography? Confession? Novel? Delusion? Many readers and critics weren't sure what they were reading when they picked up Chuck's book, Confessions of a Dangerous Mind.
AUTHOR'S COLLECTION

Anybody who met Chuck Barris could be 99% sure that this was all a crock, but what mystified the most knowledgeable readers was the amount of effort Chuck put in to make this plausible. He incorporated actual events from his life — the book gives a very real first-person account of the creation of *The Dating Game*, *The Gong Show*, and several other key milestones from Chuck's career, always including real names and job titles of the executives and stagehands he crossed paths with along the way. And for the remainder of his life, Chuck remained firmly coy, pledging never to reveal how much of the book was true, even though a decade later, he released another autobiography, *The Game Show King*, which contradicted *Confessions of a Dangerous Mind* quite a bit.

Reporters and book critics got right to work dissecting the tale, because either way it was a curious story: either a multimillionaire television producer was moonlighting as a hired gun for the federal government, or the television industry's figurehead for junk was spinning a lurid fantasy of carrying out murders. Columnist Karl Vick was quick to point out the most obvious sign that the story was fabricated: It got published. The CIA, as Vick noted, had gone to court to prevent former employee Frank Snepp from publishing a book about his experiences. That Chuck Barris' book went to press without a peep from the federal government was more than enough proof that there was no truth to the tale.

Writer Daniel Paisner investigated the tale in 1984, shortly after the book's release, and reported, with some surprise, that Chuck evidently had applied for a job at the CIA in 1959, shortly before he would have landed at *American Bandstand*. At the very least, Chuck had made it far enough in the process that he was granted access to restricted areas before he instead opted for a job at the American Broadcasting Company.

When Paisner talked to Chuck himself, Chuck let his guard down enough to reveal his mindset when he started writing the book. "I had produced more commercial television shows at one time or another than any other studio in America, and was duly castigated for it by critics the world over…I wondered, 'What if I had gone into the CIA instead and killed people?' I probably would have been given medals and presidential citations. Instead, I chose to entertain people and was nailed to more crosses than I could carry on my back."

Confessions of a Dangerous Mind is the fantasy of a man in the full throes of midlife crisis, a man who was hurting badly at the time as the success that he was awash in for more than a decade suddenly began eluding him. And so, Chuck sat down, replayed events in his life in his head, asked himself, "What if…?" and began typing.

Mike Metzger says, "I was really surprised at how people latched onto this story. For years, people would find out I used to work for Chuck Barris, and all they would say to me was, 'So…was he?' They wouldn't even ask the full question; they would just ask 'Was he?'[1]

"I began to play along with it. It was kind of fun. I would tell people, 'You know, it's weird, Chuck never came in on Thursdays. I noticed that after a while. And on Friday you'd ask where he was, and he'd always say, 'I was in Belgium, pitching a show.' And people say, 'Wait, Belgium? The book mentions a hit he carried out in Belgium!' And I'd say 'Well, I mean, I don't know anything for sure.' I'd describe a really elaborate gun that I had seen in Chuck's office, and they'd get worked up over that. I told Chuck later that I was backing up his story, and he got the biggest kick out of that."

---

1   Personal interview. 13 May 2019.

John Hill adds, "There's one thing in that story that gives it away, if you worked for the man. Allegedly, Chuck carried out the hits while chaperoning people for *The Dating Game*. Chuck never, ever, ever chaperoned the dates. That was a job that he gave to new hires."

As his attempts at reinvention stalled, Chuck looked at the ratings data for all the stations that had been airing reruns of *The Dating Game, The Newlywed Game,* and *The Gong Show* since 1980. Amazingly, in some cities, the reruns were getting higher ratings than they had when they were new. Chuck didn't need a sign from above, he just needed good business sense. He was going back to what worked for him.

In 1985, Chuck Barris Productions, now renamed Barris Industries, came back with a vengeance. A special week of *The Newlywed Game*, hosted by *Dating Game* host Jim Lange, popped up on ABC for the week of Valentine's Day 1984 and paved the way for a new syndicated version for launch in the fall of 1985, with Bob Eubanks returning as host. That same year, Chuck put on his tuxedo one last time to host an ABC prime time special, *Anything for a Laugh*, touted as a 20th anniversary celebration of his production company, with clips from all of his hit shows, interspersed by in-studio segments in which Chuck, still clapping his hands and still smiling nervously, welcomed some special guests. It was both a goodbye and a hello. Chuck Barris looked back on a prosperous 20 years of innovation and entertainment, then walked off stage, changed back into his blue jeans, and started all over again.

CHAPTER 17

The Gong Shall Rise Again

Above: The honorable Judge Chuck Barris, on the unsold pilot Comedy Courtroom. ROBERT BURROUGHS COLLECTION

It was the 1980s. Times changed. But bachelors and bachelorettes still flirted, and newlyweds still bickered. Chuck Barris could still deliver an entertaining dose of reality that ended with a prize being awarded. In 1985, *The New Newlywed Game* went on the air, five days a week, with a flashy new set, a funky new theme, but nothing new at the core. *The All-New Dating Game* (originally to be titled *We Love The Dating Game* until good sense prevailed) followed it in 1986, again very, very un-finagled-with.

Chuck even allowed himself a shot at a comeback, a pilot called *Comedy Courtroom*. Two contestants — neither of whom, the show emphasized, were experienced actors — were assigned the roles of opposing litigants and given the details of an actual small claims court case. The two contestants then had to improvise their way through a court hearing, overseen by Judge Chuck Barris, who made his entrance wearing a barrister's wig. He had a supporting cast, too. Rhonda Shear, a former beauty queen who had been a contestant on *The Gong Show* and *The $1.98 Beauty Show*, was the courtroom's buxom bailiff. Larry Gotterer wore a pair of coke-bottle glasses and played the near-sighted stenographer. Milton DeLugg and the Band with a Thugg even got back together to supply live music. NBC's verdict, however, was a hard pass. *Comedy Courtroom* never aired.

Chuck, understandably, maintained a special place in his heart for *The Gong Show* and would not let the idea die. It didn't even have to be *The Gong Show*, he just wanted a talent show, as evidenced by *Million Dollar Talent Search* and *The Original Vaudeville Show*. Chuck called Mike Metzger one day and asked him to do some research on the idea he had for a new twist.

Metzger says, "Chuck asked me to call insurance agencies and get estimates on a policy. He wanted to have a trap door that spanned the length of the stage, and that would be the new twist on the show. Instead of a gong, contestants would be disposed of through a trap door. I called Chuck a week later. The absolute best estimate I got was an insurance policy that would cost him $20 million, and he said, 'Aww, forget it.'

And then, in a surprising move, Chuck Barris departed from his own company. On March 26, 1987, Chuck Barris sold off his remaining shares — 763,546 of them — to friend and fellow producer Burt Sugarman. It was quiet and somewhat sudden. The legend was that the deal in no way resembled a business meeting. The story passed around the water cooler among Chuck's employees was that he drove to Sugarman's house one night, knocked on the door, and asked Sugarman if he wanted

to buy a company. It had been a little more than 22 years since Chuck had taken the biggest risk of his life by mounting his own production company, and now, he just walked away.

John Hill says, "Chuck pulled me into his office and personally apologized to me for what he was doing. He felt guilty, not so much about leaving, but that he was leaving all of us. I told him 'You gotta do what

By 1987, Chuck concluded that Barris Industries didn't need Chuck Barris anymore. Without the boss around, the company still thrived with The All-New Dating Game *(above left),* The New Newlywed Game *(below left), and reruns of* The Gong Show *(above), which were a big hit on the USA cable channel.* AUTHOR'S COLLECTION, ROBERT BURROUGHS COLLECTION

you gotta do, Chuck.' I understood it. Chuck made me an offer to keep me employed as his personal go-fer, but by that point, I had built a nice line-up of shows I had worked on, for his company and for other companies. And I told him that. I said I appreciated the job offer, but I didn't want the job because Chuck had already given me a career and I wanted to stay with that. Chuck said he understood, but he asked if he could still call me occasionally if he wanted a car. I said of course. And for the next few years, every couple of months, I'd get a phone call, and Chuck would tell me what kind of car he wanted, and I'd go find it for him, and he'd pay me for doing the work for him."

Chuck left the country and moved into a new home in Saint-Tropez on the French Riviera. He explained, "I was living a boyhood dream pretending to be Hemingway and Fitzgerald, writing the Great American Novel in Saint-Tropez. Della thought I was nuts to sell my company and move to Europe. She didn't know it had always been my dream to write in the little fishing village of Saint-Tropez. My dear friend Larry Collins wrote there, and I had always looked upon his life with longing. I had promised myself I would do the same thing someday. I saw the opportunity and I took it."

Larry Collins' secretary was Robin Barnes, an American who lived with Collins while working for him. She says, "We were in Ramatuelle, which is a small town near Saint-Tropez. Most people just refer to it as Saint-Tropez, but Ramatuelle is so remote, it doesn't even have a main drag. We lived on a hill at least 20 minutes from anyplace you would need to get to. Chuck and his wife rented the house down the hill from us. It had belonged to Larry's partner. I think it says something that Chuck didn't live on a yacht or in a fancy hotel. He was in this isolated area where it was quiet and where he could never be recognized. There are a lot of wealthy people and famous people who relocate to that area, and the appeal for them is that they have no identity. No one knows who they are.

"What I remember about Chuck is how consistently loveable he was. Such a nice guy. He wasn't 'on' when I knew him. I don't remember him being funny. He was never a comedian. But just a genuinely nice man. We'd spend a lot of time together; me, Chuck, his wife. We hung out by the pool, we'd drive into town, and go to the beach. Chuck didn't talk about his work at all. We never had conversations about game shows. He liked talking about books."

Without Chuck, the company's first order of business seemed to be the next logical step, after the revivals of *Newlywed Game* and *Dating Game*. Funnily, after seven years of Chuck's efforts at tinkering and reinventing, the company simply decided to stick with what was already working. Barris Industries offered a new *Gong Show* for first-run syndication. The new host was disc jockey "True" Don Bleu.

Chris Bearde returned to produce the new version. And a careful perusal of the closing credits reveals something surprising. Chuck rounded up many of his old troops for the revivals of his other shows; Walt Case, John Dorsey, Jimmy Comorre, Linda Howard, John Hill, Larry Gotterer, Rick Kates, Milton DeLugg, and even Patty Enright, who handled cue cards, all show up in the credits for *The New Newlywed Game* and *The All-New*

Dating Game. Other than Chris Bearde, only Shock Troop Johnny Michel appears in the credits for both the '70s and '80s *Gong Shows*.

It was a distinctly '80s rendering of Chuck's creation, with a pastel set and lighting. The show's theme was a rap ("We're not bad/we're not tough/but if you just ain't good enough/we're gonna gong you!") Banging the gong triggered smoke and pyrotechnics.

"True" Don Bleu, the host of the 1988 Gong Show. AUTHOR'S COLLECTION

One bit of reinvention that the new crew attempted was giving the judges a task to complete before they could bang the gong. For one episode, a pro wrestler held the gong mallets in his hands. The judges had to overpower him to get the mallet and bang the gong. For another show, a single mallet was hidden at the bottom of a trash can filled with rubber balls. The judges had to run across the stage and spill the contents, then run back to bang the gong.

Jamie Farr wasn't invited back to the judges' dais for the new version, but he found the revised role of the judges strange. He opines, "This was such a mistake. They made the judges an equal part of the show, and they made the judges as zany as the contestants. *The Gong Show* doesn't work when nobody is a straight man."

A few attempts were made to recapture the magic. Gene-Gene the Dancing Machine made a single return engagement to close out an episode. The Unknown Comic returned for a week as a judge. And even this version had a few pre-fame performances to its credit. Drag queen RuPaul and rock band Green Jelly were contestants.

Don Bleu as host was…well, actually he was good. He was polished on camera, well-spoken, smooth. It feels odd, then, to say that was a problem. It brought to light what a unique charisma Chuck possessed when he reluctantly stepped into the role over a decade earlier. In any other show, Don Bleu might have seemed like a fine host. On *The Gong*

Show, being good at the job rendered him as square a peg as Gary Owens had proven to be.

It just wasn't the same. Yes, it was zany; yes, the acts were a blend of "Good" and "Good lord!" and the celebrity judges got into the spirit. But paint on the ceiling doesn't mean it's Michelangelo. It just didn't feel like *The Gong Show*. And it was gone after one season.

The Gong Show *with host Don Bleu, which came and went during the 1988-89 season.* AUTHOR'S COLLECTION

A few years later, Burt Sugarman sold off Barris' company to Sony, which was getting a new cable channel off the ground: all game shows, all day long. Game Show Network launched in 1994, with reruns of most of Chuck Barris' shows turning up at one point or another. They even mounted their own version of *The Gong Show* in 1998, titled *Extreme Gong*, a nightly live broadcast in which home viewers called a special phone number to vote on whether to sound the gong. Like the '80s reboot, it only lasted one year. Remarkably, the channel revived *3's A Crowd* too, and seemed to figure out a way to make it palatable; on Game Show Network's incarnation, it was a contestant along with their current mate and their ex, which came off much more lighthearted.

Chuck Barris enjoyed a mostly stress-free life in France. He went to the same coffee shop every morning, took a walk in the park, and enjoyed long, long stretches of time where nobody recognized him, attempted to sing for him, critiqued his shows, or fretted to him about ratings and offensive content. It was a perfect life for him after 20 years of drowning himself in the work of running an empire.

Ellen Metzger remembers, "When Chuck turned 60, Mike and I were living in Spain. Chuck sent for us for his birthday party. We flew to France and then a helicopter took us to Chuck's home. Gorgeous house. He had a speedboat too. And the party was wonderful. Chuck's wife looked after our daughter for the evening, and he hired three bands to play music. Chuck gave everybody who attended a gift. All the women got a silver whistle from Tiffany's. And it wasn't so much in the gift as it was the presentation. It wasn't in a box or taped under your seat. Chuck went to every woman one by one, pulled each of us aside, and personally gave each of us the whistle. I still have it."

In truth, the extravagant party wasn't really Chuck's thing, even when it was in his honor. Lavish parties were a favorite indulgence of his second wife. They had met when she worked for him, and as he tells the tale in his book *Della*, she frequently traveled to Rome, Paris, and London for lavish shopping trips.

Chuck had a stormy relationship with Della, who was unrecognizable after spending a significant amount of Daddy's money on plastic surgery. She had never liked her face and underwent procedure after procedure until she had a "California look." They still spoke on the phone occasionally, and Della made it known what a low opinion she had of her father's wife. She told her father repeatedly that the frequent "shopping trips" were cover stories for secret boyfriends, a warning Chuck ignored until he found himself getting divorced for the second time, in 1995.

Chuck opted to move once more, this time to New York, hoping to repair his relationship with Della once and for all. The phone conversations since 1980 had been infrequent and argumentative. Much of what he knew about her life came secondhand from friends who were willing to tell him what they knew.

When Chuck returned to America, he was disturbed by the sight of his daughter, unhealthily thin and unrecognizable due to all the surgeries. But they were together, and they both wanted to clear the air, thick and polluted as it had become. Chuck apologized to Della for being such an inept father. Della opened up about how bad her drug addiction had truly become. She had been a prostitute (with photo evidence, which alarmed her father), and she now had HIV. Chuck dedicated himself to spending as much time with her as possible. They'd go to dinner and movies periodically. The relationship was still a contentious one. Della resented Chuck using "good drug money" to buy food for her when she didn't even have an appetite anymore.

On July 28, 1998, Della Barris died of a drug overdose at age 36. It was ruled a suicide, though Chuck maintained that it was an accident and, as grim as those final months were, when she complained that she preferred drugs to food, he believed that, deep down, she really did want to keep living.

Two years later, Chuck would be diagnosed with lung cancer. He had major surgery to remove part of one lung. The surgery was successful, but two days later, a staph infection put him in intensive care for a month.

Chuck Barris fought and won. He survived the cancer and the infection. He married for the third and final time — the marriage lasted the rest of his life. It wasn't just that he had beaten two brushes with death. In other ways, Chuck Barris was about to be revived.

The new millennium brought forth a new wave and a new genre: Reality TV. They were competitions, with winners and prizes and hosts, and yet, they weren't exactly game shows. Reality shows generally had an episodic feel to them, with a "story" of sorts guiding the season. Viewers got to know the contestants more deeply; their quirks, what made them tick. Elements of the competition were presented in the form of a documentary.

A British show called *Pop Idol* was adapted for American television and rechristened *American Idol*. Premiering on Fox in 2002, the show featured judges Simon Cowell, Paula Abdul, and Randy Jackson judging singers week after week, with viewers voting for their favorites. One by one, a singer was eliminated until only one remained and was crowned *American Idol*. There was a glitzy element to the show. The semi-finalists performed in front of a frenzied audience on live broadcasts. But before all that, each season began with the audition rounds. Anybody could audition for *American Idol*. And the one who couldn't carry a tune in a paper bag were bluntly told so. Usually by Simon Cowell.

"This has been one of the worst days we've ever had, and you are probably the worst we've had today."

"You don't sound like The Eagles…maybe an eagle, though."

"You sing like a three-year-old girl, you look like LaToya Jackson, and you've got a beard. The whole thing was too weird."

"Coaching you to sing would be like coaching a one-legged man to win a 100-meter sprint."

THE UNCENSORED HISTORY OF TELEVISION'S WILDEST TALENT SHOW   353

Cowell would go on to mount a similar series, *The X Factor*, which would similarly cross the ocean from the UK to the USA. The auditions were there, and so were the teardowns of the vocalists who didn't deserve a spot.

Another British import, *Britain's Got Talent*, made its way to the US as *America's Got Talent*. Now the judges had buzzers to sound off their

Della Barris, 1962-1998. PHOTO COURTESY OF SHELLEY HERMAN

disapproval during the performances. And while some great singers and dancers made their way onto the stage. But to get to them, viewers first had to endure the trained cats who didn't want to do their tricks, the naked man who covered himself in a tablecloth and teacups, and removed the tablecloth without touching the teacups, keyboard-playing chickens, a man who played "America the Beautiful" by making fart sounds with his hands, expert belchers, and human fountains who spat water all over the stage.

One of the stage managers for *America's Got Talent* is, fittingly, John Hill, who says, "*America's Got Talent* draws a lot from *The Gong Show*. *America's Got Talent* is a search for extraordinary talent, for people who could be stars, but we still book and showcase people whose act consists of sticking their heads in goldfish bowls. They make it on TV because it provokes people's curiosity. *The Gong Show, America's Got Talent,* and *American Idol* at their core are appealing for the same reason: these are real people. These aren't professionals that we hired. These are mostly undiscovered talent who came to those shows seeking opportunity. It's intriguing to watch these shows and think 'This person could be anybody. Maybe this contestant I'm watching is a guy who lives down the street. Maybe we've crossed paths at the store.' And what Chuck got criticized for all those years ago are the elements of what are now extraordinarily successful and well-regarded shows."

In 2002, Chuck finally saw one of his books adapted into a film. George Clooney made his directorial debut with an adaptation of *Confessions of a Dangerous Mind*, starring Sam Rockwell as Chuck Barris, with Julia Roberts, Drew Barrymore, and Clooney himself in supporting roles. Murray Langston donned the paper bag once more to play himself.

Langston says, "I found out that the Unknown Comic was going to be a character in the movie. What they didn't realize was that I owned the character. I trademarked the name and the outfit. I sent them a letter saying I expected to be paid if they used this character that I owned for their film. George Clooney himself called me and asked if I wanted to be in the movie, and that satisfied all the issues I had. I was paid and I portrayed the character that I owned. And it was a wonderful experience."

John Hill says, "The set designer for that movie clearly did a lot of homework. What really got to me were the scenes that took place in Chuck's office. Not only did it look correct, just in general, but I mean there were specific things in those scenes that I remember buying for Chuck.[1]

1. Personal interview. 14 May 2019.

"My mother saw the movie, and when she got home, she called me to say, 'I can't believe you worked for that son of a bitch! He was a murderer!'"

Confessions of a Dangerous Mind, the movie, again brought to light the outrageous claims from Chuck's original book, that he was a contract killer for the CIA. Chuck was cheerfully evasive about it when he made the rounds in the press to promote the movie, promising not to reveal if it was true.

His wife Mary kept mum too, telling the press, "Chuck and I never really talk about whether he did it."

The fact that he wanted to maintain that ruse seemed to reveal a lot about the man. Roger Ebert concluded his review by musing, "…[A]ny man who would claim 33 killings as a way to rehabilitate his reputation deserves our sympathy and maybe our forgiveness."

The criticisms that he weathered for all those years had stung him quite a bit, and the idea that you might criticize a guy who had ways of making people disappear would make you think twice about what you were going to say, and Chuck liked it that way.

Though the movie wasn't a box office smash (it just barely made back its budget and grossed $33 million at the box office), the success for Chuck Barris came in another form. All the press surrounding the movie revealed a different tone from entertainment writers than he was accustomed to. The writers who wailed and gnashed their teeth every time they had to type a review of a Chuck Barris show had been replaced by a new generation of writers who simply accepted the success of his shows as matter of fact, and who often were willing to acknowledge that, yes, they actually liked *The Gong Show*.

This sudden onslaught of respect didn't exactly overjoy Chuck the way you'd expect. It would be one thing if he felt that people were just now seeing the light and deciding he was a genius. But in Chuck's eyes, the only reason he came off so great in the new millennium was because by comparison, television had become worse.

"What we see now is so awful that people look back at me with sweet reverence," Chuck mused. "Now I'm not such a nut and crazy maniac. But I'm the pioneer of reality shows, for good or bad. *Fear Factor*, the [Jerry] Springers of the world with the screaming and yelling and slapping…if that's what I pioneered, geez, I'm not sure that's the best thing in the world."

Larry Spencer, who had departed Chuck Barris Productions in the early 1980s for a long, successful career as a sitcom writer and producer, saw the same change in perception in his own endeavors. "For the longest time I was embarrassed to say I had worked on *The Gong Show*. I kind of hid that and emphasized my sitcom work. But over the years, I've gone to social functions, and I meet new people, and when I tell people everything I've done, *The Gong Show* ends up being all they want to talk about."

So, with the emergence of so many reality competition shows where acts were presented and panned, and with all the extra attention *The Gong Show* garnered because of *Confessions of a Dangerous Mind*, surely a *Gong Show* revival was on the docket, right?

Sony tried. First, they tried with a pilot hosted by Tom Arnold. It didn't get picked up. Then they tried with a pilot hosted by Jeff Ross two years later. It didn't get picked up. Comedy Central finally picked up *The Gong Show with Dave Attell*, a joint venture with Adam Sandler's production company, Happy Madison, in 2008; it lasted eight episodes before Comedy Central opted to pick up their mallets. And then there was one more shot at it. ABC, which had tremendous success with a string of vintage game show revivals as summer replacement programming starting in 2016, green-lit a new *Gong Show* to start in the summer of 2017.

But Chuck Barris would never see the new show. He died on March 21, 2017, at age 87.

"Chuck and I e-mailed frequently for a while," says Mike Metzger. "Ellen and I had moved to New England, and I would write these long e-mails about what we were doing, and Chuck would let me know what he was doing, and what he did, mostly, was write, and that made him happy. He never talked about wanting to go back into television. Never talked about some great idea he had or how much he wanted to get out there. He was done with television. It was behind him, and he had moved on from it."

Vince Longo says, "Years after I had moved on and done other things with my career, I got a chance to tell Chuck how much I loved working for him. I thanked him for hiring me and told him what a happy experience it was for me, how it didn't feel like a job most of the time, and what fun it was. Chuck thanked me and he said, 'But you know...I could never do that today. The accountants wouldn't allow it.'[2]

"And Chuck's right. Accountants have taken over the TV business, and it's not as much fun as a result. The number crunchers now would never allow anybody to run a company the way that Chuck ran his. Chuck just came along at this wrinkle in time where everything was perfect, and he was able to do it the way he did."

2. Personal interview. 9 May 2019.

Larry Spencer says, "Chuck Barris was my mentor. My hero. He gave me a career. Handed me a typewriter and said kid, go be weird, funny and clever. Truth, I owe this man my profession as a legit writer, having written and produced a plethora of sitcoms, four feature films and two novels. God bless you Chuck if you're looking down on us."

ABC heavily promoted the new *Gong Show* in 2017, hosted by "Tommy Maitland," an alter ego of Mike Myers, who hosted the show as an aging legendary British television presenter.

Myers explained his new identity to *Vanity Fair*. "I'm an old punk rocker, and there were a few things I would watch [growing up]: *Saturday Night Live,* Toronto Maple Leafs Hockey Club TV, and *The Gong Show*... There was something punk rock about the show...It was show business, but it had absolutely no ambition in it whatsoever — it was ambition-free. The show was kind of like performance art of a talent show. It's not really taking itself seriously. I just thought, if I'm doing this almost deconstruction of a talent show, I should be the ringmaster who is also deconstructed. It should be English in that way of keeping things moving, the super-gregarious [host]."

John Hill was hired as a stage manager, giving the new version one link to the past that few viewers would recognize.

Vince Longo says, "Yvonne and I went as VIPs, and we wore our old *Gong Show* staff jackets that Chuck had made for us. An audience member standing in line offered me $500 on the spot for mine. I said no, but what does that say about the allure of the old show?"

Yvonne Longo adds, "Mike Myers asked to meet with us after the taping. He said he was a fan of the original show and he wanted to be faithful to us, and he really wanted our feedback. He asked if there was anything we weren't satisfied with because he said he and everybody else wanted to do it right."

ABC aired 10 episodes in the summer of 2017, plus another summer run the following year, but after two summers, the network opted not to go for a third season. Audiences were intrigued, then they weren't, and the show faded away.

Murray Langston theorizes, "The revivals failed, I think, because of timing. *The Gong Show* was the first show like it on television, and when they brought it back, they brought it back to a television landscape that had already seen it and already had shows like it."

Lynnette Karnes agrees. "Have you ever seen *The Wizard of Oz*? You know how Dorothy lives in that black and white farm community in Kansas, and after the twister, she opens the door and sees Oz for the first time, and it's in color? That was what *The Gong Show* was like in 1976. People were opening that door to our show and seeing something they had never seen before. And you can never create that feeling again."

But it appears that's not the only problem. When asked why the revivals haven't been able to replicate the success of the original, nearly every person interviewed for this book had the same answer.

Jamie Farr: "Chuck wasn't there."

Vince Longo: "The hosts on the revivals have been good hosts, but *The Gong Show* that people knew and loved was hosted by this unique personality who hosted the show in a way that nobody could duplicate. If you have a smooth host doing that show, it doesn't feel like *The Gong Show*. And if you had someone trying to mimic the way Chuck did it, it would come off as fake. The problem with that show overall is that it had to be Chuck Barris. It doesn't feel right when anybody else does it."

Yvonne Longo: "Chuck put everything he had into that show, so the way that everybody remembers the show is because of him."

Murray Langston: "Chuck's performance as host gave that show so much of an identity. The revivals felt too slick and too professional. Chuck had this amateurish style as host that was just so perfect, and as strange as it sounds. Hiring a host who's funny and witty and charming and good at being a host just doesn't work for that show."

The job that Chuck never wanted, the job that Chuck resisted, the job that Madeline David at NBC had forced him into, had proven to be a job that literally only one man could do.

The Gong Show's legacy is filled with irony. Its recent history of fizzling and fading is arguably due to the original version succeeding so strongly. When it premiered there was nothing else like it, but it returned to a television landscape where it somehow blended in. Chuck Barris started the project wanting to create new stars, then changed his mind, then became the biggest star to emerge from his creation. His most significant successes were ideas cribbed from other producers and older shows, but his unique imprint gave him a legacy as an innovator.

Athens Abell, whose mother was a contestant on the original show, says that *The Gong Show*'s greatest legacy was that it came along when it was needed the most. "*The Gong Show* was a release valve. It came along in 1976. I was just a teenager, but I had spent the last nine years watching this horrifying footage from Vietnam on the news. Boys who weren't that much older than me were coming back to America without limbs. Nine years of that. And *The Gong Show* comes along, and it was fun, and crazy, and silly, and we needed that. You just watched this show to laugh.

It didn't try to be about anything, it didn't try to be great art. It was just a fun show, and occasionally, you got to watch a genuinely good act that made you say wow. The good acts made you, as a viewer, feel good. *The Gong Show* helped us cope and gave us hope. I don't think it gets enough credit for that.

Jeff Schimmel, whose brother boosted his career by playing the piano with his nose, reflects, "For those of us who watched the show regularly, it was probably the funniest thing on TV at that time. We loved

ROBERT BURROUGHS COLLECTION

it and it resonated with us. We loved that anything-goes sensibility and that no one took it seriously. The sad thing is that younger people don't know what that was like. You can go on YouTube and see people do anything. There's no appreciating what it was like to have access to something like that show. When you step back and see TV as a whole, you step back and see Chuck Barris as a whole, he had his finger on the pulse. Chuck broke the mold so hard that it opened the door for reality television. Chuck showed that what network executives thought was entertainment wasn't all that there was. There was so much more out there, and Chuck saw it.

BIBLIOGRAPHY

"ABC 'Brain' Leaves Legacy of Top Shows." *The Gazette.* Montreal, QUE. 27 Jan. 1978.

"Access Leaders." *Broadcasting Magazine.* 23 May 1977.

"Association Screens Some TV Shows." *The Mercury.* Pottstown, PA. 23 Apr. 1977.

"Barris Bangs the Gong for All His Shows." *Broadcasting Magazine.* 17 Mar. 1980.

"Barris Boss on Gong." *The Newark Advocate.* Newark, OH. 20 Feb. 1978.

"Barris Industries." *The New York Times.* 26 Mar. 1987.

Beck, Marilyn. "Cosby Has Changed." *The San Francisco Examiner.* 12 Aug. 1976.

"Bottom Line: All in Family." *Broadcasting Magazine.* 21 Jul. 1980.

"Bottom Line: Gamesmanship." *Broadcasting Magazine.* 1 Sep. 1980.

Bowden, Robert. "Chuck Barris Has the Good Fortune to be Tasteless." *Tampa Bay Times.* 28 Sep. 1979.

Buckley, Tom. "Game Shows: The Payoff is Right." *The Windsor Star.* 29 Dec. 1979.

"Dick Clark Survives the Payola Scandal." 27 Jul. 2019. Retrieved from https://www.history.com/this-day-in-history/dick-clark-survives-the-payola-scandal

Dunning, John. *On the Air: The Encyclopedia of Old-Time Radio.* Oxford University Press. 1998.

Eder, Shirley. "Sills Party has a Chiming Time." *The Times.* Shreveport, LA. 4 Jan. 1977.

Espinoza, Galina. "The Spy Who Gonged Me." *People.* 13 Jan. 2003. Retrieved from https://people.com/archive/the-spy-who-gonged-me-vol-59-no-1/

Foil, David. "About Time to Chuck Barris' Rah-Rah Show." *The Town Talk.* Alexandria, LA. 22 Mar. 1978.

"Gong Gets Viewers, Reviews." *The Advocate-Messenger.* Danville, KY. 24 Apr. 1977.

"Gong Show Boosts Careers." *The Dispatch.* Miline, IL. 11 Jul. 1976.

"Gong Show is a Game Program with a Bizarre Twist." *Daily Times.* St. Cloud, MN. 1 Jun. 1977.

"Gong That Man." *Channels Magazine.* May/June 1983.

Grey, Gene. "They'll Be Gonged Tonight." *Press and Sun-Bulletin.* Binghamton, NY. 4 Nov. 1977.

Grover, Stephen. "Treasure Hunts and Culture, Too." *The San Francisco Examiner.* 18 Nov. 1976.

"High Profits from Low-Brow TV." *Broadcasting Magazine*. 16 Ju. 1979.

Hill, Michael. "Television: The Good Guys Finish First, for a Change." *The Evening Sun*. Baltimore, MD. 24 Dec. 1979.

Hiltbrand, David. "Barris Sticks to His Guns." *The Gazette*. Cedar Rapids, IA. 23 Jan. 2003.

Hoffman, Will. "Daytime Ratings War Begins." *Albuequerque Journal*. 28 Sep. 1981.

Holsopple, Barbara. "ABC Seeks Viewer Vote on Oswald's TV Trial." *The Pittsburgh Press*. 29 Sep. 1977.

Holston, Noel. "NBC Plans Amateur Hour." *The Orlando Sentinel*. 3 May 1976.

Inman, Julia. "Barris Struck It Rich in Games." *The Indianapolis Star*. 17 Sep. 1967.

"Intermedia: Low-Power Barris." *Broadcasting Magazine*. 7 Mar. 1983.

Kart, Larry. "Gong Roadshow has a Familiar Ring." *Chicago Tribune*. 18 Aug. 1977.

"Major Bowes' Amateur Hour." *Old Time Radio Catalog*. Retrieved at *https://www.otrcat.com/p/major-bowes*

"Major Bowes' Stock Up Another Point as He Gets a New Sponsor." *The Nebraska State Journal*. Lincoln, NE. 28 Jun. 1936.

Maksian, George. "Chuck Takes His Gong and It Tolls for Gary." *New York Daily News*. 3 Sep. 1977.

Maurice, Dick. "Lawsuit Claims Barris Stole 'Gong Show' Idea." *The Evening Press*. 19 Sep. 1977.

McKenne, Kristine. "Martin von Haselberg." *Los Angeles Times*. 12 Jan. 1986.

Melnick, Ross. "American idols: Roxy, Major Bowes, and Early Radio Stardom." 14 Apr. 2015. Retrieved at *http://blog.commarts.wisc.edu/2015/04/14/american-idols-roxy-major-bowes-and-early-radio-stardom/*

Metz, Robert. "Buying Stock at the Sound of the Gong." *The Evening Sun*. Baltimore, MD. 26 Aug. 1977.

"No More Self-Impressions for Chris." *Poughkeepsie Journal*. 7 Jul. 1976.

O'Connor, Bill. "Brashest of the Brash." *The Dispatch*. Moline, IL. 21 Feb. 1982.

Preston, Marilynn. "The Cornball, the Bizarre, the Crazies — That's The Gong Show." *The Daily Oklahoman*. Oklahoma City, OK. 5 Sep. 1976.

"Remembering Chuck Barris, Self-Proclaimed King of Daytime Television." *Fresh Air* (radio broadcast). 23 Mar. 2017. Retrieved at *https://www.npr.org/2017/03/23/521229061/remembering-chuck-barris-self-proclaimed-king-of-daytime-television*

Ring, Trudy. "Gong Show Trio Performs at Lounge." *Galesburg Registered Mail*. 26 Sep. 1977.

Rosenberg, Howard. "Barris, Demeanest Man in All TV, has Returned." *The Los Angeles Times*. 23 Sep. 1981.

Scott, Vernon. "I Give Viewers Some Laughs, Put Some Fun in Their Lives." *The Orlando Sentinel*. 26 Aug. 1979.

Siegel, Norman. "Hold That Gong." *The Pittsburgh Press*. 28 Oct. 1935.

"Silverman Urges Hollywood to Put Down Its Rifles." *Broadcasting Magazine*. 26 Feb. 1979.

Staten, Vince. "Gong at Last." *Dayton Daily News*. 29 Apr. 1977.

Steinhauser, Si. "Blind Date GIs Wear Hearts on Sleeves." *The Pittsburgh Press*. 4 Sep. 1944.

Stock, Craig. "Ringer on the Gong Show." *Detroit Free Press*. 1 Jun. 1977.

Stoeher, Chris. "A Question of Local Programming Taste." *Detroit Free Press*. 1 Oct. 1979.

"Super Series 76 Brings Out Best." *Star-Phoenix*. Saskatoon, SK, Canada. 9 Jan. 1976.

Swertlow, Frank. "Jaye P. Morgan Offers Viewers Shock, Schlock." *The Cincinnati Enquirer*. 11 Apr. 1978.

Swertlow, Frank. "No Cheers for Rah Rah Show." *The Missoulian*. Missoula, MT. 4 Mar. 1978.

"Talent Doesn't Pay on The Gong Show." *The Dispatch*. Moline, IL. 24 Apr. 1977.

"Television Notes." *Tampa Tribune*. 5 Feb. 1978.

"The Tightening Market for Access." *Broadcasting Magazine*. 5 Mar. 1979.

"Today's Highlights." *The Courier-Journal*. Louisville, KY. 28 Feb. 1978.

Vick, Karl. "Confessions Fits Typical Barris Mold." *Tampa Bay Times*. 30 May 1984.

"What a Way to Spend a Weekend." *The Province*. Vancouver, BC, Canada. 4 Aug. 1976.

Woods, Sherry. "ABC Makes It 26 of 30 Weeks on Top of the Ratings Heap." *The Miami News*. 13 Apr. 1978.

Woods, Sherry. "Sevareid's Retirement Will Keep Him Out of the Business." *The Miami News*. 29 Nov. 1977.

Young, Mort. "Though Others May Gong Him, Barris is Daytime King." *News-Press*. Fort Myers, FL. 10 May 1979.

INDEX

*Numbers in **bold** indicate photographs*

$1.98 Beauty Show, The 292, 301-305, **303**, **304**, **306**, 315, 323, 345
2-4 The Show Trio 220
3's a Crowd 305, 315-319, **317**, **319**, 320-323, 325
60 Minutes 213

Abell, Athens 244-246, 358-359
Abell, Kurt 241-244, **242**, 311-312, 315, 325-327
Aberg, Sivi **83**, **120**, 121, 128, 134, 137, 161
Ada and Alice 280
"Ahab the Arab" 245
"Alabamee Bound" 242
Albertson, Jack **90**
"Alley Cats" 261
"Alley Cat" **178**
All-New Dating Game 345, **346**
All-Star Gong Show, The **184**, 185
Allyson, June **233**, 256
Altman, Robin "Red" **310**, **311**, 314
America's Got Talent 353-354
American Bandstand 21-24, 31, 342
American Idol **93**, 246, 352, 354
Andrews, Patty 194
Ann-Margret 20
Anything for a Laugh 343
Archerd, Army 326
Arlen, Michael J. 317-318
Arnaz, Lucie **90, 104**
Arnold, Tom 356
Arnopole, Alan 254-256
Atkins, Chet 223
Attell, Dave 356

"Bad, Bad Leroy Brown" 232, 233
Bailey, Pearl 91
Bait Brothers, The **195**, 224, **313**, 314
Bandit Impressionist, The 224

Banks, Gene 94-95, 106, 117, 128, **143**, 143, **153**, 254
Barbeau, Adrienne 63
Barbour, John 73, 74-75, **75**, 77-78, 80-82, 83, **84**, 85, 91, 299
Barker, Bob 174
Barnes, Greg 142
Barnes, Robin 348
Barris, Della 24, 89, 161-166, **161**, 217-218, **217**, 220, 284, 314, **315**, 329-330, **329**, 348, 351-352, **353**
Barris, Lyn 19, 20, 24, 162, 163
Bay City Rollers, The 220
Bearde, Chris 58-60, **59**, 61, 63, 65, 68, 69-70, 73, 89, 91, 124-125, 126, 134, 336, 348, 349
Bearded Lady, The 283
Beatles, The 32, 170, 270
Beeker, Jefferson 91, 119, 126, 137, **138**, 139, 148, **149**, 150-152, **151**, **158**, 174, 192-193, 216, 217, **219**, 220-221, 222, 272-273, **273**, 283-287, **284**, 288, 300-301, 308, 311, 333
Bell, Bob 270
Bells, Orson 100, **103**
Bennett, Michael 87
Berle, Milton **124**, **221**, 223, 224-225
Bernardi, Jack **313**
Bernhard, Sandra 222
Betty and Eddie 260-261, 262
Bleier, Edward 26
Bleu, Don 348, **349**, 349-350, **350**
Blind Date 31
"Blue Danube" 80
Bobo, Willie 194, 300
Bolen, Lin 61-62, 70
Bonnie, Bob 68
Boone, Pat 15, 16, 228
Borge, Victor 223
Bork, Johann Sebastian **146**

Bowes, Major Edward 6, 7-16, **10**, **13**, 58, 76, 170, 340
Brecker, Renee **172**
Bricker, Steve **95**
Bridges, Bill **329**
Brill, Charlie 254
Britain's Got Talent 353
Brockman, Michael 70, 71, 200, 279, 289-290, 293-294
Brothers Vert, The 153, 154
Brown, Peter H. 219
Bryant, Anita 133, 282, **283**
Bubbles 93-94
Buffalo Chips, The **334**
Bulifant, Joyce 91
Burnett, Carol 174
Burton, Teresa 262
"Butcher Boy" 108
Butler, Rhetch 239
Buzzi, Ruth **124, 131**
Byrd, Jim 340, 341

California Zephyr 254-256
Callas, Maria 11
Calloway, Cab 19, **222**, 244
Camouflage 26, 305-306, 323
Cannon, Freddie 24
Carlin, George **48**, 220, 268, **269**
Carroll, Bob 156, 157
Carroll, Billy **147**
Carson, Johnny 63, 98, 202, 229, 236, 238, 244, 256, 264, 268, 270, 274, 305, 333
Carson, Sue 19
Case, Walt 204, 348
Cassidy, Jack 75, **76**, 78
Cato, Florence **173**
Charles, Ray 223
Chase, Chevy 174-176
"Chattanooga Choo-Choo" 117
Christina & Friend **309**
Chuck Barris Hour Talk Show 305
Chuck Barris Rah-Rah Show, The **219**, 219-225, **221, 222, 223, 226**, 229, 244, 268, **269**, 292
Church, Bubba 19
Churian, Professor Kaka **180**
Clark Twins, The **304**
Clark, Candy **93**
Clark, Dick 21-23, 24, 31-32, 338
Clark, Richard 170
Clonettes, The **188**
Clooney, George 354

Close Encounters of the Third Kind **188**
Collins, Larry 348
"Come On, Get Happy" 117
Comedy Courtroom **344**, 345
Commore, Jimmy 172, 334, 348
Confessions of a Dangerous Mind 340-343, **341**, 354-355, 356
Connor and Dalton **105**
Connors, Carol **281**
Conway, Tim 65, 269
Cook, Maurice 124
Cooper, Alice 185
Corcoran, Jr., John H. 87
Corey, Eliot 101-102
Cote, Merry Kay *see* Roxie Paramour 100, 103
Count Banjola *see* Abell, Kurt
Count Basie 157
Cowell, Simon **93**, 267, 352-353
Cronkite, Betsy 169

D'Auria, Joey 112, 265-270, **269** *see* Dr. Flame-O
D'Imperio, Chuck 229-234, **231**
Dancin' Feet 261
Dating Game, The 32-35, **33**, 38, 41, 43, 47, 88, 143, 190, 204, 211, 218, 262, 292, 301, 305, 315, 319, 323, 340-341, 343, 345, 348
David, Madeline 70, 73-74, 77, 80, 81, 82, 129, 185, 286, 289, 293, 358
Davidson, John 174
Dawson, Richard 63, 65, 68
De Fox, Fillipe 153, 299
Debin, Jonathan 34, **34**
Deeb, Gary 74, 88, 211-212
Deer, Gary Mule 271, 300
"Delta Dawn" **308**
DeLugg, Milton 63, 66, 78, 91, **109**, 121, 123, 124, 139, 153, 156, 157, 191, 227, **237**, 242, 254, 288, 302, 303, 314, 345, 348
Devo, Ron 195
Diller, Phyllis **90**, 99, **162**, 223, 245, 278
Disco Lizards, The **207**
Divorce Game, The 305
Dollar a Second 305, 336, 338
"Don't Get Up" 314, **315**
Dorsey, John 116, 118, 122, **141**, 185, 197, 288, 320, 348
Douglas, Mike 97, 131, 177, 179, 215, 218, 274
Downey, Robert 307, 308-309, 310, 314
Dr. Flame-o *see* D'Auria, Joey
Dr. Jerry the Singing Chef 146, 314
Dubert and Pucky **284**

DuBois, Ja'Net **233, 304**
Duke Ellington Orchestra, The 220

Ebert, Roger 355
Ed Sullivan Show, The 19, 65
Edwards, Geoff 49, **50,** 336
Edwards, Stephanie 335
Elfman, Danny 260
Elliott, Mama Cass 206
"Embraceable You" 128
Emmanuel 195-196
Enright, Patty 348
Eubanks, Bob **36,** 80, 170, 171, 182, 292, 343, **346**
Evans, Dale 220
Extreme Gong 350

Family Feud 199, 324
Farr, Jamie 75, 76, **76,** 77, 78-80, 83, 85, 92-93, 95-96, **97, 127,** 128, 145, 152, **168, 171,** 174, 194, 196-197, 224, 233, **233,** 238, 245, 248, **265,** 278, 295, 301, 349, 358
Farrakhan, Louis 15
Father Ed 147-148, **148,** 299, 311 *see* Holland, Ed
"Feelings" **154,** 173, 174, 195-196
Felsher, Howard 199
"Fifth of Beethoven, A" 207
Finell, "Mr." Tootie 282, **283**
Fisher, Albert 15, 58, 59
Flagg, Fannie 91
Flanders, Jerry 196
Foxx, Redd 99, 223
Francis, Arlene 31
Francis, Connie 15
Freberg, Stan 228
Freed, Alan 22
Friedman, Budd 263
Friedman, Steve 38
"Friendship" 74

Gable, Clark 150, 239
Gabor, Eva **108,** 152, 252
Gallagher 224
Game Show King, The 74, 211, 291, 341
Garner, Paul "Mousie" 123
Garvey, Steve 227, **245**
Geer, Will 238, 240
Gene-Gene the Dancing Machine **156,** 156-159, **157, 158,** 185, 204, 224, 288, 296, 299, 314, 333, 349
George Beagle and Twilight **176**

George, Susan **196**
Gleason, Jackie 47
Goldberg, Ruth 144, 272
Goldwyn, Samuel 7
Gone with the Wind 150, 239
Gong Roadshow, The 170-173
Gong Show Movie, The 306-315, **307, 308, 310, 311, 312, 313, 315,** 316, **321,** 325-329, **326, 327, 328, 329,** 330, 331, 339
Goodson, Mark 324
Gotterer, Larry 111-113, 117, 212-213, 294-296, 302-303, **303,** 321-322, 345, 348
Goulet, Robert 175
Granger, Bill 87
Granoff, Budd 134, 293, 316, 317, 322-323, 324, 336
Graveyard Grease, The 194
Greed 48
Green Jelly 349
Groundlings, The 261-262, 301

Hackett, Buddy 122, 123, 124
Hall, Monty 50-51
Halpern, Ellen 38, 40-41, 45 *see* Metzger, Ellen
Hamner, Earl 240
Hanna, Lee 277-278, 279, 280
Hannon, Sean 238-241, **239**
"Happy Days are Here Again" 160
Harris, Oren 22
Hartman, Phil 262, **312,** 314
"Hava Nagila" 139-140
Have You Got a Nickel *see* Popsicle Twins, The
Heatter, Merrill 76
Hensel, Scott Charles 195
"Here, There, and Everywhere" 270
Herman, Shelley **136,** 137, **217,** 319
Hill, John 40, 44, 96, 145, 155-156, 164-165, 167, 180-182, 202, 206, 208-209, 325, 343, 347, 348, 354-355, 357
Hilligoss, Mountain John **60,** 60-61, 66-68, 69, 123, 124
Hoboken Four 11-12, **13**
Holland, Ed *see* Father Ed
Hollywood Cowboys, The 295
Holston, Noel 74
Hopkins, Linda 174
Houston, Evelyn 128
How's Your Mother-in-Law? 37, 48, **48,** 305
Howard, Bob 70
Howard, Linda 106, 109, 307, 335, 348
Hughes, Howard 37

Hunter, Gloria **127**
Hyman, Terri 68

"I Ain't Really a Cowboy, I Just Found the Hat" 254-255
"I Can't Dance, Don't Ask Me" 239
"I Got Rhythm" 252
"I Just Want to be a Pimp" 103-104
"I'm Going Out of My Head" 185

Jackson, Andy 195
Jacobs, Johnny 32, 110, 121, 302
James, Harry 185
Jarkey, Harry 191
Jenson, Adrena 99
Joel, Billy 185
"John and Marsha" 228
"Johnny B. Goode" 224, 255
Johnson, Arte 63, 65, 68, 94, **104**, 127, **187**, 196, **200**, 227, 239, 252, 336
Jolson, Al 93, 99
Jones, Spike 220
"Joseph Make Your Mind Up" 172
Julia, Raul 15
"Jump at the Woodside" 157, 158, 159

Kanakke Kuties, The **308**
Karnes, Lynnette Pope 41, 45-46, 52, 206, 214, 224-225, 333-334, 357-358
Kates, Rick 192, 348
Katy the Caterpillar **118**
Keen, Larry 246-248
Kellard, Rick 77, 114
Kelly, Eddie 23-24
Kelly, Roz **215**
Kendall, Messmore 7
Kerns, Jocko **148**
King, Gertie **110**
King, Mabel 314
Kipper, Harry 100-101, **101**, 224
Kirk, Rahsaan Roland 250
Klein, Jaime 152-153, 196, 212, 303, 325
Klein, Robert 15
Knight, Gladys 15, 16
Krause, E. Jay 73

L.A. Knockers, The **301**
LaBelle, Patti 223
LaChance, Manette and Steve **168**
Lampkin, Al 235-236
Langdon, Verne 146

Lange, Jim 32, **33**, 35, 292, 343
Langston, Murray 142-145, **144**, 203-204, 217, 224, 273-275, **274**, **286**, 299, 308-309, 311, 314, 349, 354, 357, 358
Lapp, Ann **90**
Larry and His Magic Trumpet **155**
Larsen, Milt 268
Laugh-In 58, 63-64, 65, 121, 228
Lawford, Peter 252
Le Poof, Monsieur **285**
Leave It to the Women 335-336
Lee, Brandy 282-283
Lee, Michele 160, **247**, 271
Lehrer, Tom **165**, **212**
Leigh, Vivien 150
Lenya, Lotte 169
Les Chats 261
Letterman, David **272**, 272, 275
LeVasseur, LaVern 244-246
Levy, Lyn *see* Barris, Lyn
Lewis, Marcene **181**
Lewis, Shari 91
Lies, Danny 110-111, 112, 113, **143**, 147, 188, 189, 190, 207, 288, 290, 306, 307, 314, 334
Lisa and the Insomniacs **213**
"Listen to the Mockingbird" 101
Literatus, Nazo 153
Little El 68
Logan, Joshua 169
Longo, Vince 37-38, 42, 43-44, 45, 47, 49, 52, 78, 102, 103, 104, 105, 109, 115, 118, 134, 169, 171-173, 178, 192, 193, 204-205, 259, 281, 288-289, 292, 299, 308, 309, 321, 322, 356, 357, 358
Longo, Yvonne Tolbert 117-118, **158**, 159, 281, 309, 357, 358
Longtoe, Jay 261, **261**
"Look for the Silver Lining" 170
"Love Will Keep Us Together" 315
"Lovee's Come Back" 128
Ludden, Allen **131**, 145, 174, **215**, 272, **272**

Mabley, Moms **110**
Mack, Ted 14-16, 20, 54, 57, 58, 65, 85, 88, 230, 244, 340
Magical, Mystical Guitarist, The 128-129
Maitland, Tommy *see* Myers, Mike
Major and Minor 256
Major Bowes' Capitol Family 8
Major Bowes' Original Amateur Hour 9-16, **13**
Mama Hooch and Her Maid June 203

"Man I Love, The" 147
Marguiles, Lee 87
Marin, Jerry 121, 123, 291
Martindale, Wink **48**
Marty, Dave 241
Masini, Al 338
Match Game, The 91
Matthau, Walter 252
McCall, Mitzi 195
McCawley, Jim 268-269, 270
McClurg, Edie 222
McCormick, Pat 160, 268, 271, **304**, 305
McGinnis, Charlotte 262
McGlory, Margee 99
McKenna, Christa **106**
McMahon, Ed 333, 338
Mencken, H.L. 11
Metz, Robert 170
Metzger, Mike 26, 32-34, **34**, 38, 40, 41, 44-45, 46, **46**, 47, 96, 107, 175-176, 182, 205, 316, 317, 319, 320, 322-323, 336, 342, 345, 356
Metzger, Ellen **46**, 46-47, **142**, 166, 205-206, 317, 319-320, 351, 356
Michael, Raymond **233**, 234
Michel, Johnny 172, 195, 349
Midnight Special, The 100, 142, 273
Mike Douglas Show, The 131, 177
Miller, Chuck 271
Million Dollar Talent Search 336-337
Million Dollar Talent Show **338**
Mills Brothers, The 224
Minnelli, Liza 103
Mins, Peter 148, **149**, 150-152, **151**, 151, **158**, **219**, 220, 272-273, **273**, 284, **284**, 286-287, 299, 311

Miss Dolly 280
Miss Gigi **201**
Mooney, Paul 222
Moore's Mongrel Review **205**
Morgan, Jaye P. 74-75, 80, **93**, **97**, 97-98, **99**, 128, 145, 160, **171**, 174, **187**, 196, 220, **223**, 224, 227, 233-234, 238, 243, **245**, 247, 248, 253, 260, **265**, 268, 278, 283, 288-290, **289**, 291, 293, 296, 311, 314, 328
"Morning After, The" 94
Moy, Harold 11
Mr. Bell Jazzy **115**
Mr. Didlo **311**, 313, 314
"Mr. Frump in the Iron Lung" 271
Mrs. Klebenoff 74-75

Muchero the Clown 238
Muir, Roger 35
"Mulambo No. 1" 228
Myers, Mike 357

Nabors, Jim 268
Natividad, Kitten 312
Neale, Bill 178
Netherton, Tom **304**
New Newlywed Game 345, **346**, 348
"New Talent Time" 65
New Treasure Hunt, The 305, 336
Newlywed Game, The 35-38, **36**, 42, 43, 47, 80, 87, 88, 112, 170, 182, 218, 292, 301, 305, 315, 316, **319**, 323, 333, 337, 343, 348
Nicholson, Nick 35
Nitty Gritty Dirt Band 244
Nixon, Richard 162
"No Better Feeling" 246
Norton, Ken **108**
Noy, Yakov **190**
Nugent, Howard 139, 148, 156-157, 186
Nye, Louie 238

O'Connor, Bill 98
O'Connor, John J. 87
Oak Ridge Boys, The 223
"Oh Johnny, Oh Johnny" **181**
Oingo Boingo 259-260
"Okee from Muskogee" 69
"Old MacDonald Had a Jungle" 117
"On a Clear Day" 69, 99
"On Wisconsin!" 227
"One O'Clock Jump" 157, 159
Original Vaudeville Show, The **339**, 339-340, 345
Orth, Maureen 227-228
Oscar and Poncho **177**
Owens, Gary 63-65, **64**, 68, 73, 76, **90**, **120**, 121-122, **122**, 123-124, **123**, **124**, 126, 128-129, **129**, **130**, 130-133, **131**, **132**, 169, 229, 350

Paisner, Daniel 342
"Palisades Park" 23-24, 27
Parker, Kevin 224
Parks, Bert 303
Patton, Gene *see* Gene-Gene the Dancing Machine
Paulsen, Pat 142, 256
Paycheck, Johnny 224
Peck, Jim 316, **317**, 317-318, **319**
Phillips, Michelle 223

Pickens & Reid and the Boys with the Noise 251-252
Pickens, Rick 251-252
"Please Release Me" 280
Poker People 26-27
Pollack, Richard 246
Pop Idol 352
Popsicle Twins, The 277-279
Post, Markie 160
Presley, Elvis 68, **110, 233**, 234, 299
Prince Kenaga **116**
Professor Wolfgang Von Bimbo 267
Pryor, Richard 221-222
"Raindrops Keep Falling on My Head" **173**
Randall, Tony **184**, 185
Rayburn, Gene 20, 91, 174
Real People 228
Redford, Robert 116
Reed, Rex **90, 93, 97, 104, 108**, 128, **131, 168**, 169, **171, 196, 215, 247, 265**
Reid, Jimmy 251, 252
Reid, Tim 222
"Respect" 282
Reubens, Paul **261**, 261-262, 301
Rhett & Scarlett 150-152, **151, 158, 219**, 220, 272-273, **273**, 284, 286-287, 299, 311
Richardson, Jim 249-251
Rickles, Don **123**
Riddle, Rock **215**
Rinder Cella 254
Rockwell, Sam 354
"Rocky Raccoon" 252
Romani, Dora 108, **109**
"Root Beer Rag" 185
Rosenberg, Howard 335
Ross, Jeff 356
Ross, Marion 121, 122, 123
Rothafel, Samuel Roxy 7-8
Roxie Paramour *see* Cote, Merry Kay
Roxy and His Gang 7-8
RuPaul 349
Rupert, Penny 99, **178**
Ruthie the Stripper 153

Sales, Soupy **124**, 199
Sanford and Son 99, 119, 133, 248
Sargent, Cassius 142
Saturday Night Live 175, 262, 357
Schimmel, Jeff 263-265
Schimmel, Robert **263**, 263-265
Schneiderman, John 253-254

Schock, Daniel **209**
Schreiber, Avery 91
Scott, Maribelle **163**
Scruggs, Earl 244
"See See Rider" 68
Shales, Tom 87, 107-108, 200-201
Shamus, Sharon *see* Winningham, Mare
Shandler, Sharon *see* Winningham, Mare
Shannon, Nyna 69, 99
Shawn, Dick 256
Shear, Rhonda 345
Sherman, Michael 98-99, 228-229, **229**
Sills, Beverly 11
Silver Throated Tenor, The **88**
Silverman, Fred 293
Simons, Susan 77-78, 128, 137, 164, 165-166, 292
Sinatra, Frank 11-12, 13, **13**
"Smoke Gets in Your Eyes" 112, 268
Snepp, Frank 342
Snider, Ed 331
Solid Gold 339
Somers, Suzanne 91, **168**
"Something in the Way I Move" 281
"Sometimes It Just Don't Pay to Get Up" 314
"Somewhere Over the Rainbow" 253
"Soon It's Gonna Rain" 261
Sowell, Ron 246
"Speedy Gonzales" 228
Spencer, Fred 66, **67**, 69
Spencer, Larry 77, 109, 113-115, 128, 140-141, **143**, 154-155, **155**, 158, 159, 175, 194, 203, 208, 210, 220, 224, 259, **260**, 278, 283, 288, 292, 302, 307-308, 314, 355-356, 357
Spider Lady, The **106**
Star Search 264, 338, 340
Star Wars **188**
Stephenson, Skip 228
Stevens, Ray 245
Storch, Larry **48**, 121, 122, 123
String Bean **170**
Suave and Debonair 261
Sugarman, Burt 345, 350
Sullivan, Ed 19, 57, 65, 84, 219, 337
Sumac, Yma 228
Swan, Andy 236-238
"Swanee" 241
"Sweet Georgia Brown" 139
Sweet, Mark 191-192
Swertlow, Frank 199, 213, 281

"Take This Job and Shove It" 295
Taylor, Darvy 100
Taylor, Rip 162, 187, 220, 235, 245, 247, 301, 302, 303, 305, 306, 313, 314, 339, 339
Tedesco, Arte 252-253
Teen Tones 15
Temptations, The 224
"Tequila" 142
Texas Lil 200
"That's Amore" 108
That's Incredible! 334
Three of a Kind 37, 315
Tillis, Mel 245
Tobin, Jim 251-252
Todman, Bill 324
Tonight Show Starring Johny Carson, The 63, 236, 264, 270, 274, 275, 333
Travalena, Fred 220, 268
Treasure Hunt 49, 50, 335, 336
Trixie *see* Spencer, Fred
Tunes, Lenny 100
Turner, Lynn 94
Tuttle, Lisa 224
Two Left Feet 114

Unknown Comic, The *see* Langston, Murray

Van Doren, Tony 189
Van Dyke, Dick 119, 174
Vane, Ed 70
Vatican Four, The 165, 212
"Vatican Rag" 165, 212
Vaughn, Sarah 91
Vegas a Go-Go 111
Vick, Karl 342
Vils, Ursula 100
Voinivich, Vladimir 147
Von Haselberg, Martin 100-101, 101

Waggoner, Lyle 142
Wallace, Mike 213
Walters, Barbara 169
Waltons, The 240
Ward, Wanda 98
Warfield, Marsha 222
Warhol, Andy 174
Webb, Orma 88
Welch, Alan 38
Where the Action Is 31-32
Whispers, The 146, 299
White, Barry 185

"Why Me Oh Lord?" 314
Widoff, Gypsy Rose 279
"William Tell Overture, The" 241, 267
Williams, Anson 85
Williams, Paul 90, 196, 248, 271
Williams, Robin 222, 266
Williams, Sue 196
Willie the Juggling Ape 89
Wilson, Ron 100, 103
Winchell, Paul 11
Winningham, Mare 270-271
Winslow, Michael 271
Wizard of Oz, The 142, 253, 357
Wolcott, Nina and Robbie 68
Wolf, Esther 159-160, 264
Woolery, Chuck 162
Woo-Woo Chorus 196
Woodall, Ann 93-94
Worley, Jo Anne 63, 65, 75, 76, 78, 91-92, 101, 131
X Factor, The 353

"Yankee Doodle" 248
Yankovic, Weird Al 271
"Yellow Rose of Texas" 156
"Yesterday" 88
You and Me, Babe 53, 307, 313, 340
"You Light Up My Life" 267
Youngman, Henny 229, 233
Your Hit Parade 57, 63

Zeglar, Paul 248-249, 249

Bear Manor Media

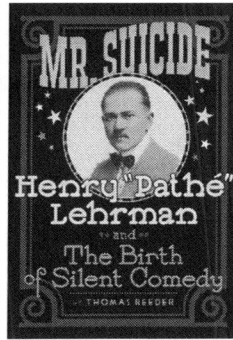

Classic Cinema.
Timeless TV.
Retro Radio.

WWW.BEARMANORMEDIA.COM

Printed in Great Britain
by Amazon

f96ad16a-3b18-4551-92f2-e7ec0c6ed737R01